Ontario

Competing in the New Global Economy

Report of the Premier's Council

Volume I

TABLE OF CONTENTS

3

PREFACE

The Premier's Council was established in the April 22, 1986 Speech from the Throne with a mandate to "steer Ontario into the forefront of economic leadership and technological innovation." A multipartite advisory body chaired by Premier David Peterson, the Council is composed of a number of cabinet ministers and leaders of the business, labour and academic communities.

When the Premier presided over the Council's first meeting in July of 1986, he challenged its members to examine the state of the Ontario economy objectively, determine how to enhance the province's strengths while addressing its weaknesses, and, based on their findings, develop policies and proposals for the province's future. The services of outside consultants were retained to assist the Council in carrying out an extensive and in-depth study of the competitiveness of the Ontario economy, the results of which are presented in this report. A special secretariat to the Council was also established within the Ministry of Industry, Trade and Technology to support the Council in this major undertaking.

During the next 18 months, the Premier presided over almost two dozen formal meetings of the Council. While the Council debated issues relating to the long-term future of the economy, it was also involved in steering the $1 billion Technology Fund, which is now providing substantial program support to several initiatives recommended by the Council. Several programs now operating successfully under the Technology Fund include the Centres of Excellence, the Centres of Entrepreneurship, the Industry Research Program and the University Research Incentive Fund. A new Council initiative, the Technology Adjustment and Research Program, has now been added to the Fund's program roster. The Council also initiated and is playing an active role in implementing a major symposium on entrepreneurship to be held in the spring of 1988.

As part of the Council's ongoing research, a selection of Council members visited Japan in early 1987 on a fact-finding mission. Consultations took place with senior Japanese government and industry officials to discuss key economic developments and assess new directions in science and technology. In keeping with this consultative research effort, the experiences of the United States, Europe and other industrialized countries were also reviewed and considered. Within Ontario, strategic analyses were carried out in key sectors of the economy, and meetings were held with over 1,000 people in business, the labour movement, colleges and universities, and government.

In examining existing government programs in Ontario, Canada and throughout the industrial world, the Council was in a unique position to view the Ontario economy in a global context. The Premier, through his personal involvement in the process, encouraged Council members to forego their private interests in order to achieve a consensus-building partnership formerly unknown in Canada. As a result, the Council's own representative makeup and broad consultative approach have enabled it to arrive at a commonly held view which forms the basis of its report.

The Council's report therefore represents a major step forward in consensus building in the public policy process. The role of the Premier in chairing the Council has been to ensure that advice from all quarters is considered and that their often diverse goals and interests are served. At the same time, however, the government stands apart from the Council as the final arbiter of the decisions it will make and the directions it will take. This separation of roles and responsibilities has been implicit in the Council's work without in any way diminishing its consensus building approach.

Volume I of this report represents the culmination of this effort. It presents a comprehensive set of proposals that have long-range implications for the province. It also calls for fundamental changes in public policies and programs, emphasizing those actions that will make Ontario more competitive in the world environment.

Volumes II and III will be companion pieces to the Council's report. These two volumes are not the report of the Council, but rather represent the reports that the consulting staff have made to the Council. They will be published in conjunction with the Council's report because they provide a unique insight into the competitive position of Ontario industry and the role and function of government programs at both the provincial and federal levels. In keeping with the spirit of consensus building that is implicit in all the Council's activities, the publication of the second and third volumes will also allow the people of the province to use this material to engage in a full discussion of our competitive future and help set the economic agenda for the next decade.

It should be noted that the work of the Council was planned and initiated well before the trade negotiations with the United States were concluded. The focus of the Council's work has been the industrial competitiveness of the province, and the proposals made have been basic to improving the trade capability of Ontario. Regardless of the trade regime that unfolds with the United States and with the world, the recommendations offered are fundamental to Ontario's future economic strength. This report is a blueprint for competitiveness in the international marketplace and the trade regimes that are part of it.

The preparation of this report was a massive undertaking involving the participation of many individuals whose contributions must be acknowledged. The Council members themselves are to be thanked for the unfailing and unstinting contribution of their valuable time, views and advice, and whose only compensation for these efforts is the excellent outcome of their deliberations. The exceptional work of the Council's consultants, Neil Paget of the Canada Consulting Group, David Pecaut and Ira Magaziner of Telesis, and their consulting associates* is gratefully acknowledged. The contributions of the staff of the Premier's Council Secretariat - Patrick Lavelle, Helen Burstyn, Gerry Pisarzowski, and Rob McLeod - also merit praise and gratitude. A further note of thanks is due to the many members of the Ministry of Industry, Trade and Technology who participated in the report's research effort.

---

* Ian Bromley, David Caldwell, Anne Donaldson-Page, Lucille Fowle, Thor Johnson, Tom O'Brien, Joanne Riccitelli, and Ed Wood.

MEMBERS OF THE PREMIER'S COUNCIL

Premier David Peterson, Chairman

Ministers

Hon. Alvin Curling, Minister of Skills Development

Hon. Monte Kwinter, Minister of Industry, Trade & Technology

Hon. Lyn McLeod, Minister of Colleges and Universities

Hon. Robert Nixon, Treasurer of Ontario, Minister of Economics and Financial Institutions

Hon. Gregory Sorbara, Minister of Labour

Hon. Chris Ward, Minister of Education

Members

David R. Beatty, President of George Weston Limited's Food Processing Group and Director of George Weston Limited.

Roberta L. Bondar, member of the Canadian Astronaut Program and a civil aviation medical examiner.

W. Edmund Clark, Senior Vice-President and Director of Merrill Lynch Canada Inc.

Susan Eng, Attorney with the law firm of Blaney, McMurtry, Stapells, Aarons and Watson.

Robert Charles Franklin, President of Ontario Hydro.

Leo W. Gerard, Director of District 6 (Ontario) of the United Steelworkers of America.

Helmut Hofmann, President and Chief Executive Officer, Devtek Corporation.

Geraldine Kenney-Wallace, Chairman of The Science Council of Canada, Professor of Chemistry and Physics, University of Toronto.

W. Norman Kissick, Chairman and Chief Executive Officer, Union Carbide Canada Ltd.

Bernd K. Koken, President and Chief Executive Officer, Abitibi-Price Inc.

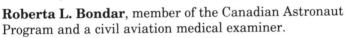

EXECUTIVE SUMMARY

The economic structure of Ontario today is a result of the opportunities and decisions of the past. Our resource-based industries are large and successful because the province had low cost raw materials and was close to the world's biggest industrial market. Many of our basic manufacturing industries, like steel and autos, owe their origins to the national decision to support domestic manufacturing through high tariffs on imported goods. Some of those manufacturing industries, such as autos, have since become part of a wider North American production system, while others continue to serve mainly local markets. In all cases our current industrial structure and economic skills are the result of our history.

The same historical factors which gave rise to our strengths in resource and basic manufacturing industries are at the root of the high level of foreign ownership in Canadian industry. The country needed capital to develop its resources, and foreign companies in Europe and the U.S. were seeking low cost sources of supply. Foreign manufacturers of consumer and industrial goods wanted to serve the Canadian market and so built branch plants to leap the tariff barriers. The country was young and resource-rich and our business culture became one mainly of living off the economic rents of the land, the forests, the waters, and eventually the captive market behind the tariff barriers. We generally did not have to invent new products, nor sell our wares in distant places, nor even manufacture very efficiently to earn a high standard of living.

The economic world is changed now, and we are no longer as naturally fortunate as we once were. A country of over 25 million cannot live well on resources alone, even ones as rich as ours. We must increasingly compete by dint of our creativity, our productivity, and our skill in working together. Success in the high-growth industries of today and the emerging industries of tomorrow will require a set of economic skills we have not yet mastered. Primarily, these are the talents required for creating and sustaining multinational enterprises which compete, not on the basis of low labour or raw materials costs, but rather through a process of continual renewal of their products, their systems, their factories, and their people.

Our research has found that Ontario is now uncompetitive in many high-growth industries like computers and may not even get out of the starting gate in many new and emerging businesses such as biotechnology. There are notable exceptions, like aerospace and telecommunications equipment, where past policy decisions and strong companies have built sustainable competitive advantages in export markets, but these exceptions are few in number.

These weaknesses in high-growth and emerging industries are especially worrisome because Ontario's traditionally strong resource and mature manufacturing businesses are coming under increasing competitive pressures due to slower market growth and new, intense competitors in industrialized and low wage countries. Many of these, our core industries, are undergoing major restructurings as the dynamics of competition are changing. Companies are moving to higher value-added products which require new skills and capabilities. The marketing of specialty papers or specialty steels is a more complicated business than selling simple commodity products. Some new businesses require applications engineering talents; others need research and development to support them. Investments in more highly automated production and new quality control systems are requiring greater skills from the workforce.

Just as the opportunities and decisions of the past have shaped the economic hand we play today, the opportunities and decisions we now face will determine the level of prosperity available to the next generation. As the Council has examined the adequacy of our current economic situation, a number of structural and competitive weaknesses have come to light. Chief among these is the lack of a healthy base of indigenous Ontario multinational companies in non-resource industries. The lack of such firms is a major reason for our poor performance in most high-growth sectors.

In addition to this structural problem, we have identified several other industrial weaknesses, including the low level of research and development spending in most industries, the dependence of too many sectors on undifferentiated commodity-type products, the presence of seriously uncompetitive plants in certain core industries, and the inadequate support climate for both entrepreneurial start-ups and larger, but not yet fully multinational threshold companies. The lack of support for threshold firms is of particular concern because it will be from the ranks of such companies that the indigenous multinationals of the future can emerge.

These industrial weaknesses are compounded by problems in the public infrastructure which supports our economic system. Our research has found that the education and training systems of the province, while strong in many respects, are not up to the levels of many of our competitors and not adequate to the economic challenges we will face. The science and technology infrastructure of the province in our universities and government labs, while achieving certain notable successes, has not focussed enough on industrial priorities and world-class performance. It is in the support systems of an advanced industrial economy that the basic abilities, specific skills, and ideas of its people will be developed. We must pay more attention to this human infrastructure in Ontario.

Our research has also found that our industrial problems are often exacerbated by a public policy base that is ill-conceived in terms of what assistance it delivers to industry and ill-equipped to manage that assistance effectively from a competitive standpoint. Government has often been indiscriminate in devoting too much of its resources to non-traded businesses which do not compete in world markets, to smaller businesses which are not the primary drivers of the wealth creation process, and to fixed asset assistance which does not benefit high-growth industries in need of more strategic investment in R&D and marketing. The regional goals of policy have often become confused with the economic development objectives.

OBJECTIVES GUIDING THE COUNCIL'S STRATEGY

The new challenges facing the Province will require new responses and initiatives. They will also require a different orientation and focus for public policy. To set the broad direction which the government should follow, we have adopted seven objectives that are the result of our analysis and deliberations. They form the basis of our strategy and underlie all our recommendations. Ontario should:

- Encourage all industries to move to competitive higher value-added per employee activities which can contribute to greater provincial wealth
- Focus industrial assistance efforts on businesses and industries in internationally traded sectors
- Emphasize the growth of major indigenous Ontario companies of world scale in those traded sectors
- Create an entrepreneurial, risk-taking culture that fosters an above-average number of successful start-ups in internationally traded sectors
- Build a strong science and technology infrastructure which can support the technological needs of our industries
- Improve the education, training, and labour adjustment infrastructure to levels adequate to sustain the province's indus-

13

trial competitiveness and help workers weather the technological change and adjustment necessary to move to higher value-added per employee activities

• Follow a consensus approach, like that embodied in the Premier's Council, in the creation of both economic strategies and specific programs and in the mobilization of public support for the new directions.

To implement these objectives, address our weaknesses, and build the economy we require, we propose the following program.

ASSISTING RESTRUCTURING IN CORE INDUSTRIES

Ontario's resource-based and mature manufacturing industries must reduce their international cost positions through continued productivity improvements. Increasingly, they will also need to move to greater product specialization and higher value-added per employee business segments. Newsprint producers may need to shift some production to the fast growing specialty papers. Chemical producers must invest in R&D and applications engineering to expand their specialty product opportunities. Food processors have to invest in expanded facilities which are closer to world scale. Steel producers must continue to increase their basic product quality and move into more specialty engineered and custom steels.

14

The core industries in Ontario in raw materials and mature manufacturing are at varying stages of restructuring and adjustment. Industries such as automotive, steel, and basic chemicals have made major investments in leading-edge facilities. Others, such as food processing, forest products, and specialty chemicals, are not as far along in the restructuring process. Industries such as rubber already bear the scars of structural change undertaken too late.

The adjustments taking place in the core industries in Ontario are driven by maturing markets and intensifying international competition. While the proposed Canada-U.S. Free Trade Agreement may accelerate the adjustment process, it will not change it fundamentally.

This process of industrial restructuring is critical to Ontario's future economic health. Some of the core industries have invested to meet these challenges; others have let the falling Canadian dollar disguise their competitive weaknesses. All will have to continue investing heavily to stay in the race.

A primary constraint to restructuring and the development of growth opportunities for small- and medium-sized Ontario manufacturers is the problem of raising new capital. Making the tran-

sition to higher value-added activities requires major investments and represents a formidable hurdle in the development of
many firms. The investment climate is bleaker today than it has
been in some time: nervous investors have pulled back from equity markets, and most new public offerings have been put on
hold.

There is a need to bring investors back into the market and
make funds available to the promising indigenous medium-size
firms in Ontario's core industries. Without new equity, these
firms will be unable to take advantage of the restructuring opportunities in auto parts, forest products, specialty chemicals, and
other industries. We have developed a specific incentive to address the critical recapitalization needs of Ontario's mid-size core
companies.

Recommendation 1: ONTARIO RECAPITALIZATION INCENTIVE PLAN
*An Ontario Recapitalization Incentive Plan should be established to at-
tract investors to indigenous mid-size exporting companies going to public
equity markets to raise new capital.*

The program would allow investors in new equity issues from
companies in traded sectors to receive a significant tax credit or
deduction (whichever the government deems most appropriate).
The investments would be restricted to a government-approved
registry of firms which met certain provincial criteria. These criteria should include the following:

15

- A listing on the Toronto Stock Exchange (or, for initial pub-
lic offerings, listing within 60 days)
- A maximum total equity capitalization (say in the range of
$100-$200 million)
- Headquarters and major strategic direction from an Ontario
base (i.e., indigenous companies)
- At least 25 percent of their world-wide employment value-
added in Ontario
- A minimum of, say, 50 full-time employees in Ontario
- A significant level of export sales.

Investors should be able to receive the tax benefits for direct
investment in the shares or in mutual funds which agreed to invest only in the qualified issues. There would need to be maximum limits on individual investor contributions and a minimum
holding period of at least one year for investors to keep their
qualified shares.

This program should benefit both mid-size companies in core

industries and manufacturers in high growth sectors. As we shall see in later chapters, the indigenous high growth firms in Ontario also require greater access to risk capital if they hope to survive and prosper. An added restructuring benefit of the incentive may be that it will encourage more Canadian entrepreneurs to buy the branch plant facilities of foreign firms and, with re-investment, turn them into indigenous Canadian operations selling to world as well as local markets.

The Recapitalization Incentive Plan can assist relatively healthy companies with foresight to restructure their operations. Nevertheless, there will be firms already burdened with unprofitable operations which may not be able to take advantage of the plan. In some of these cases, restructuring opportunities will still be present. In others, the plant and products may not be truly viable.

When significant numbers of jobs are involved, requests for government assistance will almost be automatic. In the past, the Ontario government has responded to such requests as they arise, often at the last moment and often on a case-by-case basis. The province has sometimes extended loan guarantees (e.g., Chrysler), other times lent money at low interest, and in other cases refused to get involved because the prospects for turnaround were slim. In nearly all cases, the lead time for government involvement was negligible, the expectations for results high, and the available options for action seriously diminished because of the late awareness of the need for restructuring.

In recognition of its continuing restructuring problems and appeals for government assistance, Ontario has created the office of the Industrial Restructuring Commissioner. The Council believes this is an important initiative. But based on our initial review of the restructuring experience in Canada and other countries, the Council believes that this initiative must be accompanied by a new set of guidelines that will fundamentally strengthen the restructuring effort. The Council therefore recommends that the restructuring effort in Ontario be carried out under the auspices of the Industrial Restructuring Commissioner as follows:

Recommendation 2: NEW DIRECTIONS FOR RESTRUCTURING

Ontario should put in place a sound industrial restructuring process focussed on the traded sectors, requiring the active involvement of business, labour, and government, and aimed at achieving timely and workable restructuring actions.

Several considerations enter into developing such an industrial restructuring process and should become integral parts of the approach:

- Focus on the traded sectors. Jobs lost in the traded sectors are usually jobs lost permanently to the Ontario economy
- Anticipate the declining industries and major trouble spots. Establish sufficient lead time and direct efforts towards viable restructuring arrangements, not bailouts
- When government involvement is requested, require the industry or company to put the restructuring plan together with key stakeholders (e.g., owners, workers, suppliers, and lenders) and agree on the actions to be taken
- Work from a sound basis of competitive analysis by putting together a small team of outstanding specialists from business, labour, and government to assist in company restructuring
- Deliver government support only to well-conceived and viable restructuring plans. Companies that leave restructuring until it is too late should not be automatic candidates for government bailouts. Nor should firms which have little prospect of long-term survival.

To embark on a truly new direction in industrial restructuring, the province must be prepared to address the problems of labour adjustment in restructuring industries. If Ontario intends to assist only viable firms which fall into difficulty, it must be prepared to help the workers of non-viable firms to develop new skills and find alternative employment.

The Council was not able to study the existing labour adjustment programs in the country, but a thorough review of them is in order, especially if the Canada - U.S. Free Trade Agreement is implemented. The Council is proposing that it address the labour adjustment issues associated with industrial restructuring in its next agenda. This can be part of a comprehensive and in-depth look which the Council plans to take into all the "people issues" related to its proposed economic strategy. Development of this people strategy will include not just labour adjustment, but all worker education and training issues.

Recommendation 3: A REVIEW OF WORKER ADJUSTMENT
The Premier's Council should examine the labour adjustment issues of restructuring in Ontario's core industries and work with the government to develop a comprehensive approach to meeting the adjustment needs of workers in these industries.

Specific issues which the Council believes will need to be examined include:

- The current effectiveness of labour markets in coping with worker adjustment
- The subsequent economic fortunes of workers displaced during industry restructurings, including their eventual employment situation and income levels
- The linkage between retraining strategies and adjustment strategies
- The experience of other countries in successfully meeting the adjustment needs of workers in declining industries
- The potential effects of the proposed Canada - U.S. Free Trade Agreement on the worker adjustment process in Ontario.

The Council research has also established that one of the key ingredients underlying successful restructuring efforts in other countries is a well-informed labour movement that understands the competitive situation of industry and a labour-management atmosphere where jointly held facts and perceptions of the international competitive arena can guide business and labour decisions. To assist in achieving this kind of environment in Ontario, the Premier's Council has worked with the government of Ontario to create the Technology Adjustment and Research Program (TARP), the objective of which is to encourage and assist labour and management to carry out research into:

- The effects of technological change on the worker and workplace
- The effects of technological change on the company and its competitive and working environment
- The competitive outlook and the role of technology for the industry
- The issues of adjustment, restructuring, and training in the industry.

This new program will make an important contribution to coping with the effects of technology on the part of both business and labour. Moreover, it will enhance the process of consultation between labour and management, both of whom will benefit as much from the opportunity to work together as from the information generated in the process.

Initiatives taken in Quebec through the Solidarity Fund, and more recently at the federal level through new tax incentives for national labour organizations to put in place venture capital funds, have pointed to worker ownership as a complementary component of industrial restructuring. Such initiatives are not intended as last-resort financing for failing firms. Rather, they provide labour with the opportunity to invest in healthy companies that need capital for growth, to put in place new management in restructuring potentially healthy firms, or to buy out discrete businesses from existing companies when those firms no longer have a strong interest in them. They are also intended to maintain good jobs in the country and expand the value-added capability of firms.

The Council believes that worker ownership has an important role to play in Ontario, but there is no clear answer regarding the best course to pursue for the province. One possibility is a worker restructuring investment fund like the Quebec Solidarity Fund; another is a worker equity guarantee program to guarantee loans to workers for the purpose of investing in worker buyouts.

Recommendation 4: ONTARIO WORKER OWNERSHIP INITIATIVE
The government of Ontario should initiate a full examination of the potential benefits of encouraging broader worker ownership in Ontario companies.

This initiative should be developed jointly with the Premier's Council to explore several potential mechanisms for encouraging broader employee ownership and worker investment in restructuring companies. It should carefully examine successful and unsuccessful workers ownership models in other jurisdictions, and based on those and the interests of labour and other relevant groups, formulate specific programs that could work in Ontario.

19

INVESTING IN HIGH GROWTH AND EMERGING INDUSTRIES

Ontario has a serious competitive problem in its high growth and emerging industries. In a handful of high growth sectors, like aerospace and telecommunications equipment, Ontario has a positive trade balance and relatively high value-added per employee. But in many others, like computer hardware, software, medical instruments, pharmaceuticals, and semiconductors, Ontario is suffering major trade deficits and relatively low value-added per employee compared to those industries in other countries.

In emerging industries where markets are much less developed and technological directions still largely uncertain, Ontario has a similarly weak position. In a few areas like lasers, a strong Ontario firm has emerged to become an international competitor of note. But in most emerging sectors, Ontario has virtually no participation and in others like biotechnology, only a few small start-ups struggling to gain a toehold.

The challenge for the province and the nation in the future is to develop stronger competitive positions in a larger set of high growth and emerging sectors. It will not be necessary, nor possible as a small nation, to succeed in all such industries, but it is an imperative to broaden and deepen the current high growth and emerging industrial base.

Canada has only a few world-class indigenous technology firms carrying out pre-competitive research and development and introducing advanced technological products on a world-wide basis. By indigenous we mean firms that direct their R&D, marketing, and overall strategy for their core products from a Canadian base. Other successful industrialized countries already have this technologically advanced indigenous core. Even nations as small as Sweden, Switzerland, and the Netherlands have a larger base of such companies than Canada does.

To create and sustain a core group of major technology driven multinationals we must offer greater tax-based assistance to the few we already have, share the risks of R&D with firms which could grow into those multinationals, and encourage our major indigenous companies in traditional industries to diversify into more technologically driven and higher value-added products and markets. Given that the current level of government assistance in Canada to industrial R&D seriously lags behind that of other countries, Ontario could significantly improve the competitiveness of high growth and emerging industries by offering a provincial R&D tax incentive.

Recommendation 5: INCREMENTAL R&D TAX INCENTIVES
The Ontario Government should institute a special tax incentive for incremental R&D expenditures above a company's three-year rolling average of R&D performed in Ontario.

The incentive could be in the form of a tax credit or a deduction. If it is a tax credit, it should include a provision enabling R&D performing firms which pay no taxes to take advantage of it by making it refundable. The advantage of using a deduction, of course, is that a tax credit will itself be taxed by the federal government, thus diminishing the benefit to companies receiving it.

Another important means of assistance to high growth and emerging industries is through government procurement contracts, especially in areas of new technology. Governments at all levels in Canada recognize that procurement is an important industrial development tool. With close to $80 billion in purchases annually, the public sector's combined buying power makes it the largest potential customer by far for thousands of Canadian businesses. Yet neither the federal nor provincial governments (with the partial exception of federal aerospace offsets and Quebec computer and hydro procurement policies) have effectively harnessed this purchasing power to the benefit of Canadian industry.

One of the most significant problems with existing Ontario and federal procurement efforts is that they are based on a "local content" approach of giving a price preference or quota to local suppliers. Unfortunately, such an approach does very little to build internationally competitive Canadian firms. In technologically advanced products and services, it does not even result in local procurement because very often a Canadian supplier is not deemed capable.

The Ontario approach to procurement also favours the award of many small contracts for pieces of projects rather than large awards to a few suppliers which could help those suppliers build sufficient scale to compete in export markets. This contrasts with Quebec's approach to contracting, which has played a major role in the international success of consulting engineering firms like Lavalin and in Quebec's software and systems integration industry.

The Council recommends an alternative approach to purchasing in Ontario which we call "strategic procurement." In strategic procurement the goal is to assist local suppliers through procurement to broaden or deepen their experience, improve their products, reduce their costs, and gain sufficient scale to be more competitive in world markets. Strategic procurement requires understanding the international competitive environment facing domestic suppliers and recognizing the most critical leverage points for gaining a competitive advantage in their businesses.

In some businesses, new product development is a critical competitive tool. Strategic procurement can help by funding the development of new state-of-the-art techniques, testing prototypes, and making the initial purchases of new products. In other businesses, economies of scale in production or after sales service may be critical to competitive success. Strategic procurement can assist companies in those businesses by helping them build scale.

A number of initiatives can be taken in Ontario to make procurement more strategic and effective. Specifically, the Council recommends that a strategic procurement plan be implemented.

Recommendation 6: STRATEGIC PROCUREMENT PLAN
A strategic approach to procurement should be adopted throughout the Ontario government, including Ontario Hydro. Such an approach should include three initiatives:

• *A Strategic Procurement Committee to be composed of independent business, academic, and labour leaders, as well as senior government representatives, to lead the initiative*

• *A Health Care Procurement Commissioner to focus on pulling together Ontario's substantial buying power in the health care field to assist in the development of Canadian medical equipment and pharmaceutical firms, and in attracting foreign multinationals to carry out R&D and locate manufacturing facilities in the province*

• *An Enabling R&D Contract Fund which, under the direction of the Strategic Procurement Committee, would receive proposals from all arms of the Ontario government and provide a means for developing competitive Ontario suppliers by awarding small developmental contracts prior to tendering major contracts.*

The role of the Strategic Procurement Committee would be to identify major purchase requirements of the Ontario government for the long-term (perhaps the next ten years) and develop a strategic approach to procurement in selected promising areas. This approach would involve early identification and notification of Canadian firms, providing these firms with enabling research and development contracts to expand their technical capability, and defining how Ontario's needs and the demands of the international marketplace could be meshed in the development of procurement specifications. The Committee would also act as a watchdog over the government procurement system and report regularly to government on how well industrial development objectives are being met. This would require an overall procurement plan from the government with specific goals to be achieved each year.

The Strategic Procurement Committee would use the Enabling R&D Contract Fund to award small, developmental (i.e., enabling) contracts prior to tendering a major contract. This would require anticipating major purchases years in advance and making this information known to the appropriate Canadian companies that might, perhaps with some technical help, be able to bid on the major contracts eventually. Small contracts for researching current technologies, writing specifications, and developing and testing prototype designs could then be awarded to one (or perhaps several) Canadian firms. This would give these firms an opportunity to develop a strong position in that product and increase the likelihood of their becoming the most qualified bidder once a contract is tendered to make a major purchase.

RISK SHARING WITH THRESHOLD FIRMS

Long-term economic prosperity in Ontario will depend on the

rapid growth of a number of indigenous medium-size exporters. No modern economy has been able to maintain successful industries in non-resource sectors without a core of strong world-wide indigenous firms. Ontario is lacking that core today (with a few exceptions, like Northern Telecom) and must build on the strength of dozens of medium-size ($40-400 million sales) firms which are on the threshold of becoming true multinationals. A number of large countries (U.S., Japan, U.K., France, etc.) are blessed with markets which are substantial enough to create world-scale companies on the basis of domestic sales alone. Canada faces the small country problem of needing to target export markets from an early point in the product life cycle.

Even Canadian firms of $100 or $200 million in sales find themselves to be small firms in a global sense. Ontario has probably 40-50 firms outside the resource sector which are "threshold firms". They are firms which are now becoming truly international competitors. One finds them in high growth areas like software, lasers, and telecommunications equipment, but also in auto parts, machinery, and plastics. Most have good basic technology, competitive cost positions, and proven success in exporting, but none has not yet reached a dominant position in its industry. Often they are competing against much larger, diversified multinational firms which can sustain losses in one business with cash flow from others. Typically, when they make a major new investment in a product line or opening up a new international market, it is of such significant size that they are almost "betting the company" on it.

Unfortunately, most provincial and federal programs offer little to these threshold companies. The bias toward fixed asset assistance in government programs is a particular problem since most of the strategic investments of many threshold firms are in product development, design, testing, marketing, and other areas where fixed assets are not very important.

In order to help speed the growth of Ontario threshold firms into more stable international competitors, we recommend the development of a program which will share the risks associated with these companies seeking to develop new products or markets.

Recommendation 7: ONTARIO RISK SHARING FUND
The Government should create an Ontario Risk Sharing Fund to provide conditionally reimbursable matching loans to successful, established exporting companies for investments in new product development, prototype placement in export markets, and the establishment of new marketing offices outside North America.

The fund should be focussed on threshold firms, although multinationals would not be turned away if they were indigenous and had suitable export-oriented projects. The fund would have the following characteristics:

- Loans would be available for up to 50 percent of total project costs, including new product development, design, and placement of prototypes, and/or establishment of marketing offices outside North America
- Loans would be repayable on a sliding scale, depending on the success of the project - no payback if the project fails and an above-market rate payback if it succeeds. The above-market rate would ensure that companies were not merely coming to the Risk Sharing Fund for low cost capital
- Since the goal is to build on strengths, only companies with a successful record of exporting would be funded
- The Fund should also have the flexibility to share the costs with companies (on a conditionally reimbursable basis) of feasibility studies for high Ontario value-added opportunities in new products or overseas markets
- Based on the experience of other countries such as Sweden and France, which have similar funds, such a program would aim to be self-sufficient after its initial capitalization.

24

The major industrial assistance agencies in the province are the Ontario Development Corporations. Charged with encouraging and assisting in the development and diversification of Ontario industry, the ODCs make available loans and investment monies mainly for new business start-ups, capacity expansions, and high risk ventures. They also provide a variety of business advisory services and play a major role in regional development efforts.

Unfortunately, the ODCs have exhibited many of the problems of government assistance to business discussed previously. They have assisted non-traded and traded businesses alike, focussed mostly on very small businesses, lent heavily for fixed assets and not R&D or marketing efforts, and emphasized slower growth industries and firms that have encountered difficulties. The government has already begun addressing these issues and refocussing the activities of the ODCs on middle-sized firms that have strong export performance or potential. The ODCs will continue to serve regional policy objectives, but they can and should move away from their non-traded business orientation and provide more assistance to larger businesses.

Recommendation 8: REFOCUS THE ONTARIO DEVELOPMENT CORPORATIONS

The Government should accelerate the refocussing of the Ontario Development Corporations according to the competitive priorities identified in this report.

Specifically, this will require adjusting the ODCs' own priorities to:

- Provide assistance only to businesses in manufacturing and tradable service sectors
- Build an active relationship with successful middle-sized companies and assist these firms to make the leap into world export markets
- Improve ODC response times for reviewing and processing applications to match the best industry standards
- Assist the development of Ontario's high growth industries by providing needed funds for prototype development and marketing as opposed to emphasizing fixed asset lending
- Orient all assistance to encourage companies to move to higher value-added products
- Emphasize these strategic priorities even when pursuing regional development objectives.

25

The shift in ODC priorities is already underway. Once completed the ODCs should be able to play a complementary role to the proposed Risk Sharing Fund. The ODCs could have two objectives: assisting in regional development and helping middle-sized Ontario companies in traded goods and services businesses move into world markets and over time attain threshold company status. In that sense, many firms might begin as clients of the ODCs and later, as they grew and developed, become clients of the Risk Sharing Fund. Because of their regional priorities, the focus of the ODCs will always be much broader than that of the Risk Sharing Fund.

IMPROVING THE ENTREPRENEURIAL CLIMATE FOR TRADED BUSINESSES

Ontario start-up companies in traded, high growth sectors will be important to the long-run prosperity of the province and require special attention. New businesses in Ontario, as in any jurisdiction, face a unique set of challenges that are not well addressed by broadly-based economic development policies. These businesses tend to be financed outside the mainstream of banking and other financial institutions, and they often do not have access to marketing and distribution channels routinely used by larger competitors. Yet a disproportionate share of important new products and services, as well as new employment creation, comes from these companies.

The Council conducted extensive research on start-ups in Ontario and recommends that any government assistance programs be based on the lessons drawn from that research. Ontario initiatives directed at start-ups should:

- Focus on manufacturing sectors and clearly traded services only
- Create a climate that tolerates failure; many entrepreneurs start several companies, often succeeding the second or third time around
- Support the success of growing indigenous Canadian firms which are the most likely incubators of new companies
- Encourage more venture capital to be directed to the seed and early stage financing of start-ups
- Foster a more participative venture capital industry in which fund managers take an active role in advising and sustaining the firms they fund (such participative funds are at the heart of the U.S. entrepreneurial successes in Silicon Valley and Boston).

26

Past efforts to aid start-ups have focussed mainly on a direct government role in venture capital. Such an approach does not yield much leverage on the government investment. Moreover, it does not put the emphasis on development of the participative venture capital expertise which Ontario lacks and needs. Instead of focussing on direct assistance to start-ups, the best and most highly leveraged help the government can give would be incentives to increase the sophistication of the venture capital industry and encourage its funds to flow to early stage financing in traded businesses.

Recommendation 9: EARLY STAGE VENTURE CAPITAL INCENTIVES
The Government should provide tax incentives for investments in a special class of early stage venture capital funds.

These funds would be established by private sector venture capitalists specifically to invest in qualifying businesses. Investors would receive a tax exemption on these investments. Qualifying businesses would include manufacturing or traded service businesses committed to achieving substantial export sales over the next five years.

A minimum of 20 percent of each fund would have to be set aside for seed capital investment, and the balance for investing in businesses of up to $10 million in sales (although follow-up second and third investments in firms would be allowed after they had passed that size). The fund could invest only in firms committed to maintaining significant production, R&D, and a head office presence in Ontario. Full-time professional management with an equity stake in the fund would be a requirement in order to encourage participative management assistance and oversight to the firms financed.

One of the major impediments to greater venture capital investment is the difficulty of exiting or selling a venture capital investment. In the U.S., public stock markets are the primary exit route, whereas in Canada, repurchase of shares or acquisition of the company still predominate. Making initial public stock offerings more accessible would enhance the liquidity of venture capital investment in Ontario, thereby making it more attractive to investors. The Quebec Stock Savings Plan was far too broadly designed and benefitted mainly large companies and non-traded sectors. Consequently, a much more focussed approach is recommended for Ontario:

27

Recommendation 10: INITIAL PUBLIC OFFERING INCENTIVE
The Ontario government should offer investors in the initial public offerings of Ontario companies in traded sectors a tax incentive significantly above the base level tax credit or deduction offered under the Ontario Recapitalization Incentive Plan described in Recommendation 1.

The Initial Public Offering Incentive would apply to first time offerings for firms meeting the requirements of the Ontario Recapitalization Incentive Plan. The incentive would be easy to administer as part of the plan. Its benefits would be to:

• Encourage early stage venture capital investment in traded start-up businesses by making the public share offering exit route more attractive
• Increase the capital available to threshold companies
• Foster a more entrepreneurial culture in Ontario which would lead to a higher formation of start-ups in traded businesses.

The importance of building an entrepreneurial culture to promote new business start-ups should not be overlooked. In recognition of this need to stimulate entrepreneurship in the province, the Premier's Council recommended and the Ontario government established six Centres of Entrepreneurship in provincial colleges and universities in 1987. These centres will offer programs and courses in entrepreneurial skills development. They will offer a unique learning opportunity for potential entrepreneurs to acquire the skills and knowledge needed to open and operate their own businesses.

MEETING THE SCIENCE AND TECHNOLOGY IMPERATIVE

The industrial competitiveness of a nation, today more than ever before, is influenced by its capabilities in science and technology. The industrial leadership of the United States can be attributed in large part to its research and development efforts. Japan's rise to international competitiveness required a rapid ability to adapt existing technology to new applications.

Research and development spending in Canada has not kept pace with the international requirements for competitive success. Our technological effort is too concentrated within government labs and lacks strategic focus. The industry R&D base is limited and fragile. Industry research and development is concentrated in a very small part of Canadian business, and a significant portion of it is performed by small- and medium-sized firms that must put their entire company at risk with each major technological investment.

28

There is a crisis in industrial R&D in Canada. Those few who know how serious the situation is have turned their attention to fighting to keep in place the few industrial R&D incentives which still exist, such as the federal R&D tax credit - the use of which Ottawa has now decided to limit. The widespread discussion given to setting a national R&D target of 2-3 percent of GDP draws attention to the nation's science and technology problems, but the focus on a general target has obscured the fact that the underlying crisis is really a low level of R&D in industry. Unfortunately, additional federal resources for science have generally not flowed to industrial purposes.

Compared to other countries, Canada spends a very high percentage of its government funding for science and technology in government laboratories. Some of these have well-defined public missions and do excellent research. Many, however, were set up or encouraged over time to be surrogates for the industrial research base lacking in the country. As surrogates, they are totally ineffective.

The old approaches to science and technology policy are no

longer viable. A major shift in public and private resources to greater science and technology investment will be required to meet the competitive challenges we face. However, these increased resources must be applied to the nation's industrial priorities and not used, as they were in the past, to build public surrogates for our weak corporate R&D base. The Council's recommendations for greater direct funding of industrial R&D and better procurement policies were described above. There is a need to implement these initiatives with a strong emphasis on a better defined role for university and government research.

Recommendation 11: RE-DIRECT GOVERNMENT RESEARCH TO INDUSTRY

Government should involve the private sector more effectively in university and government research and ensure that industrial priorities play a much more important role in guiding such research.

Specific steps that can be taken include:

• Ensure that 100 percent of R&D in government labs is mission-oriented, and if the R&D is oriented to business, it should be directed and co-funded by industry

• Encourage the federal government to shift a significant percentage of current government in-house research to industry under the direction of the private sector

• Where feasible, source necessary government research and development from private sector firms capable of building on it in developing commercial products

• Encourage universities to orient more research to industrial priorities; but dampen the expectations of what universities can do in short-term commercial research. Their primary role should be to train world-class graduates and be pre-eminent in longer term pre-competitive research.

A second priority in improving the science and technology infrastructure is to ensure that all companies that need it can use it. Unfortunately, among the hundreds of small- to medium-size Ontario companies in core industries like auto parts, metal fabrication, and plastics are many firms which do not yet have any substantial technological capability on staff and which are not fully aware of the technological opportunities open to them. In fact, over 70 percent of Ontario manufacturing firms do not employ any full-time engineers or scientists. In some cases, firms know they need to do more technologically but cannot justify the cost of hiring such personnel.

To address this problem and rapidly enhance the technological capability of Ontario firms in traded industries, the Council recommends the establishment of a Technical Personnel Assistance Program.

Recommendation 12: TECHNICAL PERSONNEL ASSISTANCE PROGRAM

Ontario should establish a Technical Personnel Assistance Program to encourage small- and medium-sized firms to accelerate their hiring of R&D, engineering and other technical personnel.

Qualifying firms would have less than $100 million in sales. Priority would be given to exporting firms, but it is also recognized that import replacement firms may become exporters and should also be given consideration. For each new technical job created, the employer would receive a subsidy of 50 percent of the new employee's salary in the first year and 25 percent in the second year. Positions qualifying for the subsidy would include technicians, engineers, and scientists.

In addition to reordering government priorities in research and enhancing the technological capabilities of small- and medium-sized firms, key aspects of the scientific and technological infrastructure need bolstering if Ontario is to remain competitive. In particular, the longer term pre-competitive research capability in Ontario's universities needs to be focussed and extended in those areas where the province's scientists and engineers have already attained a measure of excellence. A jurisdiction the size of Ontario cannot afford to be good at everything, but rather should strive to build on strengths and be a world leader in a small number of important new technologies.

The Premier's Council has already recommended and the government has established seven Centres of Excellence designed to stimulate advanced research in Ontario's critical areas of scientific endeavour. The Centres will draw on Ontario's best scientists and are expected to play a role in training and developing world-class researchers, both from Ontario universities and abroad.

Each Centre is comprised of both university and industry participants to encourage the transfer and diffusion of technology into industry. The Centres will receive a total of $200 million from the Technology Fund over a five-year period.

The seven Centres of Excellence are:

- Centre for Materials Research
- Telecommunications Research Institute of Ontario

30

- Centre for Advanced Laser and Lightwave Research
- Centre for Groundwater Research
- Centre in Information Technology
- Centre in Space and Terrestrial Science
- Centre for Integrated Manufacturing.

INVESTING IN PEOPLE

One of the key competitive challenges Ontario faces is developing our most fundamental natural resource: the minds and skills of our workers.

If the basic skills and knowledge acquired during early education determine the strength and competence of our workforce, then many of Ontario's students will be ill-equipped to meet the demands of the working world. Ontario student performance on basic skills tests has declined appreciably over the last two decades; their mathematical abilities are only average, according to the results of recent international comparative studies; and illiteracy rates among post-secondary students as well as the out-of-school population are alarmingly high. The 30 percent high school dropout rate for Ontario - one of the highest in the industrialized world - adds to this poor achievement record and points to the further problem of inadequate commitment to educational completion.

31

Although the Premier's Council is keenly interested in educational issues, it has been unable to pursue this area intensively given the breadth of its mandate. In its next agenda, the Council proposes to work in cooperation with the Ministries of Education, Colleges and Universities, Industry, Trade & Technology, and other relevant public policy groups to pursue an in-depth review of the education issues and devise strategic policy approaches to meet the challenges identified.

Equally important to tackling the challenge of improving educational performance is the need for more and better training of workers on the job and between jobs. Both Ontario and the federal government have major training programs in place to assist people beyond their formal schooling years. Unfortunately, because basic skills are often not mastered and more advanced technical knowledge is not introduced during formal education, much of the training effort is directed at teaching basics. This may account for the federal training strategy's concentration on access programs designed simply to facilitate entry into the workforce rather than develop industry-specific skills.

While it is essential that workers have the basic literacy and numeracy skills that will allow them to gain employment and function effectively in the workplace, their training must also be job-specific and compatible with the needs of industry. Because training undertaken by industry itself is limited primarily to major employers in only a few sectors, there is a need for government to provide incentives for increased training for industry and by industry.

The Council's work to date on education, training, and labour adjustment has only provided us with enough understanding of these "people issues" to realize that Ontario has serious problems in these areas that must be addressed. To build on that work and develop the necessary human resources strategy and programs to support the economic policy agenda we have set forth, we offer the following recommendation:

Recommendation 13: COMPREHENSIVE PEOPLE STRATEGY
The Premier's Council should work with appropriate areas of government to develop a comprehensive people strategy that will address vital education, training, and labour market policy issues as an integral part of its next agenda.

Having carried out some preliminary research into the education and training areas, the Council sees an immediate need to delve further into a number of key issues:

32

• The low literacy and basic skills levels of the workforce, and the availability of basic skills upgrading opportunities to meet their needs
• The various shortcomings of the apprenticeship system and how they can best be addressed
• Methods of increasing the amount and quality of training in industry through incentives or a regulatory framework
• The special training needs of older workers in restructuring industries and types of employment undergoing major adjustments
• The role of training in industrial adjustment, particularly in comparison to the training-for-adjustment experience of other jurisdictions.

The Council would expect that if this program is pursued, it will be able to put before the government next year a comprehensive people strategy and set of initiatives which build on the existing provincial efforts in education, training, and labour adjustment. This strategy should not be seen as a new or additional mandate for the Council, but rather as a natural and necessary complement to the economic initiatives recommended in this report.

BUILDING A NATIONAL CONSENSUS

A number of opportunities exist for bringing the provincial and national interests closer together. The Premier's Council firmly believes that building and sustaining international competitiveness must be viewed as a national goal and achieved co-operatively by the provincial and federal governments. Moving towards that goal is a matter of adopting, at both levels of public policy, a consistent, compatible, and complementary approach. We have outlined in the report a number of specific areas where such joint policies and programs could be effective.

In building public commitment for the agenda we are proposing, and in developing a consensus for similar initiatives in the nation as a whole, we are mindful of the important role that public symbols can play. The Council believes strongly that there is a need for leadership and excellence to be recognized and rewarded. Symbolic but highly visible recognition of excellence is an essential form of goal-setting that will provide a powerful incentive for those in the province who are involved in these activities to move towards higher achievement.

Recommendation 14: ONTARIO EXCELLENCE AWARDS
The Ontario Excellence Awards should be created to give recognition to individuals for their special contributions to making a better economic future for the people of the province.

33

The Council would see an annual celebration of the Ontario Excellence Awards in which people who are making outstanding contributions in their fields are recognized. This will give Ontarians whose special achievements merit acclaim an opportunity to be honoured. Areas for recognition of performance should include:

- Education
- Entrepreneurship
- Worker innovation
- Engineering
- Science

Excellence Awards in these areas would be distinct from the Order of Ontario in that they would recognize the achievements and unique contributions of people in the mainstream of their careers within strictly defined categories.

The Premier's Council is a new initiative in the public policy process in Canada. At its inception, the Council was a testing ground for the creation of a broad consensus mechanism that represented the diverse but compatible interests of the Ontario economy. The Council prides itself on having proven that such a consensus-building mechanism can indeed be effective in developing successful joint strategies.

CHAPTER I
COMPETING FOR PROSPERITY

Ontario is in the midst of an economic boom. The provincial economy has expanded at the rate of 4.4 percent a year since 1982; the total number of Ontarians employed has grown by 617,000 since that year; and real per capita income is rising. The signs of prosperity abound in heightened personal consumption, growing corporate profitability, and increasing government revenues. While some regions of the province, especially in the north and east, have not participated significantly in the economic expansion, they are the decided exceptions. In short, Ontario's record of economic growth is the envy of most of the rest of Canada.

Unfortunately, our current economic success will not guarantee our future prosperity. Indeed, there are clear signs amid this boom that many of our industries have significant competitive weaknesses in international markets. Moreover, the Council's research indicates that our scientific and technical capability, our education and training performance, and our government policies and programs as presently constituted will not be adequate to the new economic challenges we face.

35

The path to economic success is changing for Canadians. We cannot depend on our resources or our proximity to the United States for our continued prosperity. Nor should we rely on a declining Canadian dollar to keep us competitive in world markets. We have attained our present wealth by mastering a set of economic rules that are becoming steadily less relevant for our circumstances. In the future our prosperity will depend increasingly upon our ability to sustain a sufficiently large base of companies competing in world markets, not on the basis of lower labour or raw materials costs, but rather through technical innovation, skilled labour, adept marketing, and high productivity. Changes in the world economic system have forced this new reality upon us. As a small nation which must trade to survive, we cannot escape its logic.

We are now firmly ensconced in a new global economy in which our ability to compete will be increasingly called into question. Ontario is a major world trader, selling 35 percent of its goods abroad and importing about 41 percent of the goods it consumes. Our exports have traditionally been raw materials based or more recently, manufactured products, such as automobiles, produced as part of a North American production system. In both we have benefitted from our geographical proximity to the American market and from our cultural similarities with the U.S., which have allowed the production of similar products for both parts of the continent. Increasingly, though, these natural benefits of sharing geography and culture have become less important to assuring our future economic success.

The new global economy is one where the traditional barriers to international trade - shipping costs and differences in local customer tastes - have broken down. It now costs more to ship a ton of iron ore from Duluth, Minnesota to Pittsburgh than it does to ship it from Labrador or Brazil half way around the world to Japan. And the video recorder sold in Tokyo, Thunder Bay, or Tunisia is the same model for each market, though the instructions may be in Japanese, English, or Arabic. In spite of increasing non-tariff barriers in many countries, world trade continues to grow, and national economies everywhere are moving toward greater economic integration.

In this world of increasing trade, the relative industrial competitiveness of nations and provinces has become a major concern. Increases in prosperity must come from increased productivity in the creation of goods and services. But in a world of trade, absolute increases in productivity will not guarantee increases in wealth. If an Ontario automotive parts producer increases its productivity by two percent, while its international competitors increase theirs by five percent, provincial wealth in Ontario may actually decline as the Ontario parts producer loses sales and market share to its lower-cost foreign competitors.

When nations cannot maintain productivity growth in their internationally traded goods and services at rates equal to their competitors, they have only one alternative to remain viable in international markets: they must reduce their wages. The usual method for this is a currency devaluation. Devaluations boost exports because they reduce costs, but they do so at the expense of a nation's living standards. The current economic expansion in Ontario has been fueled by increasing productivity in some sectors, but much more important than productivity gains has been the falling value of the Canadian dollar. The dollar has risen somewhat recently, but our labour costs are still generally 20 percent lower than those in the U.S.

Short-term devaluations can be beneficial if used strategically to provide a breathing space for an economy when changes in international competition require a restructuring of industry and a re-deployment of investment to new opportunities. Sweden used such a short-term devaluation to good effect in the early 1980s to restructure its industrial base away from low wage businesses

EXHIBIT I.1
GDP PER CAPITA RELATIVE TO UNITED STATES
1960-86
United States = 100

	1960	1970	1986
United States	100	100	100
Japan	16	40	94
Denmark	46	65	92
Sweden	66	84	91
Ontario	90*	93	88
Germany	46	62	85
Canada	75*	79	83
France	47	56	74
Belgium	43	54	66
United Kingdom	49	45	57
Italy	26	38	51
Singapore	15	18	42
Ireland	22	27	37
Korea	6	6	18

*Ratio calculated for 1961
Sources: IMF, OECD, World Bank and U.S. Dept. of Commerce

like shipbuilding and declining resource industries like iron ore, to higher growth opportunities in manufacturing. A long-term devaluation strategy, however, is nothing more than a program of achieving international competitiveness through steady reductions in living standards.

Ontario may in effect be following such a strategy. Ontario's wealth creating capacity, as measured by gross domestic product (GDP) per person, has been increasing much more slowly than that of other countries. This problem can be illustrated by comparing Ontario's GDP per capita today with what it was in 1960 relative to major industrial nations (See Exhibit I.1). Ontario's GDP per person in 1960 was 90 percent of the U.S. rate and significantly higher than that of Canada as a whole, as well as those of other industrial countries. Sweden, with a GDP per capita of 66 percent of the U.S. rate, ranked second after Ontario.

By 1970, Ontario had improved its relative standing slightly to 93 percent of the U.S. rate, but most other countries had improved much more significantly. Most notably, Japan's GDP per capita had leapt from 16 percent of the U.S. rate in 1960 to 40 percent in 1970. As of 1986, Japan, Denmark, and Sweden had actually surpassed Ontario, and Germany had caught up to our level. The disparity between Ontario and the rest of Canada had also narrowed noticeably, even though Canada as a whole lost ground against every other nation in this group except the U.S. and the United Kingdom.

As Exhibit I.1 makes clear, the U.S. economy provides a false standard for Ontario to be measuring itself against, since most other nations are improving their output per person at a far faster rate than our American neighbours. Canada as a whole, the U.S., and the U.K. are the wrong jurisdictions with which to compare ourselves. The reality is that so far they and we have lost ground in the world economic race.

THE PROCESS OF WEALTH CREATION

Raising the value of output for every hour worked in the Ontario economy should be the primary economic goal for the province. With greater productivity, the same amount of labour can yield more goods and services. If employment levels are maintained as productivity increases, the result is greater material wealth, which in turn allows a higher standard of living.

Our standard of living is a combination of two things: the wealth we produce (GDP) and the goods it can buy (purchasing power). In Ontario, we are fortunate that our purchasing power is greatly enriched by the low cost of land, food, and certain public services such as health care (which costs Canadians a much smaller share of GDP than it does Americans). Our greater purchasing power means an Ontario autoworker can buy more with an equivalent amount of wealth than a Japanese autoworker can.

This greater purchasing power sometimes obscures our relative underperformance in wealth creation. No one can dispute that Ontarians experience one of the highest standards of living in the world, but that standard of living cannot be sustained by purchasing power alone. We must be able to create wealth at the level of other leading industrial nations. If we do not, we will find it increasingly difficult to maintain the social services and quality of life which Ontarians expect and deserve.

Increasing Value-Added Per Employee

The process of increasing productivity can be described as raising the value-added per employee in the economy. "Value-added" may be roughly defined as the cost of a finished product minus the raw materials and purchased services which were required to produce it. In a business, value-added includes payroll, profit, and capital amortization (See Exhibit I.2). Management and shareholders on the one hand, and labour on the other hand,

EXHIBIT I.2

BUSINESS VALUE-ADDED AND GROSS DOMESTIC PRODUCT

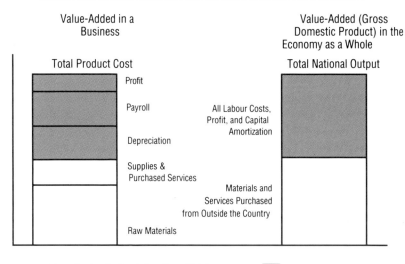

| Value-Added in a Business | Value-Added (Gross Domestic Product) in the Economy as a Whole |

Total Product Cost — Total National Output

Profit

Payroll — All Labour Costs, Profit, and Capital Amortization

Depreciation

Supplies & Purchased Services

Materials and Services Purchased from Outside the Country

Raw Materials

Source: Developed by Canada Consulting and Telesis

 Value-Added

39

may argue over how much value-added should be allocated to profits and how much to payroll, but if the total value-added per employee is increased, there is greater wealth for everyone to share.

The total value-added of all business, government, and other productive activities in the economy constitutes the gross domestic product. Just as the GDP per person is a measure of the wealth creation capacity of the province as a whole, the value-added per employee in a business or an industry is a measure of the wealth creation capacity of that business or industry.

Higher value-added per employee in the economy can come from increasing productivity in the existing mix of goods and services or by shifting the industrial structure of the province towards goods and services that are inherently higher value-added per employee activities. In the first instance, an Ontario steel producer increases its productivity in manufacturing an existing product, say basic sheet steel, thus increasing its value-added per employee. In the second instance, that same steel producer might shift its product mix more toward specialty steels, which require greater metallurgical expertise and customization of the product. These specialty steels are inherently higher value-added per employee products because of the greater knowledge and special skills required in their production and sales.

The process of continuously shifting production towards higher value-added per employee activities we call "industrial re-

structuring" - a process long underway in all advanced economies. Trade protection for low value-added per employee industries can slow the restructuring process down, but in the long
run, protecting and retaining such low wage jobs will impair the
wealth creation capability of a country. High wages require performing activities which result in high value-added per hour
worked.

But improvements in value-added per work hour are not
enough. Greater wealth can only be realized if workers displaced
by efficiency improvements or industrial restructuring find work
in other productive enterprises. Workers displaced by greater
productivity must be re-employed. This can only occur if the
economy is growing and developing new products, markets, and
businesses.

Focussing On Traded Businesses

Ontario must focus its economic policies on traded businesses -
that is, those industries which are exposed to world trade and
competition. Not all businesses in an economy play the same role
in economic development. In an open economy, some businesses
are primary to the wealth creation process, while others play a
derivative or secondary role. To illustrate the difference, imagine
an Ontario town made up of a steel mill, as well as various small
manufacturers, wholesalers, and retail stores which provide supplies for the mill and consumer goods for the employees. These
smaller firms may employ more people than the mill. But if one
of the retail stores fails, most likely the other stores will get its
business and hire some of the unemployed workers. There are no
major effects because the town's retail market is a closed system.
If the steel mill fails, however, everyone in the town will be seriously affected because it is the mill that is actually bringing in
substantial wealth to the town. The steel mill is a traded business; the wholesale and retail stores are non-traded businesses.

Similarly, the entire economy of a province or country is made
up of both traded and non-traded businesses. The traded sectors
in Ontario include most manufactured products. Only those
manufactured goods which are too costly to transport relative to
the cost savings available from increased manufacturing scale
are likely to be non-traded. Examples of such products include
fresh milk, which is difficult to transport, or large plastic mold-
ings, which are expensive to transport compared to the value of
the product. A small number of service businesses are traded:
parts of financial services, consulting engineering, software writing, and tourism are examples. By and large, however, most service businesses, including wholesale and retail trade, construction,

utilities, health care, and education are non-traded. Although an internationally-oriented hospital or university may attract customers from abroad, these are exceptions, and traded services account for a tiny fraction of total output in these sectors.

Prosperity in the non-traded sectors in Ontario will reflect the relative international prosperity of the traded sectors. A taxi cab driver or a doctor in Mexico City, whose jobs are in non-traded businesses, may be just as efficient as a cab driver or doctor in Toronto, but each will earn a fraction of what their Canadian counterparts make, in large part because of the difference in the value-added per employee in the traded sectors in Canada versus Mexico.

Moreover, only the traded sectors in overall Ontario employment are fundamentally at risk from international competition. The demise of individual firms within non-traded sectors will mean the rise of others. If one Ontario restaurant goes bankrupt, another will take its place since this service can only be provided locally. Overall employment in non-traded sectors is not directly threatened by foreign competition. However, if a traded business in Ontario goes bankrupt due to international competition, those jobs may be lost permanently and the products the business used to market will be supplied by foreigners.

For all these reasons, the traded sectors must be viewed as the fundamental drivers of our future wealth and prosperity. Unfortunately, public policies and programs intended to stimulate economic development have not recognized this necessary distinction between traded and non-traded businesses, a failing that will be discussed more extensively in Chapter III.

It is easy to understand why the non-traded sectors have traditionally figured prominently in the minds of public policy makers. After all, the non-traded sectors do account for the lion's share (at least two-thirds) of Ontario's economy (See Exhibit I.3). Furthermore, the non-traded sectors account for the bulk of new jobs and the majority of new business start-ups. But the job creation capacity of the non-traded sectors is tied to the wealth creation capacity of our traded sectors. Job creation in restaurants, hospitals, department stores, real estate, bus systems, secretarial services, law firms, accounting firms, florists, day care, delivery firms, janitorial services, and other fast-growing, non-traded parts of the Ontario economy will depend on increasing competitiveness and higher value-added per employee in our traded industries.

In focussing our research and recommendations primarily on the traded goods and services sectors, the Council has paid particular attention to the competitive performance of Ontario firms

41

EXHIBIT I.3

ECONOMIC ACTIVITY IN TRADED AND NON-TRADED SECTORS
Ontario

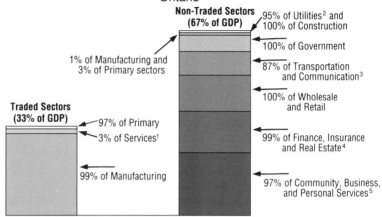

1 Traded sectors of services include parts of utilities, transportation and communication, finance, insurance, and community, business, and personal services
2 Parts of utilities - electricity generation is traded   3 Satellites and parts of shipping and air travel are traded
4 A small part of banking and life insurance is traded
5 Parts of management consulting, architects, engineers, accountants, and tourism are traded
Source: These are only general estimates derived by Canada Consulting and Telesis based on analysis of trade data, company interviews, and comparisons with similar analyses in the United States

in export markets. Although Ontario also trades with the rest of Canada, we have concentrated on Ontario's trade position with the outside world in the belief that increasing provincial wealth will require meeting international standards of competitiveness. If Ontario industries cannot compete abroad, trade within Canada alone will not preserve a high standard of living in the long run.

A FRAMEWORK FOR COMPETITIVE ANALYSIS

Evaluating the competitive health of Ontario's economy is not something which can be done effectively at an aggregate level. General economic measures offer a snapshot of the well-being of the province at any point in time, but are not likely to point to underlying systemic weaknesses or potential problems.

Statistical analyses of individual industries using the Standard Industrial Classification (SIC) code, while the stock in trade of microeconomists, are also fraught with problems of oversimplification. The process of competition differs significantly across businesses. Unfortunately, the SIC code categorization of industries makes analysis and grouping of businesses by their driving competitive factors almost impossible. Within single industries in the SIC codes are grouped many businesses with significantly different competitive dynamics.

For example, the manufacturing of airplanes is an industry that includes several different businesses, such as commercial jetliners, commuter aircraft, corporate jets, and propeller-driven two seaters. The markets, technologies, production methods, and requirements for growth will differ in each of these businesses. Their cost structures are different, as are the potential barriers to new competition. It would be extremely difficult for a manufacturer in one business to enter another's markets. Canadair with its corporate jets and De Havilland with its turboprop commuter planes are grouped together by SIC codes in the aircraft industry, but the businesses in which they actually participate are quite distinct and subject to different competitive factors.

Similarly, the chemical industry is composed of literally hundreds of different businesses, each with its own competitive dynamic. In businesses like ethylene or methanol, plant location, the scale of production facilities, and the output achieved at a given scale determine competitive success. For other parts of the chemical industry, these competitive factors are much less relevant. For example, in some specialty chemical businesses the applications engineering costs associated with developing custom formulations for different customer needs are the most important source of competitive advantage. A specific example of this type of business in Ontario is the applications engineering of specialty process chemicals for the pulp and paper industry to meet the different fibre and process characteristics of individual plants.

Specialty chemical businesses, where applications engineering costs are critical determinants of competitive success, often have more in common with specialty steel businesses requiring special formulations of steel than they do with other chemical businesses. Similarly, basic steel production may have more in common with bulk chemical manufacturing than it does with specialty steel businesses.

These differences can be critical from an economic policy point of view. Analyses of the steel industry's competitive position that do not take into account the significant competitive differences among steel business segments can be fatally flawed. Good competitive analysis must be done at the business segment level, and effective economic development policies should be grounded in an understanding of the key competitive differences that separate businesses from one another.

Naturally, it is impossible to analyze all of the hundreds of distinct traded businesses in Ontario in sufficient detail to understand their particular competitive dynamics. Instead, we have analyzed the range of competitive drivers in 15 broad industry categories[1] representing a high percentage of Ontario's traded in-

43

dustries. In each case we examined the dynamics of the most important specific business segments in addition to the general competitive problems facing the industry. We have also looked at the factors governing competition in the various products and markets of about 50 other leading Ontario exporters whose operations did not fall into the 15 categories selected for study. We have used these analyses and drawn on the experience of other countries[2] to develop a framework for examining Ontario's global competitive position. This framework groups businesses according to the broad means by which they can gain a competitive advantage over one another (See Exhibit I.4).

Gaining A Competitive Advantage

There are essentially two ways of gaining a competitive advantage in international markets:

- By producing and delivering your product at a lower total cost than your competitors can achieve
- By commanding a higher price for your product than others who produce similar goods or services.

44

Ontario newsprint producers compete on the first basis - namely, lower costs. Newsprint is a commodity which customers will purchase at the lowest price available. The relatively low cost position of Ontario newsprint gives it a competitive advantage in world markets up to the point at which transportation costs for the finished product negate the raw materials and energy advantages of the Ontario industry.

The Sony Corporation of Japan competes on a price premium basis in colour televisions. Design differences make Sony's televisions 20 percent more expensive to manufacture than its competitors' sets, but Sony's sets command prices 20-30 percent higher than other brands. Because Sony televisions are perceived as higher in quality, customers are willing to pay more for them.

To simplify our overview of Ontario's competitive position, we can characterize businesses in Ontario into three main types:

- Resource-based businesses

---

1. These industrial categories were very broad and were selected to obtain insights from a range of mature and high growth sectors. Some categories are not properly viewed as industries yet, but rather as emerging technologies. Others encompassed several industry groups. The categories studied included Advanced Materials, Aerospace, Automotive Vehicles and Parts, Biotechnology, Chemicals, Computer Hardware, Computer Software, Financial Services, Food Processing, Lasers, Nuclear Equipment, Pulp and Paper, Steel, Telecommunications Equipment, and Wood Industries.

2. In particular the framework draws upon previous economic development work by Telesis in Sweden, Ireland, France, Belgium, the United States, and Israel.

EXHIBIT I.4

A FRAMEWORK FOR ANALYSING
COMPETITIVE ADVANTAGE IN TRADED BUSINESSES

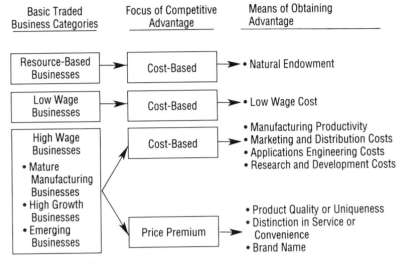

Basic Traded Business Categories	Focus of Competitive Advantage	Means of Obtaining Advantage
Resource-Based Businesses	Cost-Based	• Natural Endowment
Low Wage Businesses	Cost-Based	• Low Wage Cost
High Wage Businesses • Mature Manufacturing Businesses • High Growth Businesses • Emerging Businesses	Cost-Based	• Manufacturing Productivity • Marketing and Distribution Costs • Applications Engineering Costs • Research and Development Costs
	Price Premium	• Product Quality or Uniqueness • Distinction in Service or Convenience • Brand Name

Source: Developed by Telesis

- Low wage businesses
- High wage businesses

When we make comparisons between Ontario and other countries, we will separate high wage businesses into three sub-categories based on the state of their evolution: mature manufacturing businesses, high growth businesses, and emerging businesses.

Competitive Advantage In Resource-Based Businesses

In a resource-based industry, the relative quality of the raw material available to a company determines its competitive position. Most of Ontario's forest products and metals smelting industries, as well as segments of the food processing industry, are driven by raw materials costs. Other costs, such as labour or marketing, may play a role in competition, but in these businesses the critical determinant of competitive advantage is a company's raw materials position.

For example, in the processing of many non-branded commodity food products, the cost of raw materials determines competitive success in the long run. A quick look at the cost structure of an Ontario processed meats product illustrates why (See Exhibit I.5). About 65 percent of the cost of such a product is raw materials. Labour costs are a distant second factor at 15 percent, and no

EXHIBIT I.5
COST STRUCTURE OF AN ONTARIO PROCESSED MEAT PRODUCT

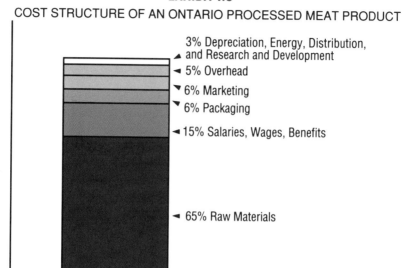

3% Depreciation, Energy, Distribution, and Research and Development
◀ 5% Overhead
▼ 6% Marketing
▼ 6% Packaging
◀ 15% Salaries, Wages, Benefits

◀ 65% Raw Materials

Source: Canada Consulting and Telesis interviews and analysis

other component accounts for more than six percent of the total. In this type of business, the cost of raw materials is extremely critical in one country's attempt to gain competitive advantage over another. Newsprint is a similar business in that the delivered cost of the raw material (wood) is the most important factor in determining relative competitive success among nations.

The key to identifying which businesses are resource-based is whether or not the most decisive factor in long-run competition is the cost of the raw material. However, analysis of cost structures alone will not determine which businesses are raw materials cost driven. For example, over 90 percent of the cost of a basic petrochemical refinery product may be raw materials, but given an open world market for crude oil and the ease of transporting crude, it may be difficult for any company to gain a materials cost advantage.

In most resource-based industries, the factor which makes resource costs critical to competitive success is the transportation costs of shipping the raw material. In the Ontario processed meats example above, the limitation would be the high cost of shipping live animals; in the newsprint business, it would be transportation of the unprocessed timber or wood chips.

Which countries succeed in resource-based businesses is very much a matter of inheritance. Such businesses depend on the physical and climatic endowments of a nation or province.

Ontario's soil and climate are favourable for softwood based newsprint production and for raising meat animals. Japan's mountain air and rocky soil are generally favourable for neither. Ontario's nickel deposits - historically the richest in the world - enabled Ontario nickel smelters to be low cost producers and capture much of the world market. In recent years, however, they have come under competitive pressure as new low cost deposits of nickel have emerged in other parts of the world. Technological ingenuity and productivity improvements have made Ontario's nickel more competitive, but in the long run the industry's success will be driven by the relative quality of its raw materials deposits.

Competitive Advantage In Low Wage Businesses

In low wage businesses, the cost of hourly labour is the most important competitive factor. Such businesses are characterized by a relatively slow pace of product innovation, production processes that are not proprietary and which can be easily standardized, and a low proportion of skilled labour in the work force.

A number of newly industrializing countries have total labour costs per hour (including benefits) ranging from Cdn.$1.75 in Korea to $.35 in China. When specific industrial activities can be carried out with sufficient productivity and quality in these countries, low wage rates become necessary to compete internationally. These then become low wage businesses. This is now the case in activities as diverse as building ships, sewing men's shirts, and assembling radios, small televisions, and some integrated circuits. It is not in the national interest, nor is it possible from a business point of view, to maintain manufacturing in these activities in a country with high living standards.

Developing countries have always had substantial wage rate advantages over the developed world, but only in recent years have they been able to use their low wages to achieve competitive success. Several factors came together over the past 20 years to assist low wage countries in developing export industries:

• World capital flows became freer and banks in developed countries became more adept at lending capital for developing country enterprises
• The concentration of retail outlets in industrialized countries greatly eased the marketing task of developing country firms, which can now sell to a reasonable share of the U.S. or Canadian market through a dozen large retail chains like The Bay or Eatons
• The latest production technology in many mature industries

is now held by engineering or construction firms that will sell it to any buyer. A developing country can purchase the world's most modern steel mills, metal smelters, paper machines, fertilizer plants, or integrated circuit insertion machines, as well as the training and technical supervision to go with them

• The falling costs and increasing reliability of high-speed communications and global transportation links have also assisted less developed countries to establish successful trading opportunities. The overseas sourcing pipeline from initial product ordering to finished goods delivery has shrunk to a very manageable length in many businesses

• Finally, all of these factors have assisted in the emergence of an entrepreneurial middle class which has become the driving force behind rapid industrialization in many developing countries.

Many of these same forces, especially greater capital flows and access to state-of-the-art technology, have also increased the competitive pressure from less developed countries in Ontario's resource industries.

It is important to note that whole businesses do not usually become low-wage driven. Often, only a portion of the production process in a business is standardized, sufficiently labour-intensive, and portable enough that it can be performed in a low wage location. Thus, integrated circuit assembly has generally been performed in low wage locations in southeast Asia, while circuit design and fabrication has remained in developed countries. Similarly, the more complex and skilled portions of the automotive industry, like automatic transmission manufacturing, have remained in developed countries, while simpler unskilled labour operations, like wiring harness production, have moved to low wage locations like Mexico.

Over time, as developing countries gain increasing experience and skills, they move to more complex manufacturing operations. Korea has moved beyond monochrome TVs to become a low cost exporter of colour TVs to North America. Korea has also successfully launched its automotive industry in world markets. In fact, Canada was the first proving ground for Hyundai's car exports with the launch of the Pony in 1985. Over the next few years, Canadian consumers will be buying economy cars made in Mexico, Taiwan, and Thailand as well.

As Korea has moved into higher value-added per employee businesses, it has begun to cede lower value-added businesses to others coming up the competitive ladder. China and Thailand, for example, have become major exporters of basic ceramics, simple clothing, and many other low wage products. In similar fashion, Japan long ago left many low wage businesses to other countries and focussed its development on high value-added activities in chemicals, computers, materials, electronics, and other areas. Those high value-added businesses which are still beyond the capabilities of most low wage countries constitute our third business category: high wage businesses.

Competitive Advantage In High Wage Businesses

High wage businesses include all internationally traded products in which competitive advantage is not gained primarily on a raw materials cost or low wage basis. In theory, any country, regardless of its raw material endowment or wage rates, has the possibility of succeeding in these businesses. In practice, these businesses are predominately in developed countries which have more of the strategic resources necessary for success in industries where wage rates are relatively less important.

Businesses consist of various functional activities, such as product and process engineering, raw material purchasing, manufacturing, marketing, and distribution. While each of these functions is present in all businesses, their relative importance varies by business. For example, in the packaged personal computer software business, product development and marketing costs are over 70 percent of the total product costs, whereas manufacturing and purchased materials costs are only 14 percent. The competitive dynamics of the packaged software business quite logically revolve around product development, marketing, and distribution. For an Ontario manufacturer of specialty engine components sold to the aerospace industry, manufacturing costs are 57 percent of total product cost, while product development and marketing accounts for less than five percent of product cost (See Exhibit I.6). The competitive dynamics of this aerospace engine component business revolve around manufacturing.

Success in high wage businesses can be based on the creation of a sustainable cost advantage or on product differentiation that makes customers willing to pay a price premium for a company's goods or services. Creating a sustainable cost advantage in these businesses is not a matter of being the low cost competitor in every element of the cost structure. In general, competition will centre on one or two key areas of cost. The largest element in the cost structure is not necessarily the one that offers the greatest opportunity for competitive advantage. As we saw earlier, raw materials account for over 90 percent of the total production cost

EXHIBIT I.6

COST STRUCTURES DIFFER DRAMATICALLY BY BUSINESS

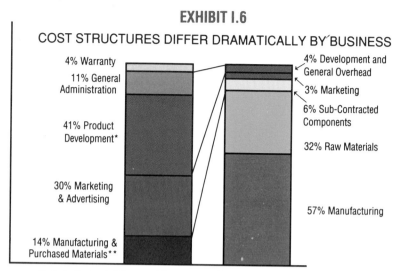

4% Warranty
11% General Administration
41% Product Development*
30% Marketing & Advertising
14% Manufacturing & Purchased Materials**

4% Development and General Overhead
3% Marketing
6% Sub-Contracted Components
32% Raw Materials
57% Manufacturing

Ontario Packaged Personal Computer Software Product Cost Structure

Ontario Specialty Aerospace Engine Component Cost Structure

* Development includes quality assurance, manual writing, and management time
** Manufacturing includes copying diskettes and manuals and packaging
Sources: Telesis and Canada Consulting Interviews and Analysis

50

of a typical refinery product, but because of the open market for crude oil, it is difficult for any company to obtain a materials cost advantage. Cost competition in refinery products thus revolves around relative production scale and output for a given scale level.

At the risk of oversimplification, there are four major means by which Ontario companies can gain a competitive cost advantage in high wage businesses. In most businesses several of these cost drivers will combine to determine overall cost leadership:

- Manufacturing Productivity - Depending on the business, competitive advantage may be realized through plant or machine scale, process yields, proprietary process technology, product design, automation, or the organization and management of the production process
- Marketing and Distribution Costs - In a business with a fragmented customer base and in which many small customers have significant requirements for after-sales service and/or spare parts, a low cost position can be achieved by obtaining a high market share in a given product line or region
- Applications Engineering Costs - In businesses where products must be engineered for specific customer uses, cost advantages can be obtained through standardization of applications

across many sales
• Research and Development Costs - When products are technologically sophisticated, have high purchase prices, and the market is fragmented, high market share can allow for wide amortization of R&D costs and a significant competitive advantage.

The Importance Of Scale And Market Share

In many of these competitive areas, scale is an important factor. Scale in manufacturing, in marketing, in applications engineering, or in R&D can all be important to competitive success. The dimension of scale which is critical will vary by business. Typically, the most important dimension of scale overall will be the share of a total product market segment that a company holds relative to its competitors. A high market share will tend to compound some of the competitive advantages mentioned above. In other words, firms with high market shares often benefit from a combination of manufacturing, marketing, applications engineering, and R&D cost advantages.

Our analyses consistently found that Ontario manufacturers which were successful exporters in high wage industries had achieved a high market share in their core product lines. Often, these were very specific niches. Exhibit I.7 lists a dozen such successful exporters and their market shares abroad. In a jurisdiction the size of Ontario, overall economic success can be based in large part on competitive dominance of several hundred product market segments in high wage businesses. Focussing on such small segments can overcome part of the small home country market problem.

Ontario firms often suffer scale disadvantages when they try to export to much larger markets against foreign competitors whose home bases give them sufficient scale to be lower cost. In small product market niches, no country, however large, constitutes a sufficient scale market. In these businesses, any successful competitor must serve many markets. Thus, a Canadian producer could be on equal footing with a U.S., French, or Japanese producer going abroad. (Naturally, such product niches are only appropriate if Ontario companies can create defensible competitive positions within them based on some factor of production).

Winning Through Price Premiums

Not all competition in high wage industries is decided on a cost basis. In some businesses, firms are able to develop a sustainable price premium in the marketplace. A higher price allows higher profits and/or greater investment in continued product

EXHIBIT 1.7

EXAMPLES OF ONTARIO FIRMS THAT HAVE DOMINATED SPECIFIC
NORTH AMERICAN OR WORLD MARKET NICHES

Industry Area	Business Segment	Company's Estimated Share of Business Segment
Plastic bottle preform systems	• Plastic bottle molds	85% of North America
Computer software	• 4th generation languages for a specific hardware environment	70% of World
Microelectronics	• Integrated circuits for miniature auditory devices	60% of World
Auto parts	• Transmission oil coolers	60% of North America
Lasers	• Industrial marking lasers	60% of World
Specialty steel	• Flat armour plate for military tanks	50% of North America
Telecommunications	• 0-100 line small PBX systems	35% of North America
Logging equipment	• Skidders	27% of World
Computer graphics equipment	• Sophisticated video post-production equipment	25% of North America
Electronic publishing	• CD ROM full text retrieval software	20% of North America
Computer graphics equipment	• Toy design software	20% of North America
Computer hardware and software	• Multi-user, library systems	15% of World

differentiation to sustain the price premium.

A company can achieve a price premium through:

- A special product quality or unique capabilities
- More convenient distribution or better service
- Creation of a brand name

There are many examples in Ontario of firms that have succeeded in world markets by achieving a price premium which often overcomes higher product costs. For instance, GEAC computers and software systems for libraries were often sold at a price premium over competitors due to the product's superior features. The Candu nuclear reactor has unique technology and superior safeguards. Some countries have been willing to pay for what they believe is a more reliable product that will have better uptime and lower operating costs.

In the food processing industry, Canada's distillers and pork producers have succeeded in selling into export markets on a substantial price premium basis. The Seagrams and Hiram Walker brand names account for Canadian whisky's ability to sell at a price premium. In the case of Canadian pork, American consumers are willing to pay more because it is a leaner product which is perceived as healthier.

53

ONTARIO'S COMPETITIVE POSITION

The high wage category of businesses described above can be further separated into three sub-categories based upon the state of evolution in each business:

- Mature Manufacturing Industries
- High Growth Industries
- Emerging Industries

Mature manufacturing industries include those high wage businesses which are fully developed and in which market growth is relatively slow. Industries which have many business segments that could be called mature include agricultural machinery, automotive, steel, chemicals, paper mill machinery, construction and mining machinery, tires, televisions, appliances, and printing and publishing. Obviously, some parts of these industries are low wage driven and others may be high growth, but on the whole they are constituted by mature manufacturing business segments.

High growth industries are fully developed high wage businesses in markets that are growing quickly. For statistical purposes, we have defined the high growth category to include all businesses which were growing by 20 percent per year in gross value-added over the period 1975-80 in the U.S.[3] Such high growth businesses can be found in areas like optical instruments, computers, medical equipment, pharmaceuticals, telecommunications equipment, aircraft, and office machinery.

Emerging industries are high wage businesses where the base of scientific knowledge is still being developed and competition mainly revolves around technological breakthroughs. Such industries have fast growth rates, but unlike those businesses included in our high growth category, well-defined markets and competitors are only beginning to emerge. Large parts of the laser and biotechnology industries are emerging industries.

The following chapters will discuss Ontario's competitive position in many industries using the framework just described. Although conventional industry categories like chemicals or automotive will be used, it must be remembered that these broad industries are made up of dozens or even hundreds of individual businesses, each with different competitive dynamics. The automotive industry will be discussed under the heading of mature manufacturing industries, but parts of it are low wage businesses and other parts are high growth. Similarly, pulp and paper will be discussed under the resource-based industry category, even though some of the high value-added business segments in the paper industry are not raw materials cost dependent. These segments would more properly belong in the mature manufacturing category. And even though we will categorize much of the clothing, textile, and footwear industries under the heading of low wage businesses, there are many segments that are not low wage driven and where developed countries can still compete effectively. High value fashion clothing, highly automated production of textiles, and specialized footwear for winter climates are all examples of such businesses in Canada.

To provide an overview in this chapter of Ontario's competitive position in world markets, we have gathered readily available statistical data on all manufacturing industries at a sub-segment level in nine countries and Ontario. This data has been reclassified according to the competitive industrial framework described above: resource-based industries, low wage industries, mature manufacturing industries, and high growth industries. Because so little data was available on emerging industries, it was impossible to provide a meaningful comparison of Ontario's performance in those businesses. Thus, emerging industries were included in the high growth business category for comparative purposes.

The Measures For Comparison

Two readily available international measures can indicate national success at achieving and sustaining international competitiveness and increased wealth generating capability:

- A positive balance of trade demonstrates competitiveness
- Total value-added per employee represents the level of national wealth creation capability.

If increasing competitiveness, as represented by a positive trade balance, is achieved by wage cuts, then value-added per employee will decline. On the other hand, if an industry becomes seriously uncompetitive, its level of value-added will be unsustainable. Prosperity depends on an increase in both competitiveness and value-added.

In Exhibit I.8 these two measures are arrayed on a single chart. The vertical axis represents international competitiveness with exports divided by imports. The horizontal axis represents weighted value-added per employee in U.S. dollars. Countries should be positioning themselves higher on the chart (for competitiveness) and to the right (for increasing standards of living).

Ontario's Position In Resource-Based Industries

Ontario's resource-based businesses are both internationally competitive and contribute substantially to provincial living standards. Exhibit I.9 compares Ontario's resource-based industries to those in Canada as a whole and in eight other countries. In addition to Ontario, only Sweden, Australia, and Canada have significant trade surpluses in their resource-based sectors.

While the U.S. has high value-added per employee in its resource-based industries, it suffers a major trade deficit.[4] The circle size in the exhibit corresponds to the proportion of total manufacturing employment in each country. Canada has the largest share of its manufacturing workers in the resource-based industries; Australia has the next largest. The high proportion of workers in the resource-based sector means that the value-added contributed by these industries in Canada is more important to

---

4. These are manufacturing comparisons only. Unprocessed raw materials are not included.

EXHIBIT I.8

A FRAMEWORK FOR INTERNATIONAL INDUSTRIAL COMPARISONS

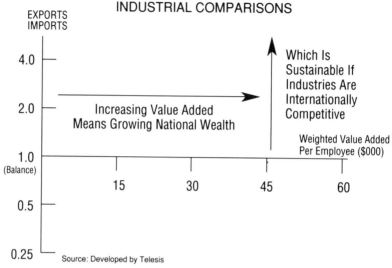

Source: Developed by Telesis

EXHIBIT I.9

RESOURCE BASED INDUSTRIES STRENGTH OF MANUFACTURING STRUCTURE

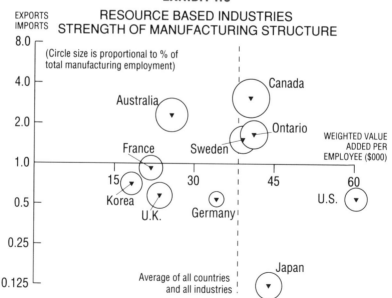

Source: Analysis by Telesis based on individual country statistical sources and U.N. Trade Statistics Yearbook.
Trade data is 1985. Value-added data is 1983 which is most recent for all countries adjusted to 1986 exchange rates

overall prosperity than may be the case in other countries.

Ontario's Position In Low Wage Industries

As one would expect, Ontario is extremely uncompetitive in low wage businesses (See Exhibit I.10). In fact, all industrialized countries except Japan have trade deficits in low wage industries. Although Japan has been exiting low wage businesses, it still maintains a low wage sector, mainly consisting of small sub-supplier businesses which are outside the Japanese economic mainstream.

Korea has a huge trade surplus in low wage industries, where a large portion of its manufacturing workforce is employed. Surprisingly, Canada still retains a significant chunk of employment in low wage businesses - more than in the high growth sectors we

will discuss below. This low wage sector owes its existence mainly to tariff barriers that limit developing country competition.

Ontario's Position in Mature Manufacturing Industries

The largest contribution to provincial wealth comes from the

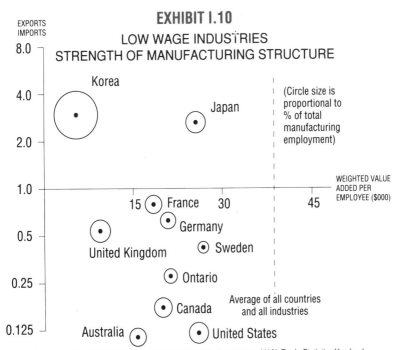

EXHIBIT I.10
LOW WAGE INDUSTRIES
STRENGTH OF MANUFACTURING STRUCTURE

Source: Analysis by Telesis based on individual country statistical sources and U.N. Trade Statistics Yearbook.
Trade data is 1985. Value-added data is 1983 which is most recent for all countries adjusted to 1986 exchange rates.

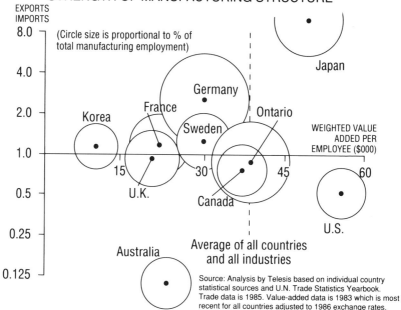

EXHIBIT I.11

MATURE MANUFACTURING INDUSTRIES
STRENGTH OF MANUFACTURING STRUCTURE

Source: Analysis by Telesis based on individual country
statistical sources and U.N. Trade Statistics Yearbook.
Trade data is 1985. Value-added data is 1983 which is most
recent for all countries adjusted to 1986 exchange rates.

58

mature manufacturing group of industries (See Exhibit I.11).
Only in Germany does this sector account for a larger portion of
total manufacturing employment. Ontario's slight trade deficit in
these industries demonstrates their moderate competitiveness.
Japan is dramatically more competitive than all other countries
and has higher value-added per employee than all but the U.S. In
Germany, Sweden, and France, the strong positive trade balances indicate a high degree of competitiveness, although their
value-added levels are below Ontario's.

The competitiveness problem facing the U.S. is starkly illustrated here. The U.S. has achieved high value-added per employee in these core manufacturing sectors, but it cannot hope to
sustain that level of wealth creation at its current level of poor
competitiveness. The steady fall of the dollar in 1987 has reduced
the relative value-added per employee in the U.S. in an effort to
improve U.S. competitiveness. All figures in Exhibit I.11 are in
1986 U.S. dollars. At end of 1987 exchange rates, the Japanese
value-added per employee would have reached U.S. levels in
these businesses.

Ontario must focus on boosting productivity in its mature
manufacturing sectors significantly if it hopes to remain competitive and raise value-added per employee in the coming years. The

dependence of Ontario on these businesses makes such improvements vital.

Ontario's Position In High Growth Industries

High growth businesses are critical for the future prosperity of industrialized countries. They include industries like telecommunications equipment, computers, aerospace, and medical equipment. Ontario has a serious competitive problem in high growth industries (See Exhibit I.12). The province has a major trade deficit here; it imports almost twice as much of these goods as it exports.

The situation for Ontario is even worse than for Canada as a whole. This is partly because Ontario's large, mature manufacturing and technology-intensive non-traded sectors import such significant amounts of these products. It is also due to the fact that other parts of Canada do have significant exports in some of these sectors, especially in telecommunications equipment and aerospace.

The seriousness of Ontario's position is demonstrated in three ways. The first is that all other countries except Australia and Korea have trade surpluses in these industries. Even Korea's

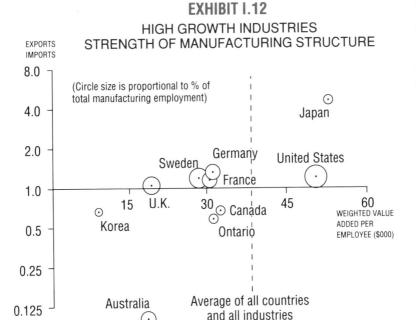

EXHIBIT I.12
HIGH GROWTH INDUSTRIES
STRENGTH OF MANUFACTURING STRUCTURE

Source: Analysis by Telesis based on individual country statistical sources and U.N. Trade Statistics Yearbook. Trade data is 1985. Value-added data is 1983 which is most recent for all countries adjusted to 1986 exchange rates.

trade position in these industries is better than Ontario's. The second is that, on a value-added basis, Ontario is at the same relative level as Germany, France, and Sweden, whereas in the mature manufacturing industries, Ontario has decidedly higher value-added per person than do those countries. Finally, these high growth industries account for a smaller part of Ontario's manufacturing employment than they do in all other jurisdictions except Japan (with its large low wage sector), Korea, and Canada as a whole.

THE HEART OF ONTARIO'S COMPETITIVE PROBLEM

The overall competitive problem facing the province is succinctly illustrated in Exhibit I.13. The resource-based industries are still competitively strong and offer high value-added per employee overall relative to the other Ontario manufacturing groups. However, their potential for expansion is limited by the quality of the raw materials in Ontario. While the province's existing natural resource base is well-established and new low cost resources may be found or become accessible, substantial growth is unlikely, especially in light of increasing competition from developing countries which are only beginning to exploit their resources fully.

The low wage businesses in Ontario, by definition, contribute very low value-added per employee and are therefore uncompetitive. They are declining and should continue to diminish in im-

EXHIBIT I.13

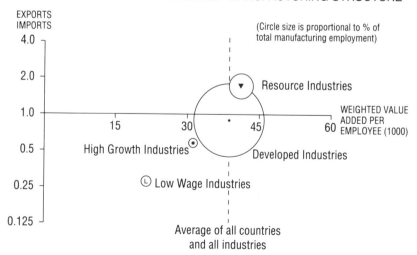

ONTARIO'S OVERALL STRENGTH OF MANUFACTURING STRUCTURE

Source: Analysis by Telesis based on individual country statistical sources and U.N. Trade Statistics Yearbook.
Trade data is 1985. Value-added data is 1983 which is most recent for all countries adjusted to 1986 exchange rates.

portance. Ontario manufacturers in these industries will increasingly focus on more defensible, higher value-added niches, such as fashion clothing, and not rely on continual tariff protection.

The mature manufacturing industries are the backbone of Ontario's economy and create most of the wealth in the traded sectors. However, these manufacturers face two difficulties: growth in their markets is slowing, and they are meeting increasing international competition. Although they will constitute Ontario's engine of wealth creation for some time to come, increasingly their contribution will need to be augmented by the value-added of high growth industries.

Herein lies Ontario's biggest competitive problem. The high growth sector as a whole is tremendously uncompetitive and has low value-added per employee relative to what one would expect from Ontario's overall value-added position. This relatively low value-added per employee results from a lack of capital intensive high growth businesses and the fact that many firms in this sector are foreign-owned and do not perform their really high value-added activities in Ontario. Such activities as research and development, product design, manufacturing engineering, corporate strategy development, marketing management, and some of the higher skilled manufacturing operations tend to be carried out on foreign-owned firms' home turf.

Ontario needs economic policies that can assist companies in all business areas to improve their competitiveness and raise their value-added per employee. But special attention will need to be paid to those high growth industries which are at the heart of Ontario's competitive problem and which must play an increasing role in sustaining prosperity over the long term.

CHAPTER II
BROADENING THE CORPORATE BASE

The preceding chapter discussed broad competitive problems facing many of Ontario's most important industries. Analyzing the competitive position of the province by business area sheds one kind of light on our current problems and opportunities. A complementary and equally important understanding of our economy can be gained by looking at the corporate structure of the province and its vulnerability to the changing demands of international competition.

THE DEPENDENCE ON MATURE MANUFACTURING

Ontario's exports are dominated by mature manufacturing businesses. Exhibit II.1 draws on a detailed analysis of the 336 leading exporters in Ontario[1], all with over $10 million in exports

EXHIBIT II.1
EXPORTS FROM ONTARIO'S 336 LEADING FIRMS
BY TYPE OF BUSINESS

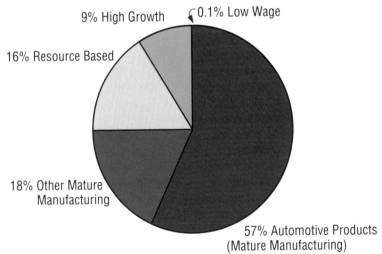

9% High Growth   0.1% Low Wage

16% Resource Based

18% Other Mature Manufacturing

57% Automotive Products (Mature Manufacturing)

Source: Telesis and Canada Consulting categorization and analysis. Information drawn from an MITT database of 336 leading Ontario exporters (over $10 million in exports), updated and classified by consultant interviews, mail questionnaires, and company annual reports

---

1. This analysis was drawn from an MITT database of leading Ontario exporters which was updated and reclassified by Canada Consulting and Telesis by type of business using interviews, mail questionnaires, and company annual reports. The total population of 336 companies exported $49 billion from Ontario in 1985 and accounted for about 83 percent of all goods exported from Ontario. Exports refers to goods sent out of the country, not to other provinces.

in 1985, to illustrate the extent of this dominance. Fully 75 percent of the exports of these leading firms were in mature manufacturing businesses; 57 percent of all exports were from the automotive industry alone. The three leading exporters were the Big Three vehicle companies - GM, Ford, and Chrysler - which accounted for 48 percent of all exports from the 336 firms.

The dominance of mature manufacturing in Ontario's exports owes both to the strength of a few mature industries, such as automotive and steel, and the comparative weakness of Ontario in high growth industries. That relative weakness is illustrated starkly by Exhibit II.2, which compares the share of value-added in high wage industries accounted for by high growth industries in Ontario and nine other jurisdictions. Only 10 percent of Ontario's high wage industry value-added comes from high growth businesses; the other 90 percent derives from mature industries. Ontario's proportion of high growth businesses is just two-fifths of the American and Swedish levels, and only Korea has a smaller high growth segment. Japan, like Ontario, is still very dependent on its mature manufacturing businesses, but unlike Ontario, it has achieved a position of world dominance in

64

EXHIBIT II.2

THE SHARE OF VALUE-ADDED IN HIGH WAGE INDUSTRIES ACCOUNTED FOR BY HIGH GROWTH INDUSTRIES

1985

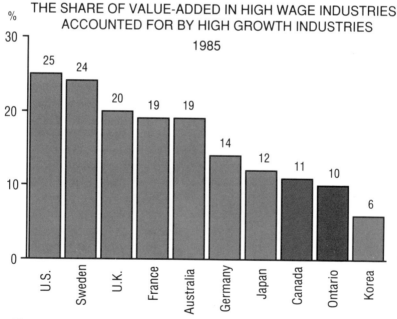

* Resource-based and low wage industries are not included

Source: Telesis and Canada Consulting based on recategorization and analysis of industrial value-added data collected from each jurisdiction

many of them. Japan is also shifting much more rapidly into these high growth sectors than is Ontario.

Ontario's high concentration of exports in mature manufacturing and resource-based industries has been an historical strength of the province. As we approach the future, our near total reliance on these traded sectors could pose several structural problems for the economy. For example, as high growth industries increase in importance world-wide and their output becomes an established part of consumption patterns in developed countries, Ontario could have a steadily deteriorating trade position. This is already the case in computer hardware, where Ontario has a nearly $3 billion deficit (up in real terms from $1 billion in 1979) and in software, where Ontario has an additional $2-3 billion trade deficit which is growing by 20-30 percent per year.

Ontario's large mature manufacturing sector has been and will increasingly be a major consumer of advanced technology as it modernizes and restructures itself. This in itself can contribute significantly to a deteriorating trade balance in the products of high growth industries. For example, most of Ontario's robots are used in the automotive industry. Unfortunately, almost all of those robots are imported.

The concentration of the traded economy in mature manufacturing and resource-based industries creates a relative growth problem as well. Overall growth in demand in most of these businesses is less than in the economy as a whole. Ontario companies can and sometimes do grow much faster than their specific industries by increasing their productivity much faster than their competitors. Magna International and Woodbridge Industries in automotive parts are two Ontario companies growing very quickly in businesses that are growing slowly. Nevertheless, over the long run high growth industries will offer the greatest opportunity for continued expansion of provincial wealth. The Ontario weakness in high growth businesses calls into question Ontario's ability to grow at a pace commensurate with leading industrial nations over the long term.

The concentration of the province in a few mature manufacturing and resource-based businesses, which are often closely linked like the automotive industry and its major suppliers in glass, rubber and steel, presents a significant risk that more diversified economies do not face. The demand for large-ticket consumer durable goods such as automobiles fluctuates more than does the economy as a whole during business cycles. Greater economic diversification would help Ontario limit its vulnerability to the continuing process of restructuring in the economy and the

65

vicissitudes of the business cycle. It would also reduce the susceptibility of the economy to changes in markets or technologies which could significantly diminish one of its core industries.

Finally, the greatest vulnerability presented by the intense reliance on mature manufacturing is the tremendous international competitive pressure on many of these industries. The automotive industry in North America must cope with the entry of substantial new capacity in assembly and automotive parts. Although the leading companies in Ontario's mature manufacturing sectors are improving their productivity and moving to higher value-added products, many of those firms are restructuring only slowly and will be increasingly vulnerable to new entrants into North America. Ontario's dependence on mature manufacturing makes this vulnerability a more serious problem than it would be if the province had a large and vibrant high growth sector.

THE NEED FOR INDIGENOUS WORLD-SCALE FIRMS

An even greater structural vulnerability of the Ontario economy is the lack of indigenous world-scale companies outside the resource-based industries. By indigenous we mean companies which direct their strategic planning, marketing, research and development, product design, manufacturing, and administration from a Canadian base. They may or may not be Canadian-owned. Most Canadian-owned firms are indigenous, but few foreign firms are. Some notable exceptions include Pratt and Whitney Canada, Mitel, and De Havilland Aircraft.

66

What determines whether a firm is indigenous is how it operates. A firm is indigenous if:

• Decisions about allocating strategic resources are made from Canada
• The R&D and marketing strategy for products made in Canada is undertaken from Canada
• The Canadian organization possesses all the fundamental operations that constitute a "whole" company in its business, (e.g., finance, marketing, R&D, manufacturing, and other functions) World product mandates do not make a company indigenous; neither does a large Canadian research and development operation. To be indigenous means to act and have the capabilities of a home-grown Canadian firm.

Traditionally, much of the Canadian public policy debate concerning corporate structure has centred on the high level of foreign ownership in Canadian industry. However, ownership is not the important factor. If foreign-owned firms operate as indigenous companies in the traded sectors, they will contribute all of the same benefits to the economy as Canadian-owned firms, except perhaps the flow of dividends to shareholders. Even in the case of dividends, foreign-owned firms that operate indigenously often allow their subsidiaries to retain most of their earnings for their investment needs.

Foreign ownership is neither a new nor a passing phenomenon. While Ontario has a high level of foreign ownership, it has also benefitted from the significant wealth generated by those foreign-owned firms that have committed themselves to exporting from an Ontario base. Many of the non-indigenous companies in Ontario are as committed as any indigenous Ontario firm to seeking new higher value-added opportunities in export markets.

But because of the huge role played by non-indigenous companies, Ontario is limited in terms of the strategic business decisions that can be made within the province and vulnerable to the strategic decisions that are made outside. It is essential that the business policy environment establish an effective balance that will encourage both the growth of indigenous multinationals and the continued commitment and expansion of the non-indigenous enterprises already here. It will also be necessary to attract new firms and investments to Ontario.

67

Why Indigenous Firms Are Critical

While the presence of any competitive multinational benefits Ontario, there are particular advantages to an industrial structure that includes a number of large indigenous firms. Indigenous multinationals enhance the stability of an economy, provide higher value-added jobs and greater indirect employment, and are more likely to create spin-off companies than are non-indigenous firms.

In a number of instances, non-indigenous multinational companies in Ontario were originally established to breach tariff or distance barriers which restricted the parent company's ability to serve the Canadian market. Many of these firms are looked upon by their parent companies as stand-alone branch manufacturing plants serving Canada as a specific region of North America. Exports from Canada in these cases are usually small and handled by the international division at each company's headquarters. Such companies are often isolated from international competition and have little incentive or the appropriate resources to perform with world-scale efficiency or to pursue significant product innovations. Even though some of these locations have now been given world-wide mandates to produce specific items from a company's product line for international distribution, they still do not provide many of the economic strengths which are associated with indigenous companies.

The indigenous multinational is a whole business entity, and as such it will almost certainly employ high value-added executive, administrative, research and development, and marketing personnel. These jobs not only add higher value per hour worked to the economy than do many other jobs, but they also create additional opportunities for small company spin-offs. International marketing jobs in an indigenous multinational, for example, allow Canadian managers to develop the skills to sell all manner of products abroad. In short, the indigenous company base is the best training ground for international managers and a breeding ground for spin-off entrepreneurs. As we shall see in Chapter VII, Northern Telecom and Bell Northern Research have accounted for over 50 spin-off new business ventures in Ontario. The non-indigenous technology firms in the province, while much larger in their total employment, have contributed only a handful.

Indigenous multinationals also create indirect employment that may be, in effect, exported. Accounting, legal, advertising, and consulting functions are often performed by firms close to headquarters. If a firm sells 80 percent of its production outside of Canada, but spends its full business services budget here, it is indirectly exporting 80 percent of the person hours it employs in business services.

Large indigenous firms are therefore well-equipped to sustain the environment required for economic growth. They develop the skills and mentality and provide an industrial base which nurtures new ventures and emerging industries. Through contracts with smaller companies close to home, they also provide the seeds of growth for sophisticated supplier and spin-off industries.

In the future, as Ontario attempts to develop a strong base of high growth industries, the development of indigenous firms will become even more important. The opportunities to attract the manufacturing plants of foreign companies in high wage businesses will be fewer in the future as those firms look to serve many markets from only a few world production bases. Ontario will also find itself in ever more intense competition with other governments to offer incentives for these new factories. Ontario will win some of these competitions, but the best hope for prosperity in the long term will be to develop a larger base of indigenous multinationals in the province.

The Importance Of Large Companies

In most major industrialized economies a core group of 40-50 multinational companies accounts for the majority of export activities. The 50 largest exporters in Sweden account for 68 percent of all exports; France's top 50 exporters account for 67 percent; Germany's for 66 percent; and Japan's for 55 percent (See Exhibit II.3). Ontario is similar in that 67 percent of all exports come from the top 50 companies. Canada is somewhat less concentrated in this respect in that 51 percent of all exports come from the top 50 exporting companies. Only Belgium, which is a branch plant location for hundreds of European multinationals, and the U.S., which has a broader group of strong multinationals than any other country, have substantially different profiles.

While small companies do play a role in exports, they are not the primary drivers of wealth creation in the traded sectors. Large companies not only export, but they represent a vast market for smaller firms. For example, General Motors of Canada buys from 7,000 suppliers in Canada, while Ford purchases from roughly 3,000-4,000 Canadian companies.[2]

Sustained success in major world markets usually requires the resources and expertise of a large multinational enterprise. As we discussed in Chapter I, the competitive dynamics of many

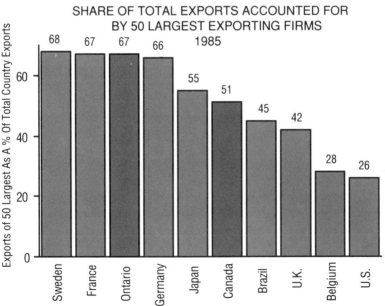

EXHIBIT II.3

SHARE OF TOTAL EXPORTS ACCOUNTED FOR BY 50 LARGEST EXPORTING FIRMS
1985

Exports of 50 Largest As A % Of Total Country Exports

Sweden	France	Ontario	Germany	Japan	Canada	Brazil	U.K.	Belgium	U.S.
68	67	67	66	55	51	45	42	28	26

Source: Telesis analysis based on the 336 leading Ontario exporters database and published sources in each country.

2. Based on the report of the Federal Task Force on Canadian Motor Vehicle and Automotive Parts Industries, May 1983. The data was adjusted downwards to reflect supplier consolidation in recent years.

international businesses tend to revolve around scale in one or more aspects of the business. Smaller companies can succeed in world markets, but only when they find a specific niche which is defensible from large firms on a cost or product differentiation basis.

Of course, one should not evaluate the importance to Ontario of small and medium-size firms solely in terms of their export capability. Such firms are also important to the province because they form the population from which large-scale indigenous firms can eventually grow. Without a healthy and sizable base of small- and medium-size exporters, Ontario cannot hope to build the multinationals required to gain major shares of high growth and emerging industry markets.

Ontario's Indigenous Firms

Ontario has a number of significant indigenous firms. Among the top ten provincial exporters are five: Polysar, Abitibi Price, Inco, Northern Telecom, and Pratt and Whitney Canada. However, of the total exports from the 336 largest Ontario exporters, only 29 percent were from indigenous firms. This number is depressed by the export dominance of the auto sector and its mainly non-indigenous structure. In the low wage sector, 100 percent of exports were from indigenous Canadian firms. In the resource sector it was 69 percent; in high growth industries it was 60 percent; and in other mature manufacturing businesses (non-automotive), it was 58 percent (See Exhibit II.4). The automotive industry is where non-indigenous firms dominate. Only four percent of automotive exports were from indigenous firms in the auto sector. However, this four percent understates the role of indigenous firms since a large share of their output is assembled into Canadian vehicles made by the Big Three, which are then exported.

Our most important concern about indigenous companies in Ontario is that there are so few large ones in high growth businesses. Among the top exporters there are only eleven non-resource based indigenous firms (See Exhibit II.5). Of these, only five are in high growth businesses, and only one of these - Northern Telecom, with nearly $6 billion in sales - could be considered a large world-scale multinational. Pratt and Whitney Canada, Mitel, and De Havilland all have substantial sales in world markets, but in their respective global industries they are still only middle-sized firms. All three do have corporate parents (Pratt & Whitney U.S., British Telecom, and Boeing respectively) which can provide assistance in research and development and marketing, thus giving them some of the reach and stability of their ma-

EXHIBIT II.4

EXPORTS OF INDIGENOUS COMPANIES AS PERCENT OF TOTAL EXPORTS OF 336 LEADING ONTARIO FIRMS BY BUSINESS CATEGORY

* A significant portion of the auto parts made by indigenous Canadian firms are exported in cars made in Canada by non-indigenous firms. Thus, the 4% figure understates the true level of indigenous activity in the auto industry by a few percentage points.

Source: Telesis and Canada Consulting - See Exhibit II.1

71

jor multinational competitors. CAE Electronics does not have that luxury and must generally "go it alone" in world markets.

The simple fact is that Ontario does not have the indigenous corporate infrastructure which it will require to be successful in the high growth traded industries of the future. The rapid growth of a Magna International in auto parts indicates that some future world scale multinationals can also emerge from the mature manufacturing sectors. But long-term economic prosperity in Ontario will depend disproportionately on developing in high growth industries another four to five firms of the scale and success of Northern Telecom.

ENHANCING THE CONTRIBUTION OF NON-INDIGENOUS FIRMS

While the development of indigenous multinationals should be a major focus of Ontario policy, the province cannot afford to ignore the huge contribution of non-indigenous firms to provincial wealth. The importance of the largest non-indigenous firms to Ontario is graphically illustrated in Exhibit II.6. Fully 75 percent

3. If one takes the Big Three automakers out of the statistics, 40 percent of the remaining Ontario exports would be accounted for by non-indigenous firms.

EXHIBIT II.5

72

THE 12 LARGEST INDIGENOUS EXPORTERS IN ONTARIO AMONG NON-RESOURCE INDUSTRIES

Company	Business	1985 Rank in Ontario Exports	Mature Manufacturing or High Growth Sector
Polysar	Resins, Synthetic Rubber	4	MM
Northern Telecom	Telecommunications Equipment	9	HG
Pratt and Whitney	Aircraft Jet Engines	10	HG
Stelco	Steel	13	MM
Magna International	Auto Parts	15	MM
Mitel	Telecommunications Equipment	21	HG
De Havilland	Commuter Aircraft	27	HG
Dofasco	Steel	28	MM
Algoma	Steel	29	MM
Petrosar (Now with Polysar)	Petrochemicals	30	MM
CAE Electronics	Avionics, Simulators, Auto Parts	44	HG/MM

Source: Telesis and Canada Consulting - See Exhibit II.1

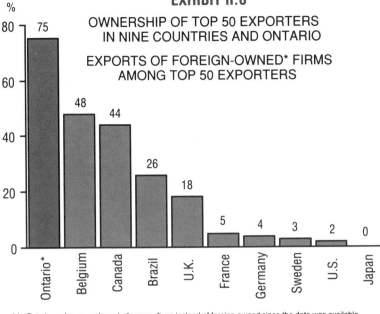

%

EXHIBIT II.6

OWNERSHIP OF TOP 50 EXPORTERS IN NINE COUNTRIES AND ONTARIO

EXPORTS OF FOREIGN-OWNED* FIRMS AMONG TOP 50 EXPORTERS

* In Ontario we have used non-indigenous firms instead of foreign-owned since the data was available

Source: Telesis and Canada Consulting based on the 336 leading Ontario exporters
database and published sources in other countries

of the exports of Ontario's 50 largest exporting companies are from non-indigenous firms[3]. This level is substantially higher than all the comparison countries, including Canada as a whole which is at 44 percent. The strong indigenous company base of nations like Japan, the U.S., Sweden, Germany, and France is illustrated by the fact that foreign-owned firms account for less than 5 percent of the exports of the 50 leading exporters in each of those countries.

Ontario must seek ways to enhance the competitive viability of its non-indigenous corporate base, and if possible to encourage it to become more indigenous in its behavior. Many of Ontario's most important non-indigenous firms are in the midst of major world-wide rationalizations of facilities and business lines. As we will see in Chapter IV, implementation of the proposed Canada-U.S. Free Trade Agreement would accelerate these restructuring activities in Ontario. The province must seek opportunities to encourage foreign multinationals to make Ontario their base for consolidating manufacturing facilities. Where feasible, Ontario should encourage the expansion of indigenous-type activities by foreign firms. This can be through the creation or expansion of R&D facilities, the development of international marketing units based in Ontario, or the general devolution of strategic responsibility for decisions directing the Canadian business to local management.

Some of Ontario's most important indigenous firms, like Northern Telecom and Pratt and Whitney, were at one time dependent on foreign technology and strategic direction. Their evolution to fully indigenous firms capable of achieving success in international markets on the strength of their own resources was gradual and in each case took more than a decade. There are non-indigenous firms in the province today which could be encouraged to follow that path in the future.

The key to successful provincial policies in dealing with non-indigenous companies will be to develop a flexible approach which recognizes the different international strategies of various firms. With many foreign companies, the main opportunity for Ontario will be to capture new higher value-added investments in plant and equipment. Some of these will be greenfield investments in totally new facilities like the recent GM/Suzuki, Honda, Toyota, and AMC (now Chrysler) car assembly plants in Ontario. Others will be upgrades of existing products and facilities. And still others will be repatriated products which had once moved offshore to low wage countries, but which with new automation or product re-design can now be manufactured for lower cost in high wage nations. Ontario must ensure that it can offer a sufficiently attractive environment relative to other jurisdictions to attract its share of all of these types of investments.

A second broad type of investment which Ontario should be alert to will be the creation of stand-alone R&D facilities by multinationals in high growth industries. IBM, for example, has built a world-wide system of large software laboratories that bid on projects and receive work from IBM divisions all over the world. The Toronto IBM laboratory is such a stand-alone facility. It is one of the five largest company R&D laboratories in Canada and has over 1,200 researchers working on projects related to IBM products under development all over the world. Many governments target such multinational R&D facilities and the high value-added work they bring through tax incentives, procurement, and education policies. Zurich, Switzerland, for example, has become an international centre for such stand-alone facilities, as has Nice, France. With the changes in drug patent legislation in Canada, at least a few pharmaceutical firms may be willing to build such stand-alone facilities in Ontario.

ONTARIO'S UNIQUE CHALLENGE

Economic policy in Ontario must take account of both the need to foster the development of world-scale indigenous multination-

74

als in the province and the need to enhance the competitive success and value-added contribution of non-indigenous companies. Ideally, Ontario should aim for an industrial structure more like Sweden's. Sweden has about the same population as Ontario and a raw materials sector of about the same size as Ontario relative to its total manufacturing sector. Swedish prosperity depends primarily on a group of 10-15 indigenous multinationals, each of which is among the world leaders in its specific business segments. Companies like Volvo and Saab in automobiles, ASEA in electrical machinery and robots, Electrolux in appliances, Ericsson in telecommunications equipment, Astra and Kema Nobel in chemicals, Sandvik in cutting tools, and Atlas Copco in machinery are all world leaders in their industry segments. However, it is important to note that many of these firms, large as they are by Ontario standards, are often still focussed on smaller niches in their industries. Volvo and Saab compete in the luxury and performance car specialty segments world-wide; they do not attempt to compete head-on with the much larger mass market manufacturers.

The development of new large multinationals anywhere in the world is not a common phenomenon. Sweden has an industrial history going back 400 years. These major Swedish multinationals were already well-established in international markets before World War II. The world is much more competitive now, and it is much harder to establish new successful world-scale competitors. Even in the U.S., only a dozen or so new world-scale multinationals have become established in the past twenty years. The challenge for Ontario is to advance the process of multinational creation and work towards having a few more indigenous Canadian world-scale firms emerge over the next ten years.

75

Critical as it is to broaden the indigenous base of companies in the province, it will also be important to broaden and deepen the commitment of non-indigenous firms which are willing to locate high value-added per employee activities here and export from this base. Ontario's unique challenge is to accelerate the growth of its indigenous companies in traded sectors while building upon and expanding the strengths in its non-indigenous base. Few of Ontario's international competitors will be grappling with quite the same problem.

CHAPTER III
REALIGNING THE GOVERNMENT FOCUS

Industrial assistance at both the provincial and federal levels is provided either directly through grant and loan programs or indirectly through tax incentives.[1] Provincially, the Ontario Development Corporations (ODCs) are the main vehicles for delivering assistance to industry. Federal assistance to business is delivered through two distinct mechanisms: grant programs residing in various industry departments and Crown agencies, and corporate tax incentives. In addition to these regular assistance routes for industry, the federal government also provides ad hoc assistance to business in the form of corporate bailouts and short-term restructuring programs to prop up troubled companies and industry sectors.

Ontario and federal government industrial incentives, whether provided through direct programs or through the tax route, often focus on assistance to economically disadvantaged regions and smaller (and thus assumed to be "needier") business interests. While this tendency to assist the have-not areas and businesses may provide for more even distribution of wealth, and may therefore serve a necessary "social" objective, it often does little to enhance the competitive strength of industry.

In the preceding chapters, we have outlined several strategic directions for improving the wealth creation capabilities of Ontario industry. We have emphasized the need to move to higher value-added manufacturing, to focus on traded goods and services, and to foster those larger, indigenous firms that could achieve multinational status from an Ontario base. In this chapter, we will examine how the government role in assisting industry usually falls short of meeting these objectives.

THE CURRENT FOCUS OF GOVERNMENT ASSISTANCE

A brief overview of key government industrial assistance programs or incentives, their mandates, and, where applicable, their expenditures in Ontario is provided in Exhibit III.1. This snapshot of public sector support to industry, though selective, covers

---

1. The following description and assessment of public sector assistance to industry excludes specific consideration of vehicles for promoting R&D and education and training. These areas and the policy and program support they receive are reviewed extensively in later sections of this report.

EXHIBIT III.1

Selected Industry Programs	Mandate	1986 Funding in Ontario ($ millions)
Ontario		
Ontario Development Corporations	• Encourages and assists in development and diversification of industry in Ontario through lending and investment activity; focus on business start-ups, expansions, high risk ventures and regional development	112
Innovation Ontario	• Assists newer ventures requiring funds for new product and prototype development	7
Canada		
Federal Business Development Bank (FBDB)	• Promotes the development of small and medium-sized businesses through financial and management services	106
Small Business Loans Administration (SBLA)	• Guarantees loans of 85 percent of the value of chartered bank loans to businesses with under $2 million in revenue	N/A
Industrial and Regional Development Program (IRDP)	• Promotes regional industrial development through financing to private sector; responds to needs of small and medium-sized businesses in particular	33
Export Development Corporation (EDC)	• Provides incentives for foreign purchasers to buy Canadian capital goods and services by financing up to 85 percent of the Canadian contract value	559
Program for Export Market Development (PEMD)	• Encourages firms to export by sharing the risks of entering new export markets	13
Defense Industry Productivity Program (DIPP)	• Develops and maintains strong Canadian defence-related industries capable of competing in domestic and export markets	33
Other Assistance		
Corporate Bailouts/Industry Restructuring	• Provides short-term assistance to individual companies undergoing financial difficulties using grants, low-interest or interest-free loans	N/A
Tax Incentives	• N/A	N/A

Source: Canada Consulting and Telesis interviews and analysis

the main provincial vehicles for delivering assistance to industry (the ODCs and the newly-created Innovation Ontario Corporation, which falls under the Development Corporation's administration); the core federal program for delivering industrial support (the Industrial and Regional Development Program); the two federal small business loan programs (the Small Business Loans Administration and the Federal Business Development Bank), the main sectoral support program (the Defence Industry Productivity Program); and the export assistance programs (those administered by the Export Development Corporation and the Program for Export Market Development). Non-program support mechanisms, such as corporate bailouts, and indirect assistance measures, such as tax incentives, are also included in this exhibit to indicate the range of industrial support options, but their ad hoc or indirect delivery precludes any attempt to attach a funding figure to such initiatives.

Our review of government support for industry suggests that there are three basic problems with the way such assistance is determined and delivered:

- The problem of indiscriminate focus is reflected in the failure to take into account the vital distinctions between high and low value-added businesses and traded and non-traded businesses in making lending or granting decisions
- The problem of mixing social and economic objectives refers to the tendency of governments to confuse even distribution of wealth with strategic generation of wealth in their incentive programs
- The problem of misapplication is a matter of funds being made available for the wrong purpose; fixed asset contributions often represent an ineffective type of assistance, while corporate bailouts or other ad hoc solutions to industry problems often provide for the short-term viability of a company or industry, while failing to address the long-term restructuring needs.

Exhibit III.2 breaks these broad problems in program delivery into more specific components. The discussion that follows explains and elaborates on this exhibit.

THE PROBLEM OF INDISCRIMINATE FOCUS
Missing Higher Value-Added Opportunities

As a general rule, both provincial and federal government programs have made no distinction between low and high value-added per employee businesses in determining where support should be directed. One good example of this was the industrial

EXHIBIT III.2
EMPHASIS OF SELECTED GOVERNMENT PROGRAMS

Program	Small Business	Non-Traded Industries	Lack of Incentive to Higher Value-Added Initiatives	Fixed Asset Bias	Lack of Assistance to High-Growth Industries	Regional Bias
Ontario Development Corporations	✓	✓	✓	✓	✓	✓
Federal Business Development Bank	✓	✓	✓	✓	✓	✓
Small Businesses Loans Administration	✓	✓	✓	✓		
Defense Industry Productivity Program			✓	✓		✓
Industrial and Regional Development Program			✓	✓	✓	✓
Export Development Corporation			✓			
Program for Export Market Development	✓	✓	✓			
Corporate Bailouts			✓		✓	

assistance provided by the federal government through the Industrial and Regional Development Program (IRDP) to the pulp and paper industry. Monies were provided for purposes of modernizing equipment, much of it dating back to the pre-1930s. Rather than tying the assistance specifically to the purchase or enhancement of equipment that would allow the industry to compete in higher value-added segments, the funding was granted for the restoration of old equipment that would enable the industry to remain in the lower value-added commodity products end of the business. Even then, the productivity improvements from these upgrades was not nearly as significant as what could have been achieved had all new machines been purchased.

Similarly, in chemicals, most government assistance has gone to commodity production and not to those high value-added activities which require greater knowledge intensiveness and special skills in production and sales.

Funding For Non-Traded Businesses

Compounding the problem of indiscriminate resource allocation to businesses, regardless of their value-added potential, is the tendency to direct assistance to non-traded businesses. The ODCs, for example, provide a major portion of their loans to non-traded businesses in the service sector. In 1985-86, 26 percent of the Corporations' loan dollars went to the recreation, accommodation, and food services sector (See Exhibit III.3). Of loans made under the New Ventures Program of Innovation Ontario, 80 percent have been for companies in the service sector. Even with the Development Corporations' large agency loans, tourism represents a major focus. Although tourism can be a traded business when foreign tourists are involved, the ODC's lending policies do not include an assessment of the level of traded activity in reviewing loan candidates.

The Federal Business Development Bank (FBDB) also provides substantial assistance to non-traded businesses. During fiscal 1986, almost two-thirds of the total number of loans authorized by the FBDB in Ontario went to services businesses, and only 34 percent of those were made to companies in the restaurant, hotel and recreation businesses which might have some traded tourism component. Because of their explicit small company client orientation, the FBDB and the Small Business Loans Administration (SBLA) tend to support companies involved in non-traded businesses.

EXHIBIT III.3

INDUSTRIAL ASSISTANCE BY COMPETITIVE INDUSTRY TYPE
ONTARIO
1985/86

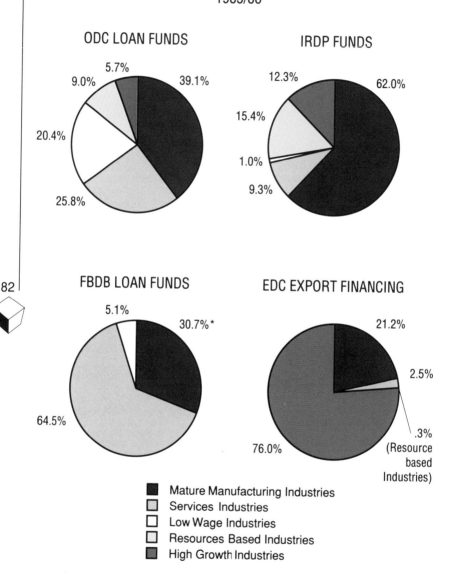

* Based on Canada Consulting and Telesis Analysis

Lack of Assistance For High Growth Sectors

The industrial assistance effort has also been too broadly focussed to provide much-needed support for the most promising growth sectors. High growth sectors have received much less attention at both provincial and federal levels than their economic importance would suggest. The ODCs have provided less than six percent of their loan dollars to these sectors (See Exhibit III.3). The largest chunk of ODC funding by business segment (40 percent) goes to mature manufacturing businesses, followed by service businesses at 26 percent. The IRDP loan portfolio follows a similar pattern, with only 12 percent of its assistance going to high growth industries, while 62 percent of IRDP expenditures in Ontario during 1985-86 were devoted to mature manufacturing industries.

Only two federal programs stand out as exceptions to the indiscriminate focus problem. The Export Development Corporation (EDC), in providing low-interest loans to foreign purchasers of Canadian capital goods and associated services, is totally focussed on traded industries and mostly high growth areas. In 1985/86, 76 percent of EDC's funding went to support the sales of high growth industries.

The federal Defence Industry Productivity Program (DIPP) is also well-targeted. Most of DIPP assistance is for R&D, and almost all of it is focussed on high growth, traded industries.

83

THE PROBLEM OF MIXED OBJECTIVES
The Regional Orientation

Another shared tendency of many federal and provincial industrial assistance programs is the mixing of regional development and wealth creation objectives. Regional programs are important, but their objectives need to be understood separately from economic development objectives of the province or the country as a whole. Much of the monies that are said to flow to economic development are really being used to meet regional development needs.

Promoting regional development has been a priority of the ODCs, which are mandated to stimulate investment on a regional basis. This has led to an increased allocation of loan dollars to the less prosperous parts of the province, namely the north and east. Assistance to Northern Ontario, for instance, has risen from 16 percent in 1981/82 to 20 percent in 1985/86.

The regional focus of federal industry programs is evident in the fact that Ontario receives only 28 percent of total IRDP money, even though its population size is 40 percent of Canada.

But Ontario's designation as a TIER I region of the country (the most economically prosperous tier) limits the province's funding prospects. The tier system is based on a complex formula involving levels of unemployment, income distribution, and the fiscal capacity of the province; thus the more economically disadvantaged an area is, the more funding it receives.

The FBDB's term lending activity provides another example of the federal government's strong regional focus. In TIER IV areas, those most economically disadvantaged, the FBDB accounts for eight percent of total banking business, or about twice the business it accounts for in other regions. Funding priorities are thus geared to regional development more than economic or industrial development.

Even the DIPP demonstrates a regional orientation that has worked to "prosperous" Ontario's economic disadvantage. Ontario has witnessed a considerable decline in the number of projects accepted under the DIPP program from 110 in 1981/82 to 26 in 1985/86. While this downsizing may have occurred in other areas of the country as well, the decline is particularly dramatic in Ontario. Ontario used to represent almost 40 percent of total Canadian assistance under this program, but it currently receives only 13 percent of all DIPP assistance. Because DIPP represents one of the only programs which provides assistance to promising industries like aerospace, the withdrawal of support to Ontario has been keenly felt. The shift in DIPP funding away from Ontario and into Quebec has affected companies' decisions regarding where to locate or expand facilities. Quebec has benefitted significantly as a result.

The Unaddressed Needs Of Larger Business

By focussing extensively on small businesses, regardless of their value-added or traded orientation, government programs again illustrate the tendency to mingle competing social and economic objectives in their industrial assistance. Small businesses, simply because they are small and suffer scale disadvantages, have become major beneficiaries of government largesse. This is not to suggest that small business is not highly deserving of public support. But because that support is often based too much on the "small" and too little on the "business" element, it should be understood as primarily social in nature. The role of small business in job creation should not override its less critical role in driving wealth creation. It should also be remembered that many of the new jobs created in small businesses depend ultimately on the international competitive success of larger Ontario companies in traded businesses.

At issue is whether much of the government funding for small business stimulates new activity that would not have happened otherwise. Service businesses, by their very nature, enjoy ease of entry to consumer markets. Many of these firms may fail, but new ones will emerge to replace them. This process will take place largely independent of what government makes available in support or incentives.

Two programs at the federal level, the FBDB and the SBLA, specifically target small businesses. Of the almost $500 million in annual assistance provided by the federal government to Ontario industry in the form of loans and grants, these two programs accounted for over 60 percent of the funding. This marked emphasis on small business in total federal funding to Ontario recognizes and supports the province's entrepreneurs, but it falls short of providing an environment in which internationally competitive firms can emerge.

One of the federal government's programs for export development also has a clear focus on small business. The Program for Export Market Development (PEMD) is used extensively by small companies. In 1985/86, over half of PEMD applications approved in Canada were for companies with less than $2 million in sales. Very few of these small businesses are likely to be capable of entering and sustaining their presence in export markets. PEMD funds are spent in ways that offer dubious assistance to businesses in establishing a strong export capability or an overseas presence. Program funds are used mainly for participation in trade fairs abroad and industrial exhibitions overseas - not activities associated with building a sustained market presence. In the end, nothing is built and the experience is sometimes more harmful than beneficial.

At the provincial level, the ODCs are actively involved in providing assistance to small business. In 1986 almost 80 percent of the Development Corporations' loans were provided to companies with ten or fewer employees, which received almost half of the Corporations' loan dollars. With this small firm focus comes a focus on service-oriented businesses. As employment levels decrease, the amount of loan dollars directed towards service firms increases.

Unfortunately, very small companies are not going to play a major role in exports. The primary focus on small business should be on those firms that might be successful in export markets. Yet little of the assistance monies devoted to smaller enterprises serve this objective since most of it goes to very small firms of less than 25 employees. (See Exhibit III.4).

EXHIBIT III.4
INDUSTRIAL ASSISTANCE BY SIZE OF BUSINESS
ONTARIO 1985/86

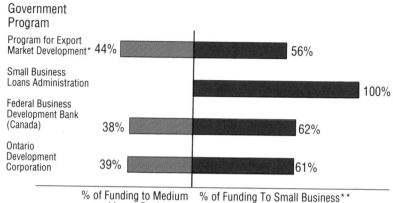

Government Program

Program		
Program for Export Market Development*	44%	56%
Small Business Loans Administration		100%
Federal Business Development Bank (Canada)	38%	62%
Ontario Development Corporation	39%	61%

% of Funding to Medium and Large Business   % of Funding To Small Business**

* Applications Approved
** Those companies with less than 25 people or less than $2 million in sales
Source: Canada Consulting and Telesis analysis, based on categorization of new data on funding allocations by company

THE PROBLEM OF MISAPPLICATION
The Fixed Asset Bias

Fixed asset financing is a major preoccupation of Ontario and federal assistance programs. During 1985/86, fixed asset financing for equipment, buildings, and machinery represented almost 50 percent of the ODC's funding dollars, while other important areas of activity, including research and development and marketing, each accounted for less than one percent of funding dollars.

The federal industry program dollars show an even higher concentration of fixed asset funding. Almost 60 percent of the amount of authorized loans of the FBDB in Ontario have been used for fixed assets, and under the SBLA, loans must be made for the purpose of purchasing equipment or for buying or renovating premises. In 1985-86, 58 percent of IRDP expenditures were used for fixed asset investments. Although 82 percent of the authorized assistance provided by DIPP in Canada in 1985/86 was earmarked for research and development activity, roughly 75 percent of these R&D monies were used for the purchase of equipment to conduct R&D (See Exhibit III.5).

The problem with a fixed asset orientation for industrial assistance is that it is inappropriate for many types of traded busi-

EXHIBIT III.5
THE FIXED ASSET BIAS
ONTARIO 1986/86

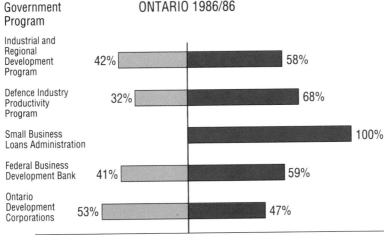

Government Program

Government Program		
Industrial and Regional Development Program	42%	58%
Defence Industry Productivity Program	32%	68%
Small Business Loans Administration		100%
Federal Business Development Bank	41%	59%
Ontario Development Corporations	53%	47%

% of Funding To All Other Categories   % of Funding To Fixed Assets

Source: Based on Canada Consulting and Telesis analysis and categorization or raw data on funding allocations by type of assistance

nesses. Exhibit III.6 illustrates investment profiles of three very different business products: a commodity steel product, an electronic component, and an end-user software based electronic system. The fixed asset requirement varies from 55 percent in the commodity steel business to 13 percent in the electronic component business, and seven percent in the electrical systems business. The electrical systems business cannot make much use of a fixed asset incentive, but it could very much use assistance in engineering and marketing. This holds true for many of the high growth businesses where Ontario needs to become more successful. For these companies, fixed assets are much less important to their competitive capability than marketing, R&D, engineering, or other strategic investments.

Temporary Support For Troubled Firms

Some government assistance to industry has the specific aim of providing temporary support to firms on the verge of collapse. Corporate bailouts are government's quick fix response to pressures from failing companies to rescue them from extinction. Decisions to bail out companies are often made for social and political reasons when a large employment base is involved or when the company's survival is critical to the well-being of a small community. In most cases, government assistance is linked

EXHIBIT III.6

PROFILE OF INVESTMENT REQUIREMENTS IN NEW
PRODUCTS FOR THREE DIFFERENT BUSINESSES
(Assuming: 10% Sales Growth/Year)

Business Investment Area	Commodity Steel Product	Electronic Component	End-user Electronic System
Fixed Assets	55	13	7
Working Capital	42	32	15
R&D and Engineering	3	55	45
Marketing & Sales	Minimal	Minimal	33
Total Investment	100%	100%	100%

Source: Telesis Client Studies

to commitments from the company to undertake activities which have a local development significance. The immediate exigencies of staving off a crisis often take precedence over economic development or long-term industrial restructuring considerations.

Other countries - West Germany, Japan, and France for instance - seem better prepared than Canada or Ontario to intervene through an early warning system. In these countries, governments' rationale for involvement is to facilitate industrial adjustment that will be sensitive to the long-term competitive circumstances rather than serving only the immediate or regional needs. The problem with corporate bailouts in Canada is that they represent the wrong kind of crisis intervention: they are a last-minute and short-term solution to deeper structural problems that should have been anticipated and addressed more comprehensively. The problem is not the government involvement per se, but the timing and method of involvement.

A BETTER FOCUS FOR PUBLIC POLICY

The problems identified in this chapter result from a lack of recognition of the need at the public policy level to synchronize industrial program delivery with sound competitive objectives. The industrial assistance base must be strengthened through policies and programs that recognize the importance of and promote higher value-added activities in industry, the traded sectors of the economy, and indigenous firms that are capable of becoming multinationals. Continuing prosperity for the Ontario economy depends heavily on the sustained growth and competitiveness of firms with a demonstrated capability in these areas.

Government can facilitate the development of these critical firms and capabilities by altering its focus. This is not a unique opportunity for Ontario but rather a catch-up response to the policy environments which exist in many competitor countries. The value-added and traded nature of businesses should be factored into lending or granting decisions; the regional and small business considerations that dominate many government program criteria, while important, should not overwhelm those considerations that are based on competitive analysis; and funding should concentrate on points of competitive leverage, such as product and market development, rather than being used to finance fixed assets or provide stop-gap assistance to failing firms.

In order to move in these directions effectively, it is essential that government begin thinking more in terms of cost sharing with industry. Instead of maintaining its traditional role as a lender and grant-giver to industry, government must begin to portray itself and function in partnership with industry. Encouraging more private sector involvement in program design and project cost is critical to the realignment of the government focus, as later chapters in this report will confirm. Specific recommendations for achieving this realignment and strengthening the government industry partnership will be provided in the chapter that follows.

89

CHAPTER IV
RESTRUCTURING IN CORE INDUSTRIES

Ontario's resource-based industries, such as forest products and food processing, and Ontario's mature manufacturing industries, such as automotive, steel, and chemicals, continue to form the backbone of the economy. They provide the bulk of manufacturing employment, account for 95 percent of all capital investment, and produce nearly 90 percent of the province's exports. We call these resource and mature manufacturing industries Ontario's core industries because they are the current foundation of Ontario's wealth creation capacity.

A number of Ontario companies enjoy a strong competitive position in many of these core industries. However, every one of them has faced increasing competitive pressures in recent years from a variety of quarters. In the resource industries, the pressures have come from slower growth in traditional markets for resource-based products, the exploitation of new low cost resources in other countries, and the consequent need for Canadian firms to add more value to resource products to achieve sustainable competitive advantages and adequate levels of profitability in international markets. In the mature manufacturing industries, the increase in competition has resulted from the entry of new players into existing markets, more aggressive and effective competitors in high wage countries, and new low wage competitors moving into higher value-added per employee activities and products.

Thus, both resource-based and mature manufacturing industries in Ontario are in the throes of industrial restructuring processes driven by increased international competition. The restructuring process is similar in most industries in the sense that it usually entails capacity reductions, a shift to higher value-added per employee businesses, and stable or declining levels of employment. In fact, employment levels have fallen in many of these industries despite Ontario's overall economic expansion (See Exhibit IV.1). This restructuring also requires greatly increased investments in capital equipment, marketing, R&D, and other areas fundamental to building a renewed competitiveness.

Firms in Ontario differ in the degree to which their industries are changing and the extent to which they themselves are restructuring to enhance their competitiveness. The automotive

EXHIBIT IV.1 EMPLOYMENT GROWTH IN SELECTED MATURE MANUFACTURING INDUSTRIES Ontario 1983-86	
Industry Sector	Growth/Decline Between 1983 and 1986 %
Automotive	+12
Chemicals	+7
Metal Fabricating	+2
Woods/Sawmills	-1
Food and Beverages	-2
Iron and Steel	-2
Paper and Allied	-2
Machinery	-7

Source: Survey of Employment, Payrolls, and Hours, Statistics Canada.

92

firms and steel companies, for example, have invested massively in new and refurbished plants, making their facilities the equals of international competitors. The forest products and food processing industries, on the other hand, are not as far along in the restructuring process and by and large do not have world leading technology or economies of scale.

The proposed Free Trade Agreement with the United States will accelerate the industrial restructuring process. In some industries, like bulk chemicals and pulp and paper, it may result in expanded Canadian market opportunities without introducing new lower cost U.S. competitors to Canada. In others, like many specialty chemicals businesses and food processing activities, free trade will pose dramatic competitive difficulties as companies are forced to invest in new world-scale capacity, move to more specialized products, or cease operations altogether.

Given these differences, we will examine the international competitive pressures and level of restructuring underway in each of these industries separately in this chapter. In doing so, however, we will also emphasize the similarities that cut across these industries as well as those features that distinguish them from one another. In the policy prescriptions that follow, we will argue that the similarities are powerful enough that a single set of policies can be implemented to address the problems of restructuring in core industries as a whole.

RESTRUCTURING IN RESOURCE-BASED INDUSTRIES

Ontario's resource-based industries have remained generally competitive in world markets. As we saw in Chapter I, Ontario has a significant overall trade surplus in these sectors and they contribute a high rate of value-added per employee - higher than that in either mature manufacturing or high growth industries in Ontario. Their competitive strength stems from the quality and accessibility of Ontario's resources, which makes them lower cost than those of many competitors. In pulp and paper and the lumber industry, the cost, quality, and accessibility of the timber is the most important competitive factor. In gold, copper, and nickel, it is the accessibility, size, and purity of the deposits which tend to determine competitive advantage.

Because the competitive strength of Ontario's resource industries is based on the natural endowment of the province in soil, climate, and geology, it will not diminish precipitously. But a number of market-based and competitive factors have combined to constrain the prospects of these industries in their current structures and states of development.

93

The market demand for most basic materials is slowing in all developed countries. This is due to product designs that use less materials of any kind, the introduction of advanced composite materials that use less raw materials, and the increasing knowledge content as opposed to the materials content of products.

Automobiles provide a useful example of all three phenomena. Cars today weigh about 600 pounds less than they did seven years ago, having been redesigned for greater energy efficiency. They also use more advanced materials, such as high strength plastics and ceramics, which have replaced more traditional materials like steel and copper. Moreover, an increasing proportion of a car's value is accounted for by knowledge intensive features, such as on-board engine diagnostic systems, intelligent controls, and a wide array of other microprocessor and memory-driven electronic systems. Estimates are that by 1990 about $1,800 of the value of the average automobile will be in electronic systems. Increasingly, when one buys a car, one is buying a system of computers as well.

Materials intensity of industrial production is declining dramatically, as illustrated in Exhibit IV.2. Whether one looks at steel, copper, pulp and paper, zinc, or cement, the raw materials

EXHIBIT IV.2

INTENSITY OF ALUMINUM, PULP AND PAPER, ZINC, STEEL, COPPER AND CEMENT CONSUMPTION PER UNIT OF INDUSTRIAL PRODUCTION*
1961 and 1986, Canada

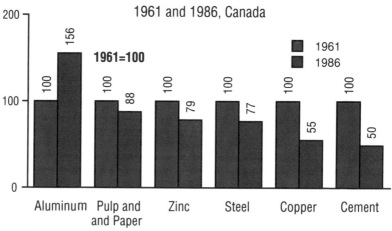

* Metric tonnes consumed in Canada per billion constant dollars of industrial production. Industrial production refers to manufacturing, mining, construction, and utilities which use these materials.

Source: Canada Consulting and Telesis analysis, based on Energy, Mines and Resources, industry association, and company data.

EXHIBIT IV.3
RELATIVE COSTS OF SHIPPING IRON ORE FOR THREE STEEL COMPANIES

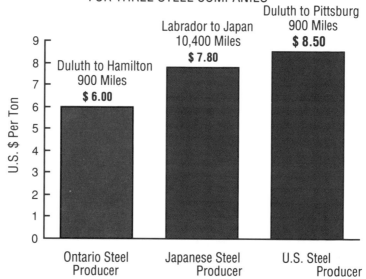

Source: Premier's Council Staff Interviews with Hanna Mining, Ontario Steel Companies, and reports from World Steel Dynamics.

required per unit of industrial output in Canada have fallen since 1961. Only demand for aluminum has continued to grow faster than industrial output. Of course, the demand for specialty steels or high grade papers is also increasing rapidly, but the demand for bulk commodity materials relative to the growth in industrial production has declined for all of the reasons enumerated above.

Compounding the difficulties presented by this slowdown in raw materials demand is the increasing international competition in resource products. Many parts of the world have been far less explored or prospected than Canada and have lacked the physical infrastructure and financial resources to develop the resources they do have. These underdeveloped resources have often proved to be highly competitive. Chile in copper, Brazil in iron ore, forest products and oranges, Zambia and Peru in copper, zinc, and lead, and Thailand in rice are all examples of countries with extremely competitive resource positions which have been known for some time but have only become well-developed in recent years. Three factors made the development of resources in these countries possible:

• The steady reduction in ocean transport costs, which has eliminated the traditional cost penalty of distance from the market. It now costs about as much to ship iron ore on the Great Lakes from Duluth, Minnesota to Stelco's mill in Hamilton as it does to ship it from Labrador halfway around the world to Japan (See Exhibit IV.3). Ocean-going shipping costs have fallen relative to other transport costs due to increased use of larger scale ships and the development of dedicated port facilities at both the raw materials and market ends of transportation links. Japan's major steel mills, for example, were built on deep water ports to allow low cost off-loading of imported iron ore and coal at dedicated facilities.

• The development of international capital markets and the increased role of multilateral lending agencies like the World Bank which have greatly increased the availability of capital at a reasonable cost for less developed countries.

• The development of greatly improved infrastructure in less developed countries. This includes both large scale physical infrastructure like roads, dams, and railways, and also systems infrastructure, like the development of fertilizer distribution networks for farmers, which has greatly boosted agricultural productivity in many countries.

Responding To Cost Pressures

Ontario's resource industries have responded to these slower growth markets and competitive pressures in different ways. In most cases resource industries have moved to cut production costs by improving productivity. Usually, this has entailed investing in more advanced equipment and reducing labour costs. Sometimes, process improvements have reduced other input costs for energy or supplies or have improved the utilization of the raw material itself. Inco, for example, has boosted the labour productivity of its nickel mining operations by 70 percent since 1980 through application of innovative vertical retreat mining techniques.

These efforts at cost reduction will make Ontario's resource industries more competitive, but they can only go so far. Ultimately, the cost of the raw material itself will determine long-run competitiveness. Foreign producers with good resources can usually adopt much of the same advanced technology as Ontario does and improve their production costs to similar levels.

As a result, the competitive response for a number of Ontario resource firms under significant international cost pressures is to shift production to higher value-added segments of their businesses where competition can be based on other factors not related to raw materials cost, such as marketing costs or manufacturing productivity. In paper production, the direction is towards specialty papers. In food processing, this means shifting to more branded products and specialty food items.

96

The Council research effort looked at two resource industries in depth: pulp and paper and food processing. Each will be discussed briefly to expand on the themes cited above.

Pulp And Paper

The Ontario pulp and paper industry appears quite healthy. The industry has a positive trade balance and currently is running at close to capacity. Ontario's wood resource, which is the most important component of total product costs, is much lower in cost than Scandinavia's, comparable to Quebec's, and higher than that of British Columbia, the U.S., and Brazil (See Exhibit IV.4). Ontario's disadvantages in wood costs relative to U.S. producers are made up partly by lower energy costs; Ontario's disadvantage relative to B.C. is partly compensated for by transportation cost advantages Ontario has in relation to eastern U.S. and European markets. The total cost picture for Ontario depends on the specific product, but generally Ontario is cost competitive in bleached kraft pulp, newsprint, and all forms of printing and writing paper where energy costs are critical (i.e., mechanical fibre based printing papers).

Despite these apparent strengths and the current industry profitability, there are important reasons for concern. The On-

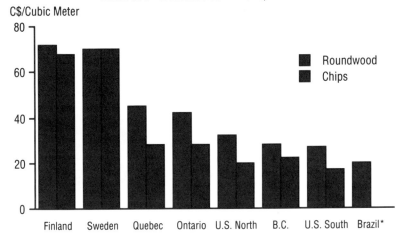

EXHIBIT IV.4
WOOD COSTS
Softwood - Delivered to mill site, 1987

C$/Cubic Meter

Legend:
■ Roundwood
■ Chips

Categories: Finland, Sweden, Quebec, Ontario, U.S. North, B.C., U.S. South, Brazil*

* Chips not available
Source: Price Waterhouse FSAC Study, Woodbridge Reed Associates research and estimates

tario industry has not kept up with fundamental technological and product mix changes in the world industry over the past twenty years. It operates almost exclusively in the commodity lower value-added end of the industry, which includes newsprint and bleached kraft pulp. Ontario has only a tiny share of the lucrative U.S. market in the higher value-added uncoated free-sheet, coated groundwood, and coated freesheet markets . This is despite the fact that in coated groundwood Ontario could be the most cost competitive supplier in the U.S. market (See Exhibit IV.5).

The higher value-added products, where Ontario is weak, are generally growing much faster than bleached kraft pulp and newsprint, where Ontario is strong. Ontario's competitors in Europe and the U.S. have taken advantage of new technologies and products (e.g., chemi-thermomechanical pulping, supercallendered and lightweight coated papers) to capture significant shares of these higher value-added specialty paper segments.

Within eastern Canada, the investment in new technology and new products has taken place outside of Ontario, primarily in Quebec. This is primarily because of the higher fibre species of wood available in Quebec, which lend themselves to specialty products, and the fact that energy costs and provincial taxes are lower in Quebec. The result is that Ontario plants have been

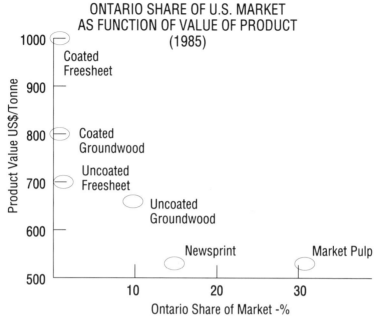

EXHIBIT IV.5

ONTARIO SHARE OF U.S. MARKET AS FUNCTION OF VALUE OF PRODUCT (1985)

Product Value US$/Tonne

- Coated Freesheet (1000)
- Coated Groundwood (800)
- Uncoated Freesheet (700)
- Uncoated Groundwood
- Newsprint
- Market Pulp

Ontario Share of Market -%

Source: Woodbridge Reed Associates

regularly maintained and modernized, but have never been entirely rebuilt or replaced by new facilities. Ontario has become the location for maintaining the production of existing high volume commodity products. This also means that Ontario producers are operating with old and higher cost plant and equipment. Sixty percent of the processing equipment in Ontario's newsprint industry was installed before 1930. Only three of twenty newsprint machines in the province are at world standards of economy of scale. The industry has tried to upgrade these, but upgrades never equal the efficiency of wholly new machines.

The Ontario industry has also been much slower to exploit new technology like thermomechanical pulping (TMP) than competitors have. Most producers consider TMP to have both cost and quality advantages over the traditional stone groundwood pulping process. Although adoption of TMP requires high energy usage and involves switching costs, most jurisdictions have adopted it to a far greater extent than Ontario has. In Sweden, 75 percent of all newsprint is produced using TMP versus only ten percent in Ontario. Ontario's reliance on TMP is also low relative to the rest of Canada: in British Columbia 60 percent and in Quebec 40 percent of newsprint production is through TMP.

Because of its smaller scale machines, older plants, and lack of advanced technology, Ontario lags behind all its competitors in the productivity of its newsprint mills as measured by man hours per ton of product. The future success of the Ontario newsprint industry is thus highly dependent on shifts in exchange rates, despite the high quality of the province's wood resource.

The Ontario pulp and paper industry's emphasis on bulk commodity products and its lagging technology put it in a vulnerable position for the future. The industry will be more at risk from exchange rate movements than industries in countries which have moved heavily into the higher value-added specialty segments of the market where product quality, manufacturing productivity, and other factors have become more important to competitive success.

The Ontario industry is also vulnerable to new low cost producers. As Exhibit IV.4 illustrated, Brazil's wood costs are half of Ontario's, and Brazil will be a formidable competitor as it develops its paper capabilities. The Swedish and Finnish industries, despite their high wood costs, have made themselves more secure against low cost suppliers like Brazil by shifting production to the high value-added printing and writing segments.

The contrast between the Swedish and Ontario pulp and paper industries could not be starker, especially given their respective exchange rate histories. In the late 1970s, the strength of the Swedish Kroner against North American currencies created major competitive difficulties for the Swedish paper industry. It lost share in world markets and many firms suffered large financial losses. In 1982 the government took a major devaluation to restore competitiveness to a number of Swedish industries. As part of the government-industry-labour consensus behind the devaluation, the pulp and paper industry was expected to use its windfall profits to restructure and invest in new higher value-added production. The industry did just that, and in the last two years has fairly successfully weathered a steady revaluation of the Kroner upwards.

The Ontario industry, on the other hand, benefitted greatly in the 1970s and again in the last few years from the devaluation of the Canadian dollar relative to the Kroner, and since 1975 has also benefitted from a low exchange rate relative to the U.S. dollar. As we have seen, the Ontario industry has not used these periods of relative advantage to invest in higher value-added product segments in this province. The pulp and paper modernization and financial assistance programs run by the federal and Ontario governments have usually resulted in investment in the existing product and technology mix. Consequently, the central challenge facing Ontario is how to increase the value-added contribution of the province's forestry resource. This challenge has yet to be addressed.

Food Processing

Although the restructuring problem in food processing is different from that in pulp and paper, there are striking similarities. Ontario's food and beverage processors have been part of a large government-regulated food chain which, until recent years, had been mostly insulated from international competition. In many product lines, government controlled marketing boards set prices and often controlled the quantity of production of raw farm products. Processors have been strictly limited in their ability to obtain access to lower cost farm produce and in return have been largely protected from foreign competition. There were some decided exceptions to this in processed meats, distilled spirits, and sugar, for instance, but most of the food processing system has been operated under input price and volume controls.

These controls have enabled the governments in Canada to subsidize farmers and support their incomes through higher food prices. This Canadian system of farm income support is significantly different from the situation in the U.S. and Europe, where the farmer is subsidized directly through general revenues, and not so much through higher prices passed through to the consumer. Under the proposed Canada - U.S. Free Trade Agreement, some Canadian food prices would fall to world levels, and tariffs that currently protect domestic processors would be eliminated.

In any case, the proposed Canada-U.S. Free Trade agreement would result in substantial restructuring in Ontario's food processing industry. In many food processing businesses, the Ontario facilities are well below world scale efficiency. For example, U.S. meat processing plants are five times Ontario scale; U.S. beer plants are three times Ontario scale; and U.S. sugar and spice plants are twice Ontario's average scale (See Exhibit IV. 6). In a few packaged goods food subsegments, one additional work shift a week by a U.S. plant would be sufficient to satisfy the Canadian market, for the same branded products. In addition, many U.S. plants in the food industry are operating well below capacity. These scale differences can compound the competitive difficulties Ontario producers already face from higher average raw materials costs.

The Ontario industry does have a few strong indigenous firms which have the financial resources to invest in new world scale facilities (See Exhibit IV.7). However, such investment is very risky, given that much of the output of any new plants will need

EXHIBIT IV.6

FOOD PROCESSING SCALE COMPARISON
Ontario Versus U.S.
(Average Scale)

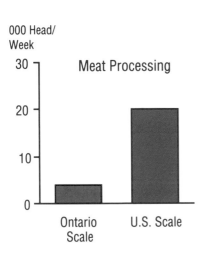

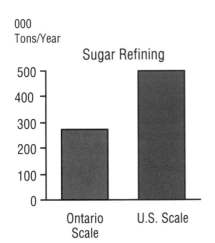

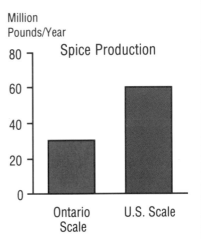

101

Source: Canada Consulting and Telesis based on industry interviews and analysis

to be exported to the U.S. Unfortunately, most food product segments are slow growing and will not easily absorb major additions in output. In any case these Canadian companies have invested heavily on both sides of the border, and plant locations will be rationalized in the future according to where costs are lowest, particularly if the Canada-U.S. Free Trade Agreement occurs. The non-indigenous food processors in Canada are even less likely to take the risks inherent in new plant investment here since they generally have larger scale facilities in the U.S. which are already operating below capacity. As Exhibit IV.7 illustrates, the non-indigenous food processors in Canada export very little, if any, of their Canadian output.

Whisky, beer, and pork represent food products where Ontario producers have established successful competitive positions in export markets on a price premium as opposed to low cost basis. In whisky, Hiram Walker and Seagram's have established major brand franchises and command high prices from U.S. consumers relative to competitive products. In beer, Canada has established the number two position behind the Netherlands in the U.S. imported beer market. The 20-30 percent price premium Canadian beers achieve over U.S. domestic beers more than compensates for the higher costs of production in Canada. In pork, Ontario now exports over 50 percent of total production, mostly to the U.S. The leaner pork produced in the province is recognized as higher quality by U.S. consumers who are willing to pay a price premium for it.

In many other product areas Ontario companies may be able to establish export opportunities through a higher value-added approach. However, the investment costs can be high in product development, advertising, and marketing. In many cases, raw materials costs will still be an important competitive factor, even when a brand or other advantage can be secured.

The similarities between the industrial restructuring process underway in food processing and those beginning in pulp and paper are several:

- New world-scale investments will be high risk because markets are not high growth
- New competitors with lower resource costs are threatening the industry
- Current company profitability may not last long
- Depending on the industry sub-segment, many plants are subscale and operating with old equipment
- Although there may be a need to shift to higher value-added products where competition is based on factors other than re-

EXHIBIT IV.7
THE TOP TEN ONTARIO FOOD PROCESSORS

Name	Sales ($ millions)	Exports as % of Sales	Products
John Labatt Ltd. (Cdn.) (U.S.-based operations contributed 25% of company sales)	2,802	10%	• Ale, beer, butter, cheese, cream, flour, gluten, ice cream, wines, wheat starch
Canada Packers Inc. (Cdn.)	2,600	12%	• Canned meat, cooked meats, peanut butter, animal feed, frozen vegetables, fresh pork, poultry, lamb, beef, edible oils, cheese, milk, pickles
Weston Foods (Food Processing Group)[1] (Cdn.)	1,380	1%	• Bread, rolls, crackers, cookies, chocolate bars, dairy products, wide range of foods, specialty high-quality products under private label
Nabisco Brands (U.S.)	786	3%	• Cereal, biscuits, coffee, popping corn, rice, oils, peanuts, brandy, rum, sherry, raisins
General Foods (U.S.)	731	2%	• Cereal products, confectionery, flavour crystals, food coatings, jelly powders, pudding mixes, snacks, soft drinks and concentrates, toppings
Coca-Cola (U.S.)	550	0	• Non-alcoholic beverages
Molson Ontario Breweries (Cdn.)	425	16%	• Ale, beer
Nestle Enterprises (Swiss)	380	2%	• Baked beans, chili con-carne, cocoa powder, coffee, desserts, frozen dinners, drink mixes, mustard, pasta, relishes, sauces, fruit juices
Robin Hood Multifoods (U.S.)	370	0	• Shortening, cheese, hams, lard, sausage, bacon
Carling O'Keefe (Cdn.)	260	10%	• Ale, beer, stout

1. 30% of total sales are in the U.S. and this activity is generated through U.S. based establishments.

Source: Canada Consulting and Telesis interviews and analysis

103

source cost, entering higher value-added segments requires new skills in product development and marketing which many firms lack.

These features are present in varying degrees and combinations in most of Ontario's resource businesses, including those we did not study in depth.

RESTRUCTURING IN MATURE MANUFACTURING INDUSTRIES

Ontario's mature manufacturing industries have retained much of their vitality but are also undergoing major restructurings. In the automotive and consumer electronics sectors, increased competition has come mainly from overseas. In the printing, specialty chemicals, and appliance industries, the competition has been most intense from the U.S. In many business segments, low wage competitors are beginning to develop strong footholds. The only visible response in high wage countries is for mature industries to invest in higher value-added per employee products and processes. In most of the mature manufacturing sectors, rapid technological change is also increasing turmoil. The application of microelectronics to products and manufacturing processes continues at an ever accelerating pace, necessitating increasing investments in equipment that rapidly reaches obsolescence. In addition, new competitive standards of quality have been introduced in many industries, thus creating a need for more effective designs, better production technology, and greater skills and commitment from workers. The Council analyses of the steel, auto, and chemicals sectors illustrate the restructuring underway in response to all of these changes.

Steel Industry

The Canadian steel industry, with more than 80 percent of its activity in Ontario, has been a successful manufacturing industry for decades. Historically, much of its competitive strength was based on the proximity of low cost, high grade raw materials. In more recent times, as shipping advances have cut transportation costs and newly industrializing countries have developed substantial iron ore and coal deposits, the basis of competition has shifted to proximity to the major steel markets, especially the North American automobile industry.

Ontario's steel industry has been more successful than its U.S. competitors in keeping its facilities close to world-class standards since the 1950s. At least three factors have been at the base of the industry's competitive strength:

104

- Continued adoption of technological advances, originally from the U.S. and more recently from Japan and West Germany
- Maintenance of a relatively high level of capital investment which in recent years has been aimed at quality and efficiency improvements rather than capacity additions
- Focus of the Ontario corporate leadership on the challenges of the core steel businesses without indulging in distracting diversifications into other industries.

For the past two decades, however, the international steel industry has been affected by over-capacity, which increased import pressures on North American markets and decreased the opportunities for the Canadian industry to export its products. As a result, Canada's small overall steel trade surplus is due only to its U.S. trade, and the country is in a trade deficit position with the rest of the world. Worldwide over-capacity has resulted both from a decreased demand for steel and the development of modern low cost steel facilities in developing areas such as Korea, Taiwan, Brazil, and Eastern Europe.

Canada has retained a favoured position in U.S. trade and is one of only three countries which has not been required to sign a voluntary restraint agreement (VRA) limiting steel exports to the U.S. However, this position has been maintained only with an understanding from major Canadian steel producers that efforts would be made to keep exports to about three percent of U.S. consumption. It is unrealistic to expect that trade to the U.S. will be allowed to grow in terms of total tonnage even under the proposed Canada-U.S. Free Trade Agreement. The existing voluntary restraint considerations will continue to be the dominant influence on the nature of steel trade with the United States. If growth in the industry occurred, it would be in value-added terms rather than tonnages.

105

Nevertheless, the Ontario steel industry has made considerable investments in restructuring its facilities during the 1980s and has vastly increased both its economic efficiency and its ability to produce a higher quality product. With its high operating capacities (80 percent) and its lower wages relative to the U.S., Ontario steel producers are among the cost leaders in the developed world, although their costs are still higher than Korea's and Brazil's (Exhibit IV.8).

The ongoing investment which has occurred in the Ontario steel industry since World War II makes it among the healthiest of the province's core industries today. Steel should be able to make a growing contribution to Ontario's economy as a high

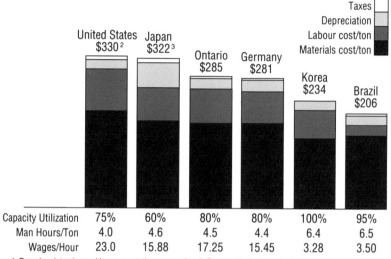

EXHIBIT IV.8
COMPARATIVE COSTS TO PRODUCE HOT ROLLED STEEL PRODUCTS[1]
1986, U.S.$/Ton

	United States $330[2]	Japan $322[3]	Ontario $285	Germany $281	Korea $234	Brazil $206
Capacity Utilization	75%	60%	80%	80%	100%	95%
Man Hours/Ton	4.0	4.6	4.5	4.4	6.4	6.5
Wages/Hour	23.0	15.88	17.25	15.45	3.28	3.50

Legend: Taxes, Depreciation, Labour cost/ton, Materials cost/ton

1. Based on interviews with representative companies, 2. Does not include marketing or overhead costs
3. Japan's man hours per ton is relatively low because capacity utilization is low.
Source: World Steel Dynamics

106

value-added, traded industry. Unfortunately, however, there are important constraints which will limit the scope of opportunities for expansion. Protectionist barriers erected in response to over-capacity have severely reduced the ability to trade steel internationally, regardless of competitive cost position. The rationalization of the U.S. steel industry is rapidly making it more difficult for Ontario mills to compete, especially if exchange rate advantages lessen. Meanwhile the Ontario steel industry is heavily dependent on the strengths of the Canadian automobile industry and the parts sector, which is facing increasing competitive pressure. Automation advances, particularly in the automobile industry, have put new quality demands on the steel industry to improve existing capabilities substantially. Expansion of the industry beyond current levels of tonnage output is not likely, but continued reinvestment in specialty products and higher quality steels should allow value-added to increase despite these constraints.

Automotive

The automotive industry, Ontario's largest manufacturing

sector, accounts for 15 percent of shipments, 60 percent of exports, and seven percent of manufacturing employment. After several years of growth, vehicle production appears to be levelling off largely due to a reduction in the demand for new cars in North America. Future demand is expected to grow at a rate of one to two percent annually.

Since 1982 Canada has enjoyed a surplus trade position with the U.S. in automotive products. The specialization of the Canadian assembly industry in certain high-selling models, the lower value Canadian dollar, and the relative strength of the U.S. economy continue to have positive effects on the Canadian industry. Unfortunately, the trade deficit in automotive products with overseas countries has increased due to high levels of vehicle imports and rising levels of parts imports.

The automotive assembly industry in Ontario has changed markedly in the last five years. What used to be mature product lines and older facilities are now new products and rebuilt assembly plants. General Motors, Ford, and Chrysler have all invested heavily in modernizing their facilities and now some of their most modern plants are in Ontario. At the same time, Honda, Toyota, and GM-Suzuki have added new greenfield plants in the province.

The new investments in assembly in North America, especially by Japanese producers, have led to over-capacity that is projected to reach five million units. This means major restructuring looms ahead and the Big Three will be closing down some operations as well as modernizing others. General Motors has announced the closing of a number of facilities in the past two years; Chrysler is closing its American Motors facility in Kenosha and a casting plant in Sarnia. While these companies are rationalizing their operations, Japanese car companies are bringing in new capacity next year: both Toyota and Mitsubishi will be opening new plants.

The Ontario assembly industry is as well positioned as any to ride the coming wave of restructuring in relatively good shape. At the same time, though, it will have to make strides in terms of quality and productivity, not just to hold its current position, but to become a strong competitor for the next round of investments.

The automotive parts industry faces severe pressure from Japanese and European parts companies entering the Canadian and U.S. markets. These foreign companies start with an assured market from their parent assembly companies and compete for the rest of the North American business from this base. These foreign parts manufacturers are prepared to forego short-term profits in order to gain market share selling to North American car companies. The available parts market is being shrunk by the new Japanese assembly entrants, while at the same time competitive pressures are intensifying. The standards for competitive survival in the Ontario auto parts industry are being rewritten daily in terms of both cost and quality.

While the competitive pressure grows, parts companies are having to take on entirely new functions. Where previously they simply built to specifications, parts companies are now being required to take greater responsibility for such activities as R&D and parts design. This has brought about consolidation in the industry as competitors seek to build the scale necessary to fund their technological efforts. For many companies, product design is a new undertaking and is proving to be a difficult capability to build. In many cases, the technological skills do not exist in the company, nor does the experience in integrating product development and manufacturing.

Another result of competitive restructuring is technological change in the workplace. Such changes are taking place in automation through computer numeric controls, computer aided design, automated guided control vehicles, and robots. More important are the attendant changes that are taking place in the skills required by the workforce. Statistical process control has heightened the need to have analytical skills. Effective worker involvement demands a new level of communication and problem solving skills. Changes in the management environment mean that the old authoritarian roles are being replaced by an emphasis on leadership and team building.

Restructuring will accelerate in the automotive parts sector. Those firms that can adopt the new technologies quickly will widen their edge over their competitors. In many cases, this means the quality of management and the skill of the work force will make the difference. It also means that policies will need to be in place to build rather than lose scale. Moreover, rationalization will mean greater needs for worker retraining and additional incentives to advance the product development capability of companies.

Chemicals

As the world chemical industry has matured in recent years, the chemical industries of many high wage countries have responded by rationalizing their capacity in high volume bulk commodity chemicals while shifting their competitive focus toward the production of higher growth specialty chemicals. Ontario's chemical companies have not followed this trend of shifting significantly into specialty chemicals due to the small scale of the domestic market and the lack of clear access to the much larger U.S. market. While the Ontario industry accounts for 59 percent of Canadian chemical production, it remains uncompetitive in large parts of the market, especially in R&D intensive specialty chemicals. As a result, Ontario's trade position in chemicals seriously lags behind that of the U.S., Japan, U.K., Germany, and France. The lack of domestic producers in specialty chemicals is a major reason why Canada's chemical trade deficit more than tripled from 1983 to 1986. The market for bulk chemicals, in which Ontario currently has a moderately competitive position overall, will grow more slowly in years to come. The major issue for Ontario is whether the industry can transform its capabilities in higher growth specialty chemicals.

The chemical industry's production can be divided into distinct business segments, each with its own competitive dynamics. Competitiveness in high volume commodity products and petrochemical products such as fertilizers and synthetic resins are primarily cost driven, require relatively low expenditures in research and development, are cyclical and generally provide low profit margins. The inorganic chemical industry, which manufactures such products as sulphuric acid and caustic soda, is influenced by the cost of power and transportation. Low volume specialty chemical products such as advanced plastics and pesticides are primarily applications driven, involve relatively high levels of R&D, and allow for high profit margins. Attaining the higher profits involved in specialty chemicals production, which on average yield nearly double the return on shareholder equity of bulk products, generally requires a different set of capabilities and skills. Competitive advantage in specialty chemicals can come from proprietary products and processes, special formulation skills, applications engineering, and marketing coverage of specialty markets. But in commodities, raw material costs, plant scale and efficiency, and transportation costs are the key competitive factors.

By about 1980, the world chemical industry reached a turning point; basic chemical industry growth had matured and the innovation rate for both products and processes had slowed. Rising raw material prices, capacity expansion in lower wage countries, and slower growth rates for bulk chemicals forced higher wage countries to restructure their commodity segment and to shift their emphasis toward specialty chemicals. Since 1980, one quarter of the world's commodity chemical capacity has been retired or mothballed as major U.S., Japanese, British, and Italian firms increased the proportion of their assets dedicated to the production of specialty chemicals. In the U.S., chemical firms have increased their spending on R&D from 2.5 percent of sales

109

in 1979 to 4.4 percent in 1986 in order to develop new specialty chemicals. By 1986 the restructuring had begun to pay off as capacity utilization had risen to 80 percent and profitability had rebounded. Prior to 1980, the chemical industries of most high wage countries were not well positioned in the high growth specialty segments.

While the Canadian industry also rationalized to improve bulk chemical capacity utilization in the 1980's, it has not kept pace in the shift toward specialty chemicals. In 1986, the production of specialty chemicals still represented only 12 percent of total Canadian chemical production. Canada's competitive strengths in chemicals are in raw materials and abundant sources of energy. These strengths are reflected in Canada's disproportionately high production and export of basic industrial chemicals, plastics, and resins in which raw material and energy are important costs. Unlike other countries, chemical industry restructuring in Canada has not resulted in the increased R&D required for competitiveness in many specialty products.

Clearly, the major issue for Ontario is the growth of capabilities in specialty chemicals. While Canada remains competitive in commodity chemicals and world demand for commodity chemicals is once again rising, prospects for growth in Ontario's commodity chemical production are poor. Because lower energy costs in western Canada provide a competitive advantage over Ontario locations, future additions to Canada's commodity chemical capacity will likely be located there. The fast growing, high value-added per employee specialty chemicals segment is the opportunity sector in chemicals for Ontario. But capturing this opportunity will be difficult, especially if the proposed Canada - U.S. Trade Agreement is implemented. Many of the specialty chemical segments in Ontario have significant tariff protection and new North American plants will need to be built if Ontario hopes to increase exports.

THE IMPLICATIONS FOR PUBLIC POLICY

The process of industrial restructuring in the core industries of Ontario revolves around several common themes. These include:

• The shift to higher value-added per employee products and businesses
• Increasing investment in R&D, applications engineering, and marketing to effect the move to higher value-added activities
• Investments in new equipment for quality and cost improvements but not generally for capacity expansion

- International competition increasingly taking place in a world of managed trading relationships (e.g. steel or car import quotas)
  - Increasing use of high technology in products and processes
  - Much greater demands placed on the workforce for increased job flexibility, higher skills, and greater involvement in solving production problems
  - Stable or declining levels of overall employment
  - Corresponding needs for worker training and policies and programs that encourage effective adjustment to technology and workplace transition.

Each of these developments is at a different stage in each industry. In some sectors, the Canadian industry is keeping pace with the world leaders in restructuring to higher value-added opportunities; but more often Canadian firms are lagging behind their international competitors. The devaluation of the Canadian dollar has benefitted mature manufacturers just as it has resource-based firms. In the case of the car companies, the lower dollar has been a spur to investment in higher value-added production facilities. In many other sectors, the devaluation has enhanced Ontario's competitiveness mainly through comparative wage reduction with other countries. The recent rise in the dollar is now giving some of these companies cause for serious concern about their continuing competitiveness.

111

The restructuring issues for mature manufacturing industries are not significantly different from those which emerged in our discussion of resource-based industries. In the resource sectors, the plant and equipment investment issues are paramount. In the mature manufacturing industries, the issues relating to workers' skills are equally critical. In all businesses, the development of new higher value-added products and markets is essential. High value-added investments, training, and research and development will thus become increasingly important to competitiveness in all of these industries as companies try to move beyond commonly available technology and low value-added products.

A NEW PROVINCIAL APPROACH

Industrial restructuring and adjustment are the inevitable responses to the forces of international competition. Some industries, like automotive and steel, have made massive investments to upgrade their facilities to improve the productivity of their manufacturing processes and the quality of their products. Other industries, such as forest products, chemicals, and food products, have generally maintained the same product focus while seeking significant productivity improvements. In the case of rubber or agricultural equipment, restructuring has meant closing Ontario operations altogether and passing on to the government the problems of worker adjustment.

From the provincial perspective, restructuring works best when companies seek out and invest in new opportunities in maturing markets and shift production to businesses where sustainable competitive advantages can be obtained from factors other than wage costs. But companies do not always solve their restructuring problems on their own, and the public interest dictates that the province assist in creating an environment that offers a constructive approach to restructuring and adjustment.

Recapitalization for Growth

A primary constraint to restructuring and the development of growth opportunities for small- and medium-sized Ontario manufacturers is the problem of raising new capital. Making the transition to higher value-added activities requires major investments and represents a formidable hurdle in the development of many firms. The investment climate is bleaker today than it has been in some time as nervous investors have pulled back from equity markets, and most new public offerings have been put on hold.

There is a need to bring investors back into the market and make funds available to the promising indigenous medium-size firms in Ontario's core industries. Without new equity, these firms will be unable to take advantage of the restructuring opportunities in auto parts, forest products, specialty chemicals, and other industries. Various share issuing incentives have worked in Canada in the past in mining, oil and gas, and other industries and could be an important element in the recapitalization and restructuring of core industries in Ontario. We have developed such an incentive to address the critical recapitalization needs of Ontario's mid-size core companies.

Recommendation 1: ONTARIO RECAPITALIZATION INCENTIVE PLAN
An Ontario Recapitalization Incentive Plan should be established to attract investors to indigenous mid-size exporting companies going to public equity markets to raise new capital.

The program would allow investors in new equity issues from companies in manufacturing and specific traded services to receive a significant tax credit or deduction (whichever the government deems most appropriate). The investments would be restricted to a government-approved registry of firms which met certain provincial criteria. These criteria should include the following:

- A listing on the Toronto Stock Exchange (or, for initial public offerings, listing within 60 days)
- A maximum total equity capitalization in the range of $100-$200 million
- Headquarters and major strategic direction from an Ontario base (i.e., indigenous companies)
- At least 25 percent of their world-wide employment value-added in Ontario
- A minimum of, say, 50 full-time employees in Ontario
- A significant level of export sales.

Investors should be able to receive the tax benefits for direct investment in the shares or in mutual funds which agreed to invest only in the qualified issues. There would need to be maximum limits on individual investor contributions and a minimum holding period of at least one year for investors to keep their qualified shares. (Mutual funds would need to be able to trade their investments without a holding period to ensure fund liquidity, but all investments would have to be in qualified firms.)

This program should benefit both mid-size companies in core industries and manufacturers in high growth sectors. As we shall see in later chapters, the indigenous high growth firms in Ontario also require greater access to risk capital if they hope to survive and prosper. An added restructuring benefit of the incentive may be that it will encourage more Canadian entrepreneurs to buy the branch plant facilities of foreign firms and, with re-investment, turn them into indigenous Canadian operations selling to world as well as local markets.

In addition to reducing the cost of raising new capital for Ontario manufacturers, the program would also enhance the venture capital environment for small firms. As we shall see in Chapter VII, the attractiveness of a venture capital investment is affected by the availability of exit routes, particularly the opportunity to take the investee company public. The recapitalization program will ease this transition from venture capital financing to public equity markets.

Expanding Market Opportunities

In many of the core industries we have examined, the shift to higher value-added products will require new competencies in product development, applications engineering, and marketing. Even some of the largest firms in these core sectors will have difficulty in developing the required expertise. One area of particular concern to the Council is the development of market opportunities abroad for higher value-added Ontario products. In some selected areas where a commonality of interest among firms exists and the barriers to entry in overseas markets are formidable, it may be possible to formulate joint marketing approaches.

The Council research program has found that in other countries, co-operative marketing efforts have provided an effective vehicle for large firms, serving mainly local markets, and small exporters to work together to mount successful export initiatives. Denmark in pork products and Italy in clothing are examples of such efforts.

Based on discussions with Ontario food processors, large and small, the Council thinks there may be an opportunity to create an Ontario food products trading company which could target export opportunities outside North America. The food processing industry has some of Ontario's largest indigenous companies, but most of them export only a small percentage of their output and most of that goes to the United States. There are also small food processors in Ontario with successful niche products, say in jams or relishes, which export successfully but to very limited markets like a few New England cities.

Ontario government participation in a high value-added food products trading company could be valuable. In some countries, like Japan, a trading company with government participation is much more likely to be able to break down the multiplicity of non-tariff trade barriers and restrictions. In other countries, particularly in the Third World, government involvement can help facilitate the establishment of marketing offices and local linkages.

The Council believes the Ontario government should explore with the food processing industry the feasibility and potential benefits of such a trading company specializing in exporting non-commodity food products to overseas markets. The government should also discuss similar opportunities with other industries that would benefit from a collective marketing approach. These might include construction materials, furniture, and high value fashion clothing.

A Better Approach to Restructuring

The Recapitalization Incentive Plan can assist relatively

healthy companies with foresight to restructure their operations. Nevertheless, there will be firms already burdened with unprofitable operations which may not be able to take advantage of the plan. In some of these cases restructuring opportunities will still be present. In others the plant and products may be truly not viable. When significant numbers of jobs are involved, requests for government assistance will almost be automatic. In the past the Ontario government has responded to such requests as they arise - often at the last moment and often on case-by-case basis. The province has sometimes extended loan guarantees (e.g. Chrysler), other times lent money at low interest, and in other cases refused to get involved because the prospects for turn-around were slim. In nearly all cases, the lead time for government involvement was negligible, the expectations for results high, and the available options for action seriously diminished because of the late awareness of the need for restructuring.

Restructuring undertaken too late is difficult, if not impossible. However, the experience of other countries shows that more lead time in the process can result in a more effective adjustment approach. The Japanese systematically monitor a series of competitive factors that indicate industries facing trouble and companies where restructuring is likely to be required. The French government assembled a highly talented team of people to deal with companies already experiencing difficulty rather than offering last minute bailout solutions. British Columbia now relies on an industrial restructuring commissioner to help encourage positive adjustment, specifically in the forest products and mining industries.

115

In recognition of its continuing restructuring problems and appeals for government assistance, Ontario has created its own Industrial Restructuring Commissioner. The Council believes this is an important initiative. But based on our initial review of the restructuring experience in Canada and other countries, the Council believes that this initiative must be accompanied by a new set of guidelines that will fundamentally strengthen the restructuring effort. The Council therefore recommends that the restructuring effort in Ontario be carried out under the auspices of the Industrial Restructuring Commissioner as follows:

Recommendation 2: NEW DIRECTIONS FOR RESTRUCTURING
Ontario should put in place a sound industrial restructuring process focussed on the traded sectors, requiring the active involvement of business, labour, and government and aimed at achieving timely and workable restructuring actions.

Several considerations enter into developing such an industrial restructuring process and should become integral parts of the approach:

- Focus on the traded sectors. Jobs lost in the traded sectors are usually jobs lost to the Ontario economy; they are either gone permanently or are very difficult to recapture. Jobs lost in non-traded business are, in most cases, replaced by similar jobs in the domestic economy
- Anticipate the declining industries and major trouble spots. Establish sufficient lead time and direct efforts towards viable restructuring arrangements, not bailouts. Established criteria exist for identifying industries in decline. These have been used to good effect by other countries and should become part of a regular monitoring process in Ontario
- When government involvement is requested, require the company and key stakeholders (e.g., owners, workers, suppliers, and lenders) to put the restructuring plan together and agree on the actions to be taken. In the end, positive action will result only if companies in difficulty are committed to resolving structural problems in their industry and if companies commit themselves to making fundamental changes in their own operations
- Work from a sound basis of competitive analysis. Other governments have had success in putting together a small team of outstanding business, labour, and government specialists to assist in company restructuring, and Ontario could follow a similar approach
- Deliver government support only to well-conceived and viable restructuring plans. The strategy must be to identify problems early and gain the support of all major parties before government financial assistance is extended. Companies that leave restructuring until it is too late should not be automatic candidates for government bailouts. Nor should firms which have little prospect of long-term survival. Workers are not assisted by bailouts which allow firms to limp along until finally collapsing a few years later.

Successful restructuring depends on a coordinated and responsive approach within government. The issues cut across many ministries and frequently present a maze through which business and labour have difficulty manoeuvering. For this reason, the Council also proposes that a committee of deputy ministers representing areas relevant to restructuring be struck to meet regularly with business and labour on restructuring and adjustment policies and issues.

Labour Adjustment

To embark on a truly new direction in industrial restructuring, the province must be prepared to address the problems of labour adjustment in restructuring industries. If Ontario intends to assist only viable firms which fall into difficulty, it must be prepared to help the workers of non-viable firms to develop new skills and find alternative employment.

The Council was not able to study the existing labour adjustment programs in the country, but a thorough review of them is in order, especially if the Canada - U.S. Free Trade Agreement is implemented. The Council is proposing that it address the labour adjustment issues associated with industrial restructuring in its next agenda. This can be part of a comprehensive and in-depth look which the Council plans to take into all the "people issues" related to its proposed economic strategy. Development of this people strategy will include not just labour adjustment, but all worker education and training issues.

Recommendation 3: A REVIEW OF WORKER ADJUSTMENT
The Premier's Council should examine the labour adjustment issues of restructuring in Ontario's core industries and work with the government to develop a comprehensive approach to meeting the adjustment needs of workers in these industries.

117

Specific issues which the Council believes will need to be examined include:

- The current effectiveness of labour markets in coping with worker adjustment
- The subsequent economic fortunes of workers displaced during industry restructurings, including their eventual employment situation and income levels
- The linkage between retraining strategies and adjustment strategies
- The experience of other countries in successfully meeting the adjustment needs of workers in declining industries
- The potential effects of the proposed Canada - U.S. Free Trade Agreement on the worker adjustment process in Ontario.

We will expand on the training aspects of this program in Chapter X.

Technology Adjustment

Restructuring to maintain or increase competitiveness nearly always implies technological change. The experience of industry is that the key to effective technological change lies in the training and adaptability of the workforce. Too often, technology has been introduced without a full understanding of its effects on the workforce and workplace and the results have been disappointing.

The Council research has also established that one of the key ingredients underlying successful restructuring efforts in other countries is a well-informed labour movement that understands the competitive situation of industry and a labour-management atmosphere where jointly held facts and perceptions of the international competitive arena can guide business and labour decisions. To assist in achieving this kind of environment in Ontario, the Premier's Council has worked with the government of Ontario to create the Technology Adjustment Research Program (TARP) the objective of which is to encourage and assist labour and management to carry out research into:

- The effects of technological change on the worker and workplace
- The effects of technological change on the company and its competitive and working environment
- The competitive outlook and the role of technology for the industry
- The issues of adjustment, restructuring, and training in the industry.

This new program will make an important contribution to coping with the effects of technology on the part of both business and labour. Moreover, it will enhance the process of consultation between labour and management, both of whom will benefit as much from the opportunity to work together as from information generated in the process.

Worker Ownership

Initiatives taken in Quebec through the Solidarity Fund, and more recently at the federal level through new tax incentives for national labour organizations to establish venture capital funds, have pointed to worker ownership as a complementary component of industrial restructuring. Such initiatives are not intended as last resort financing for failing firms. Rather, they provide labour with the opportunity to invest in healthy companies that need capital for growth, to put in place new management in restructuring potentially healthy firms, or to buy out discrete businesses from existing companies when those firms no longer have a strong interest in them. They are also intended to maintain good jobs in the country and expand the value-added capability of firms.

The Council believes that worker ownership has an important role to play in Ontario, but there is no clear answer regarding the best course to pursue for the province. One possibility is a worker restructuring investment fund like the Quebec Solidarity Fund; another is a worker equity guarantee program to guarantee loans to workers for the purpose of investing in worker buyouts. The Premier's Council believes that an Ontario worker ownership initiative needs to be fully examined at this time.

Recommendation 4: ONTARIO WORKER OWNERSHIP INITIATIVE
The government of Ontario should initiate a full examination of the potential benefits of encouraging broader worker ownership in Ontario companies.

This initiative should be developed jointly with the Premier's Council to explore several potential mechanisms for encouraging broader employee ownership and worker investment in restructuring companies. It should carefully examine successful and unsuccessful workers ownership models in other jurisdictions, and based on those and the interests of labour and other relevant groups, formulate specific programs that could work in Ontario.

119

CHAPTER V
INVESTING IN HIGH GROWTH AND EMERGING INDUSTRIES

Ontario has a serious competitive problem in its high growth and emerging industries. In a handful of high growth sectors, such as aerospace and telecommunications equipment, Ontario has a positive trade balance and relatively high value-added per employee. But in many others, like computer hardware, software, medical instruments, pharmaceuticals, and semiconductors, Ontario is suffering major trade deficits and relatively low value-added per employee compared to these sectors in other countries.

In emerging industries where markets are much less developed and technological directions still largely uncertain, Ontario has an even weaker position. In a few areas like lasers, a strong Ontario firm has emerged to become an international competitor of note. But in most emerging sectors, Ontario has virtually no participation and in others only a few small start-ups struggling to gain a toehold.

There are historical reasons that Ontario has not developed a stronger presence in high growth and emerging industries. The province's dependence on resource-based industries and the branch plant investments of foreign multinationals did not foster a fertile business climate for many technologically advanced industries. Government policies were not generally effective at remedying the voids left by history, although there were exceptions. For example, the development of Canada's aerospace industry owes much to the skillful use of offset policies by the federal government in its defence purchases, and the success of Canada in telecommunications equipment was based in part on the natural monopoly given for many years to Bell Canada and its manufacturing arm, Northern Telecom.

The challenge for the province and the nation in the future is to develop stronger competitive positions in a larger set of high growth and emerging sectors. It will not be necessary, nor possible as a small nation, to succeed in all such industries, but it is an imperative to broaden and deepen the current high growth and emerging industrial base.

The Council analyzed several high growth and emerging areas in depth. The competitive dynamics of each are different, but as we found in the resource and mature manufacturing sectors, a number of common themes emerge. All of these industries are tied together by the central competitive role which technology plays in each. In most of them, technology is changing rapidly and advanced technical competence is an absolute requirement for staying in the game. But the competitive requirements for success go far beyond good technology, and as we saw with mature manufacturing businesses, long-term success often revolves around manufacturing costs, marketing capabilities, applications engineering skills, corporate scale, or the ability to differentiate one's product sufficiently to obtain a price premium for it. We describe the interplay of some of these factors in looking at the telecommunications equipment, aerospace, computer hardware, software, laser, biotechnology, and nuclear equipment industries.

ONTARIO SUCCESSES: TELECOMMUNICATIONS AND AEROSPACE

Within the group of established high growth industries, the two obvious major success stories are telecommunications equipment and aerospace. Their success is evident in the existence of a full Canadian industry structure that includes diversified multinationals, niche or single product companies, and a network of sub-suppliers. There is also a healthy contingent of indigenous Canadian firms at all levels in these sectors. In fact, telecommunications is dominated by indigenous firms.

Telecommunications Equipment

Canada exports nearly twice as much telecommunications equipment as it imports. The primary market for Canadian telecommunications products is the U.S., which buys roughly double the amount of equipment from Canada as it sells. Other export markets for Canadian products are Japan and the U.K. Because telecommunications products are considered strategic by many countries and telephone companies are usually government-owned or closely regulated, governments often protect their domestic markets from outside competitors. In fact it was a regulatory change which opened up most of the U.S. market to Canadian products, creating Canada's first really big opportunity in telecommunications exports.

Northern Telecom, a $6 billion Canadian multinational, is the critical player in the Canadian telecommunications industry. It is impossible to tell the story of telecommunications in Canada without dwelling on it. Northern Telecom has been the breeding ground for a whole generation of telecom entrepreneurs and has directly or indirectly (through vendor relationships) opened world markets for much of the Canadian telecommunications industry.

Altogether 66 companies, including the forerunner of Mitel, have spun off from the Northern Electric Company, Northern Telecom's forerunner.

Ironically, Northern Telecom was the indirect creation of a U.S. antitrust decision which, in 1956, severed the design and development links between Northern Electric, Bell Canada's equipment manufacturer, and AT&T. Rather than simply licensing foreign technology, Bell Canada and Northern Electric agreed to conduct their own R&D. With a small team of researchers they adopted a strategy of cloning existing AT&T technology and products for sale to one customer - Bell Canada. This strategy was at the centre of R&D development efforts from 1958 to 1968. As the R&D team grew and became more familiar with the needs of its customer and the evolution of technology, they began to explore innovative applications for existing technology. During this second era, which lasted from roughly 1968 to the mid-seventies, the small home market for the company's products dictated a strategy of launching new technologies only when their application and usefulness became indisputably clear. The company did not take major risks during this period.

Northern Telecom's early success gave them the confidence to take a major innovative risk in 1976: the large scale launch of digital systems, a technology that most of the world's telecommunications manufacturers felt would not be introduced for several years. As Northern Telecom began to develop the product in its small home market, something timely happened. AT&T, which at the time was the world's largest corporation, had its U.S. phone service monopoly broken by a 1978 court ruling. The opportunity this presented to Northern Telecom ushered it into its third stage of development, which was to consolidate its digital innovation by becoming a highly productive design factory producing the myriad software programs and related products that could allow customers to customize their systems and connect a variety of product options. It also created the need to develop sophisticated international marketing and applications engineering capability to sell central office switches to local telephone companies and private branch exchanges (PBXs) to large corporate purchasers.

As one of the world's leading suppliers of digital equipment, Northern Telecom moved to develop a global customer base, but its new position required a more complex set of management skills. The new strategy involved balancing full lines of interconnected products at "technology plateaus". Because Northern Telecom was no longer selling to a captive customer, it also had to become more market-oriented and responsive to different customer needs.

Today, Northern Telecom is moving into a fourth phase of technology development which requires yet another strategy and set of skills. As other companies have developed digital capabilities, Northern Telecom has had to begin anticipating entirely new businesses. One of the most lucrative markets in telecommunications is office switching systems. Northern Telecom and some large competitors are now rushing to introduce a complete voice and data transmission system for the office market. Just as complete systems to service this market are becoming available, however, sub-components that perform some of the same functions as these costly systems are appearing and may be able to fill this market need at lower cost. Northern Telecom has found that the scale and pace of each new technical generation of their equipment is accelerating rapidly. Yet there is no assurance that major new products will succeed, and in fact, as the new voice-data systems are finding, the severest competition may come from firms which are developing very different solutions to the same problem.

Other firms have grown up in Northern Telecom's wake, developing substantial competitive positions in their own right. Mitel, for example, became the North American leader in small analog PBX telephone systems of less than 100 lines. When Mitel attempted to move to much larger digital PBX systems like those sold by Northern Telecom, it suffered a major set-back. Unfortunately, the development costs and complexity were significantly greater than Mitel's previous efforts. Perhaps more importantly, the marketing channels for large PBXs were entirely different than those used for small PBXs. Mitel's small PBX systems had been sold heavily through many small interconnection companies which in turn were served by a few large distribution companies. Mitel could serve the market by servicing a few of these large distribution accounts well. Large PBXs were much more likely to be sold directly to end users and thus required a larger company sales force and capability in applications engineering. Mitel found it difficult to sustain the investment required to develop the product and build an adequate field sales force at the same time. Mitel has since retrenched under new (British) ownership and is trying to consolidate its position in smaller systems markets with new digital products.

Aerospace

In aerospace, Ontario is also a net exporter, although Canada as a whole is a small net importer. Part of this favourable trade position is due to offset agreements, but the Canadian industry also has labour cost advantages and some strong indigenous firms. Aerospace engineering costs in Canada are 23 percent lower than in the U.S. and wages are lower by $7.00 per hour. Two indigenous firms, De Havilland and Pratt & Whitney, have been particularly successful at developing world competitive products. De Havilland, recently acquired by Boeing of the U.S. but still managed as an indigenous firm, is a successful manufacturer of commuter aircraft. Pratt & Whitney is a successful indigenous manufacturer of small jet engines.

International competition in aerospace revolves around technological, political, and market share factors. Technological capability is a critical entry ticket to the aerospace industry and in some cases products can be differentiated on a technological basis. In most business segments, however, the key success factor is gaining adequate product sales to amortize huge fixed R&D and product launch costs. High market share and long individual product runs can result from a combination of advanced technological capability, reliability, service coverage, aggressive pricing in expectation of experience curve cost reductions, and a willingness to meet the political needs of buyers. These political needs can include offset purchases, local content provisions, and technology transfer. All military sales and most civilian sales outside of North America entail such requirements.

For most aerospace companies, military projects provide a technological cushion to support civilian production. The relatively risk-free profits from military work enable firms to take on the extremely high risk of civilian projects while maintaining an acceptable overall risk profile. The fact that the U.S. and most European militaries subsidize R&D, tooling, and other product launch costs related to defence purchases provides significant competitive advantages to firms in those countries relative to their competitors in the Canadian industry, which have fewer costs covered by Canadian government assistance. Companies in these countries can recognize economies of scale in amortizing the large fixed costs of R&D across related products, both civilian and military.

The Canadian industry has a stronger orientation towards civil aircraft than does the U.S. industry. While products for military application account for only 34 percent of Canada's aerospace output, they account for 64 percent of U.S. production. This means that Canadian manufacturers do not have as large a risk-reduced military base upon which to build civilian businesses.

Individual companies in the Canadian aerospace industry owe their existence to a variety of competitive factors. Some Canadian firms, such as De Havilland and Pratt & Whitney, have a long history as independent proprietary prime aerospace contractors competing in world markets from Canada. Others, such as McDonnell-Douglas, established Canadian operations mainly because of offset requirements. Many Canadian-owned and a few foreign component manufacturers have been nurtured through offsets but are now becoming increasingly competitive firms selling on their own merits. These indigenous firms represent the most exciting growth opportunities in the industry.

Because governments account for such a large proportion of aerospace equipment purchases, they have traditionally taken an active role in aiding the development of domestic aerospace industries. Procurement is an effective lever for development. Canada has been particularly aggressive in using defence purchase offsets to foster the development of aerospace component firms.

Canada's position in aerospace is further strengthened by the Defence Industry Productivity Program (DIPP), one of the few federal assistance programs which focusses mainly on a specific industry primarily to bolster its export capabilities. The program's objective is to help Canadian companies compete in relatively risky defence-related enterprises against foreign companies which are often directly aided or subsidized by their governments. Unfortunately, DIPP funds make up for only a fraction of the competitive disadvantage of low Canadian defence funding relative to the U.S.

126

Although the aerospace industry in Ontario should continue to grow and prosper, several constraints will need to be overcome:

- There is a shortage of highly skilled machinists and related tradespeople vital to the industry
- The growing protectionism in many markets requires ever greater offsets in those countries by Canadian exporters, thus diminishing Canadian jobs and value-added
- Ontario's fast-growing indigenous aerospace component firms need to develop greater R&D capability to expand their market opportunities and secure more sustainable competitive positions
- The federal government intention to make Montreal Canada's aerospace centre - an initiative it has supported by channeling over 85 percent of DIPP monies to Quebec firms - puts Ontario firms at a competitive disadvantage.

IMPORT DOMINATED SECTORS: COMPUTER HARDWARE AND SOFTWARE

Most other industries in the established high growth category are far from internationally competitive. Industries such as pharmaceuticals, which play a major role in other countries, barely exist in Canada. Other industries, such as computer hardware, are heavily dominated by foreign owned multinationals. Both of these industries have such high R&D and product launch costs that only a small number of world-scale firms can sustain the level of investment necessary for success. Canada has not been able to develop world-scale pharmaceutical or computer hardware firms in this country. Other high growth industries, such as computer software, are not as investment-intensive, and single product niche firms have a better chance of surviving the long-term. The handful of Ontario software firms selling in world markets is growing.

Computer Hardware: A Missed Opportunity

Computer hardware has been a global industry almost since its inception. Local firms in Canada, as in other countries which launched products on the basis of technological innovation, soon found themselves in competition with major multinationals. Today there are almost no computer hardware firms serving only local markets. Even niche players have become essentially suppliers to original equipment manufacturers (OEMs) depending on long-term contracts with multinationals for their survival. The high cost of developing and distributing products for this market, combined with short product life cycles, has made scale the overriding competitive requirement. Today, 90 percent of Canada's $5 billion computer hardware market is held by non-indigenous multinationals. These multinationals import most of their requirements, leading to a $3 billion trade deficit.

The apparent inevitability of the Canadian computer industry's dominance by non-indigenous firms is open to question. Since the 1950s, Canada has had computer systems capabilities, and a number of small Canadian firms tried to develop successful market niches in the fifties and sixties. It is not clear whether these firms could have succeeded, but it is evident that they were at a competitive disadvantage in terms of the government assistance they could receive in Canada. In the U.S., computer manufacturers and semiconductor makers received very significant development assistance from the Department of Defense. In Japan, the Ministry of Industry and Trade had a special program for computer development including a large scale leasing subsidy which successfully accelerated the sales of Japanese computer makers by encouraging buying firms to turn over their computers more quickly than they would have otherwise. The program, which was not open to IBM, allowed Fujitsu and others to pro- gress along the experience curve more quickly, build scale and market share, and develop successive product generations faster. France, the U.K., and other European countries also had procurement policies which significantly favoured local firms and poured large public sums into computer research and development.

Procurement can be a major policy lever in those high growth businesses where governments are major purchasers. Computers are such a business. Governments and public institutions constitute 40 percent of the market for computer hardware and have requirements for a size and level of sophistication not often found in the private sector. During the 1970s, the Canadian government did introduce a computer procurement policy, but it was geared more toward encouraging foreign firms to locate manufacturing and R&D here than focussing on assisting indigenous companies. Lists of what were called "rationalized" companies were drawn up and used in the selection of government suppliers. Rationalized firms were those deemed to be making a significant commitment to Canadian manufacturing or R&D. The approach showed promise in encouraging major multinationals to invest in Ontario. One that did was IBM, which today operates a large Ontario manufacturing facility (also one in Quebec) and one of the five largest private R&D laboratories in the country located in Toronto.

128

In spite of Canadian content policies and good intentions, federal government procurement has been largely ineffective. In recent years, procurement policy has become much more relaxed. Each company is now considered on a case-by-case basis, taking into account overall employment, sales, and future investment plans. Almost 50 percent of federal mainframe and minicomputer purchases in 1986 were from non-rationalized suppliers. Over 50 percent of microcomputers were purchased from Olivetti - an importer with no manufacturing or R&D presence in Canada. As the president of one major computer supplier with no R&D or manufacturing in Canada put it, "Your government is very fair. As long as we have a good price and a good product, they still buy".

The current strategy at the federal level is to encourage increased foreign multinational presence in Canada by relaxing the requirements to become fully rationalized suppliers. Fostering of local firms - the Canadian-owned ten percent of the market - is expected to happen as a secondary result of the increased multinational presence. For example, supplier development programs which will provide incentives to multinationals to use Canadian suppliers are under consideration. Multinationals are also being encouraged to enter into marketing and distribution agreements with Canadian manufacturers.

Canadian hardware manufacturers are cynical about this approach. Entering into OEM contracts and becoming dedicated suppliers to foreign-owned multinationals is considered a self-limiting strategy by these firms. They lose touch with their end-users and become simply a production line dependent on the fortunes of another company. Product development and marketing activities are minimal in companies competing almost entirely on price for OEM contracts. In the long run, many such suppliers become subject to low wage competition in developing countries since their products are not sufficiently skill-intensive.

In Ontario, as in the federal government, procurement decisions are not adequately related to industrial development objectives. The Ontario government usually selects the "lowest priced technically compliant bid" but adds a ten percent price premium to bids lacking Canadian content. There is also a policy of awarding many small contracts rather than a few larger ones. The Ontario approach has fragmented purchasing to the point that a 1985-86 analysis found there were 4,000 separate procurements for $138 million in computer goods. Small-scale contracts spread among hundreds of Ontario government computer suppliers clearly does not promote the creation of a few world-scale firms. Only large contracts allowing for world-class product development can foster the consolidation necessary for growth in the small provincial industry.

129

The few Canadian computer hardware manufacturers that do sell directly to end-users face major challenges, especially due to problems of scale. Generally, they have focussed on specific niches: Gandalf specialized first in modems and now in networking systems, and GEAC developed proprietary hardware for large data base/large terminal transaction data processing. GEAC targetted two specific markets: library automation and small financial service businesses, especially credit unions and trust companies.

These firms have encountered major competitive difficulties in trying to overcome their scale disadvantages. By 1983 it was clear that the Canadian market would not be able to continue to support GEAC's growth. The company targetted U.S. banks as its next market and for the next four years spent over $30 million on product development. The resulting Advanced Banking System product was one year late, $5 million over budget, and failed in its first installation. In a large company, the scale of these problems could have been easily handled. However, GEAC, already financially precarious, was almost pushed into bankruptcy.

Computer Software: Still An Opportunity

Unlike the highly consolidated computer hardware industry, the computer software and service segment does provide growth opportunities for a number of smaller firms focussed on niche markets. The capital requirements are much lower, and it is possible to create competitive advantages through customer service, specialty product innovations, custom applications, and other points of competitive leverage.

Players in the software service industry include the multinational hardware manufacturers (like IBM and Digital Equipment), foreign-owned software and service suppliers (such as Lotus and ADP), and Canadian-owned firms (such as GEAC, Cognos, and Systemhouse), some of whom sell hardware as well as software and services. Unfortunately, though indigenous Canadian firms have met with export success, Ontario suffers a trade deficit in software of $2-3 billion that is growing at a rate of 20-30 percent/year.

The software and computer services industry is made up of four distinct market segments, each with unique competitive dynamics (See Exhibit V.1). Packaged software is the most

130

EXHIBIT V.1

MAJOR SEGMENTS OF CANADA COMPUTER INDUSTRY
1986 Revenues

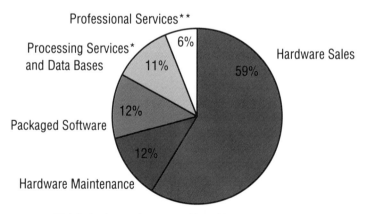

Professional Services**

Processing Services* and Data Bases 11%

6%

Hardware Sales 59%

Packaged Software 12%

Hardware Maintenance 12%

* Includes batch processing, remote problem solving, remote automated transactions

** Includes contract programming, facilities management, DP consulting

Source: International Data Corporation

traded sector and the one in which the highest percentage of value-added in the business returns to Canada from sales in export markets. Two other sectors, professional services and data bases, are also traded but as service businesses require substantial local participation in export markets, thereby reducing the value-added back to Canada. The fourth segment of the market, processing services, is traditionally a local business, although leading firms today are seeking new opportunities to diversify.

In the packaged segment, marketing scale and access to distribution channels are vitally important. For this reason well-focussed Canadian firms have been able to achieve substantial success by dominating a specialized niche market throughout the world. For example, Cognos, Canada's largest packaged software company, has achieved a 70 percent world market share in fourth generation language software for Hewlett Packard computers. Having solidified its position in that market, Cognos is now expanding to provide the same product for other selected hardware environments.

Many other Canadian packaged software companies are able to survive in the $5-15 million sales range by following a similar niche market strategy. However, as GEAC demonstrated with its U.S. banking product, a niche strategy can be risky, too. A niche market, by definition, is limited in sales growth potential. If it does grow to substantial size, it will attract large competitors; if it stays small, a firm's growth will depend on constantly identifying and moving into new niches. The investment required to make the transition to a new niche is substantial; for a small firm it can mean "betting the company" on every new product. For these companies, each new generation of product costs more to develop than the last, and a small firm cannot withstand the cost of failure. However, not investing in new products is certain failure.

131

Computer services is an entirely different business from packaged software and one that depends largely on the experience curve. Systems integration, the fastest growing segment of the services sector, illustrates the experience curve dynamic very well. Because the major cost component in a systems integration project is skilled programming labour, a firm experienced in a particular type of installation can gain significant cost advantages over its competition in subsequent contracts.

Canada's two largest systems integration firms, DMR (a Quebec firm) and Ottawa-based Systemhouse, have both achieved sales of over $50 million. Each has effectively used government procurement in various provinces (though not Ontario) and at the federal level to move along the experience curve and later sell similar systems in other domestic and foreign markets. Systemhouse, for example, has used the experience gained on provincial contracts in Saskatchewan and Nova Scotia to sell major projects in Los Angeles and Hong Kong.

The Quebec government has purposely used procurement to create a private sector computer services industry that now exports from a Quebec base. Large government contracts have given Quebec firms the scale to develop major competencies and reduce their costs on similar subsequent projects. This has given them a major competitive advantage. As a DMR senior executive put it, "DMR is a product of the buy against build policy of Quebec".

The lack of any world-scale systems integration firms based in Toronto is due in large part to the Ontario government strategy of building an internal software capability and only outsourcing overflow requirements in small contracts. Ontario government procurement policies emphasize internal control of information systems, increasing the use of inside staff, and spreading the limited number of external contracts among many small suppliers. In fact, Ontario is sourcing increasing amounts of software internally (See Exhibit V.2). The average computer software and

132

EXHIBIT V.2

ONTARIO GOVERMENT SYSTEMS DEVELOPMENT EXPENDITURES

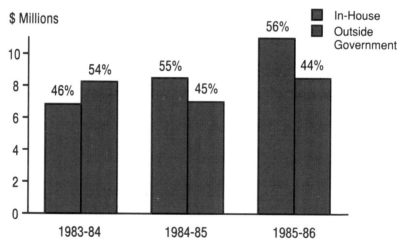

Source: Strategies for the Management of Information Technology in the Ontario Government, Management Board of Cabinet, Ontario

service contract for the Ontario government is only in the $20-50,000 range. This approach creates an Ontario industry made up of many small firms selling their services on a short-term basis. Without large, challenging contracts, there is not enough pressure on the industry to consolidate and gain the economies of scale needed to make Ontario companies competitive internationally. Software is one high-growth industry where better government policies could have a substantial effect on long-term success.

EMERGING INDUSTRIES

Emerging industries share a set of characteristics that clearly distinguishes them from the established group of high growth industries described above. Their most fundamental common features are that the scientific basis for these industries is still being developed and technology - having the latest breakthrough - is often the major competitive driver. In most emerging industries important applications of the technology are not yet known and current uses may later prove to be stepping stones to the ultimate products and markets.

These characteristics have a profound effect on the structure of emerging industries. Small research companies, years away from launching a first product, survive on consulting contracts or other financial backing but are still considered by more advanced players to be part of the industry. The few proven new companies that do exist are usually in a rapid-growth phase and financially precarious. Large multinationals, if they are involved, are usually funding the work of outside firms as well as internal R&D efforts. The ultimate industry leaders are still unproven and current leaders will not necessarily be the long-term players. Examples of these industries in Canada today include lasers, certain advanced materials, and biotechnology.

133

From a public policy point of view, these industries present a unique challenge. Despite their small size and high risk of failure, firms in these industries are critical to Canada for several reasons. First of all, they are at the vanguard of segments of the economy in which new wealth and jobs will be created. Secondly, many of the products of traditional Canadian industries will be threatened by the products of these emerging sectors. For example, some Canadian steel products are already being replaced by advanced composite materials, and nitrogen fertilizers could be threatened by advances in biotechnology. In some cases, products from emerging industries will become the enabling technologies which stimulate the future growth of established industries, as is the case with the advanced semiconductor materials now being used in telecommunications, computers, and elsewhere. The Council studied several of these emerging industries to understand how they are developing, to identify policy needs, and to measure our relative success to date.

Lasers: An Emerging Success Story

Canada is a relatively small player in the global laser industry. Whatever presence we have achieved rests primarily with the success of one firm, Lumonics, which at $65 million in sales is the third largest laser company in North America. Other than Lumonics, the Ontario industry is primarily made up of research houses generating revenue from consulting contracts, grants, and testing services rather than from product sales. Ontario firms operate mainly in industrial and scientific markets, producing lasers for materials processing, scientific, and medical uses.

The laser industry is really many individual business segments, some of which are now shifting away from being primarily technology driven to other competitive factors, such as applications engineering, service coverage, and product reputation. A shake-out is now taking place in the industry and firms without strong marketing and operations expertise are finding they are ill-equipped to survive. Lumonics, like other leading firms in the industry, has been acquiring smaller firms to broaden its capabilities and accelerate its entry into new markets.

Export markets are critical for Canadian firms. Although Lumonics exports 94% of its production to the U.S., the company faces two competitors several times its size (Spectra-Physics and Coherent) whose R&D is fuelled by large U.S. defence contracts and grants. Lumonics and other Ontario laser companies have received R&D grants from the National Research Council (NRC) and other financial support from the Ontario Development Corporations. Lumonics has also been successful in acquiring access to publicly funded research from universities and the NRC. Both the University of Toronto and McMaster University do significant research in the laser field, and the fruits of their work have been incorporated into products developed by Lumonics.

Establishing linkages with the public science and technology infrastructure is a key factor in the success of emerging industries. As Chapter IX will describe, Canada's R&D resources are heavily concentrated in government departments and public institutions. Technology transfer problems abound, and unfortunately, Lumonics' success story is the exception rather than the rule.

Biotechnology: Weak Industry-Buyer Linkages

Biotechnology is emerging as an increasingly important segment of several industries: pharmaceuticals, chemicals, agriculture and food processing. The challenge for small Canadian biotechnology firms is to develop linkages with more mature firms in these industries that can become buyers of their innovations. Unfortunately, Canada's lack of large firms in areas like pharmaceuticals clearly constrains the growth of biotechnology firms.

In a world context, Ontario is a bit player in biotechnology. Measured in terms of R&D investment, the industry is dominated by the United States. Canada's total investment in 1986 of $190 million was equal to only three percent of the $6 billion U.S. commitment. The level of R&D investment is a critical factor in the biotechnology race because of the almost unprecedented research intensity of this industry: individual product development costs can be as high as $100 million (See Exhibit V.3). To date, all significant new medical products applying biotechnology have come out of the United States.

The players in Canada's biotechnology industry are the federal government, supplying 55 percent of the R&D funding,

135

EXHIBIT V.3

BIOTECHNOLOGY-BASED PRODUCT DEVELOPMENT TIMEFRAME
Pharmaceuticals

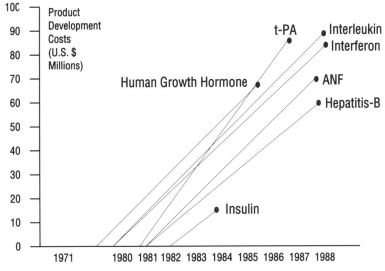

Source: Canada Consulting and Telesis

provincial governments supplying ten percent, and industry funding 35 percent. Within industry, 80 percent of R&D funding comes from small start-up companies led by the Ontario-sponsored Allelix Corporation. Federal government funding of biotechnology is almost completely internally focussed: less than ten percent of federal R&D funding goes to industry.

Ontario has approximately 45 biotechnology firms, the majority of which are in medical or agricultural biotechnology. Although some of these firms can point to examples of successful commercialization on a small scale, the industry as a whole suffers from Canada's lack of entrepreneurial infrastructure. Government support of the industry is small and poorly targetted; few venture capitalists in Canada are willing to invest in local biotechnology firms; and most critical of all, Canada lacks large research-intensive pharmaceutical and chemical companies to commercialize and distribute new products.

Ontario has addressed the lack of a domestic biotechnology industry by setting up a company, Allelix, and staffing it with world-class scientists. However, the track record of this company to date shows that, while biotechnology products are scientifically based, they require a market pull, not just a research push for their development.

Ontario's future in biotechnology will depend on forming more effective linkages between publicly funded research institutions and private sector companies, and between the companies and world-scale corporations with the means to commercialize and market their products.

Nuclear: Restructuring In High Growth Industries

The nuclear equipment industry in Canada had many of the characteristics of an emerging industry in the 1960s and 70s, but counter to expectations, it did not mature into a stable high-growth industry. Canada made a massive $4 billion investment in nuclear technology and now, as reactor sales world-wide have slowed to a trickle, the country is faced with a major dilemma as to what to do about its nuclear capability. The industry's recent experience demonstrates that restructuring and downsizing can be an issue even in high growth sectors.

The story of nuclear energy in Canada is one of substantial financial commitment, clear technological success, and massive frustration. The Canadian decision to build a nuclear supply industry was based on the country's own domestic electricity needs. The industry has successfully met Ontario's need for a substantial new source of generation capacity, but with the exception of one reactor in New Brunswick and another in Quebec, the rest of Canada's energy needs are still being met by hydro and thermal power.

From the outset it was intended that Canada's product, the Candu, would be exported to other countries which did not have domestic nuclear industries. However, export sales have been hard to win, as French, German, and U.S. competitors have scrambled after a limited number of opportunities. Declining prices for thermal energy sources and environmental concerns have greatly slowed the market demand for reactors in most parts of the world, and all major competitors have found themselves forced to cut costs, restructure, and fundamentally decide how much to participate in this industry in the future.

Since its inception, the Canadian nuclear industry has concentrated on one distinctive technology and emerged with a highly effective heavy water reactor - the Candu. In contrast, the rest of the world has concentrated on light water reactor technology originally developed in the U.S. for military applications which, unlike the Candu, has an expensive fuel cycle and relies on a few foreign sources to produce enriched uranium. The Candu reactor has built an international reputation for technical excellence, efficiency, reliability, and flexibility. In fact, the Japanese are seriously considering adopting heavy water reactors to augment their existing nuclear program and have spent $30 million over the last 10 years in support of Candu-related research.

137

In the mid-1950s, Atomic Energy of Canada Limited (AECL) and Ontario Hydro set out together to develop the Candu technology. Ontario Hydro decided on a four unit station to achieve economies of scale, while AECL opted for a single unit 600 MW design more suited to export markets and the needs of other provinces in Canada. Historically, AECL has also been an active supplier of nuclear design services to Ontario Hydro, but this relationship has declined. Over the years, Ontario Hydro has progressively established a comprehensive design capability to meet the demands of its projects. With the separate market focusses of AECL and Ontario Hydro (Ontario Hydro serving Ontario, and AECL everywhere else) two separate nuclear organizations have emerged based on the same technology. Today, both organizations have expertise in design, project management, and construction. No such duplication exists in the supplier network as the pressure has been towards rationalization and maintaining adequate strength for survival. Today, no suppliers rely solely on the nuclear industry, but view it as add-on business to their operations in related industries and technologies.

The federal government continues to fund research in nuclear technology, some of which has helped to diversify AECL away from nuclear energy into medical applications, food irradiation, and other areas. AECL's research company also continues to do about $80 million a year of Candu related research. The emphasis has been entirely on safety and fuel channel design. Critical competitive needs, such as fundamental cost reduction of mature products as well as tailoring the product line to meet specific market niches, have been given only secondary attention.

The nuclear policy dilemma facing Canada today has been brought about by a dearth of nuclear reactor market opportunities. Energy demand in the domestic market has slowed substantially, postponing the need for new capacity. International market opportunities have been even more scant. However, Ontario Hydro's $30 billion investment in the Candu reactor needs substantial continuing technological support regardless of the world market prospects for reactors. Meanwhile, any hopes we have of continuing as a presence in the international market will require significant research and development activity to reduce capital, construction, and operating costs of our reactors. The domestic market has been quality rather than cost driven, so the necessary cost cutting expertise has not been acquired at home. Furthermore, the supplier base, while shakey at present, could be lost altogether if there is no ongoing work.

If the Canadian nuclear industry is to be a successful competitor in the international market in the future, it must move from a capital projects orientation to one of a product orientation. This will require a re-focussing of the nuclear program and a co-operative commitment on the part of government and industry to achieve a standardized and lower cost Candu reactor. Given current technology and expertise, this challenge can probably be met, but it may require the privatization of Canada's nuclear program to achieve the necessary entrepreneurial and marketing flexibility.

In spite of the technological quality of the Candu reactor, Canada still faces the possibility that its investment in nuclear energy technology may not survive the pressures of the international marketplace. In the domestic market, Ontario already relies on the Candu for 50 percent of its electricity; it is unlikely that political and environmental interests will allow this proportion to increase substantially in the near future. If international markets recover, a lower cost and more standardized Candu may have a chance at commercial success, but we must first invest significantly in R&D to achieve that cost reduction. The Japanese and French are already making that investment.

The duplication of resources at AECL and Ontario Hydro has

also led to unnecessarily high costs, and a fragmented approach to the market. Rationalization of Canada's nuclear infrastructure will require the commitment of both the federal and Ontario governments to a common set of objectives that are based on a realistic assessment of the Candu's future domestic and export prospects and the technological support Ontario Hydro will need in any case for its already extensive nuclear program. It would be unfortunate for Canada and Ontario, where most of the industry is based, if an effective restructuring strategy were not developed to capitalize on the remaining opportunities inherent in Canada's largest-ever technological investment.

HIGH TECHNOLOGY IN A SMALL COUNTRY

In all of the high growth and emerging industries we have discussed, several common themes for future competitive success have emerged. Most of these can be grouped under the general problem of competing in high technology markets from a small country base.

The markets for the products of high growth industries are global, and new technological developments spread quickly across the world. Even in emerging industries, where market needs are still being defined, technologies, once introduced, move rapidly from one country to another. The international nature of competition in these industries parallels that in mature manufacturing and resource-based industries, but with one crucial exception: the industrial base of high growth and emerging firms in most countries is much less stable than the core industries base. Thus, the destabilizing potential of rapid technological change and diffusion is compounded by the relative vulnerability of many of the firms which are developing and marketing the high technology products.

139

Of course, this is not a problem for all countries to the same extent. In Japan, the U.S., and parts of Europe, large indigenous multinationals in the core industries are also leaders in high growth and emerging sectors. These firms can be funders, customers, and eventually friendly suitors and rescuers of smaller companies. Ontario does not have this resource to any marked degree. Northern Telecom, Pratt and Whitney, and perhaps a few core industry multinationals can play an anchoring role in advanced industries. By and large, though, Ontario firms in high growth and emerging industries face tough international competition without the assistance of larger parent companies to fall back upon.

There are at least four specific characteristics of high growth and emerging industries which pose tremendous challenges for companies competing from an Ontario base. Each of these are described below.

Innovation Is Only The Beginning

Many companies achieve their initial success through a technological innovation or creation of a new product which captures the support of a significant proportion of the potential market. This initial product, however, rarely gives a company a sustainable competitive advantage. Typically, management must transform the company's technological edge into lasting competitive strength through efforts such as serving a wider market than the competition, building manufacturing scale, developing an image by which they can command price premiums, or providing applications engineering that competitors cannot match.

The Pace And Scale Of Technology Are Increasing

With the achievement of each new technological plateau, the pace and scale of technology increases in most high growth and emerging industries. The cost of new products can range from a few million to hundreds of millions of dollars in the pharmaceutical and aerospace industries. (See Exhibit V.4). For small compa-

140

EXHIBIT V.4
THE COST OF DEVELOPING SELECTED NEW
CANADIAN PRODUCTS

Product	Cost
	($ Million)
Candu Reactor	$4,500
Small Commercial Aircraft	$500
Mid-range Private Branch Exchange (PBX)	$150
Canadarm for NASA	$130
Complex Minicomputer Software	$30
Multi-user Database Computer	$30
Hybrid Canola	$20
Cable Television Software Delivery System	$7
Specialized Jet Engine Component	$5
On-line Retail Pricing System	$3.5
Diagnostic Test Kit	$2.7

Source: Canada Consulting and Telesis based on company interviews

nies with limited resources this can be an explosive combination. It means that in the face of increasing R&D investment, the length of sales life in which to earn a return on that investment is contracting. In some industries, such as computer hardware, this effect is so extreme that only the largest companies with the resources to reach thousands of customers around the world in a short period of time are able to stay in the game.

The pattern is even more pronounced in second and third product generations. A company can spend years developing a biotechnology or software product only to find that its sales are cut short by rapid introduction of a second generation product by a larger competing firm.

R&D is Only A Small Part Of Getting A Product To Market

Research and development costs are often viewed as the major basis of competition in high growth industries. However, in many businesses they are only a small fraction of the total cost of bringing a new product to market. Even more critical can be the prototype costs, product testing, final design for manufacture, packaging, and market launch costs. In microcomputer software these costs can be up to ten times the development cost of the original software. In pharmaceuticals the costs of product testing are usually five to eight times the cost of the original product development. For small companies with few product lines, sustaining a new product through actual market launch can be financially debilitating.

141

Companies With Small Domestic Markets Are Disadvantaged

Companies competing from a small domestic base face special problems in gaining world scale. Because the home market for their product is small, or in some cases non-existent, a firm in a high growth industry must begin exporting at an early stage in the product life cycle, often while it is still financing initial growth. This puts added strain on the cash flow of the firm so that it enters export markets often lacking adequate marketing and sales staff. Even large firms in small domestic markets can confront this problem when they enter new product lines that may require a different sales approach.

THE ROLE OF GOVERNMENT

In every country in the world governments play a major role in fostering the development of high growth and emerging industries. The mechanisms used and their relative effectiveness differs. At least three distinct types of assistance are especially important for these industries:

- Government financed public science and technology infrastructure in laboratories and universities
- Direct financial assistance to industrial R&D in the form of contracts, grants, and tax incentives
- Procurement contracts to develop new advanced technologies and build economies of scale in them.

The Public Science And Technology Infrastructure

Public sector technological capabilities must be tailored to the specific competition, positions, and needs of individual industries (See Exhibit V.5). In areas such as biotechnology, where the public research infrastructure is larger than industry research efforts, policies should focus on increasing private sector capability. In strong industry sectors such as telecommunications, public sector resources should complement private sector requirements in areas that the industry identifies as important. The best opportunities for effective public-private sector linkage are when both are strong, as in the Ontario laser industry today. When each is strong, linkages tend to be established more easily and informally. The need to refocus Canada's science and technology infrastructure will be discussed more extensively in Chapter IX.

142

Government Assistance To Industrial R&D

Overall government assistance to industrial R&D in Canada seriously lags behind that available in other major industrial nations. This means that the private sector is at a severe competitive disadvantage versus other countries in terms of the level of government funding for R&D carried out in industry. Taking non-tax support (grants, R&D contracts, etc.) and tax credit support together, about 20 percent of all R&D performed in Canadian industry is financed by government (federal and provincial). This is half of the level of support in the U.S., where 40 percent of all industrial R&D is financed by government. In the U.K., it is 37 percent, in France 29 percent, and in Germany 24 percent (Exhibit V.6).

A primary form of government R&D assistance to industry is through tax incentives. Canada's R&D tax incentives have been at least as generous as those in other countries. However, recent cuts in federal tax support for R&D will eliminate this position of advantage. The federal government is introducing a limit on R&D tax credits to 75 percent of taxes payable, which will have the effect of reducing the cash flow of Canadian R&D performing companies by $30-40 million/year. It will particularly affect the few large firms doing substantial R&D in Canada. For some of

EXHIBIT V.5

MATCHING SUPPORT TO INDUSTRY CAPABILITY

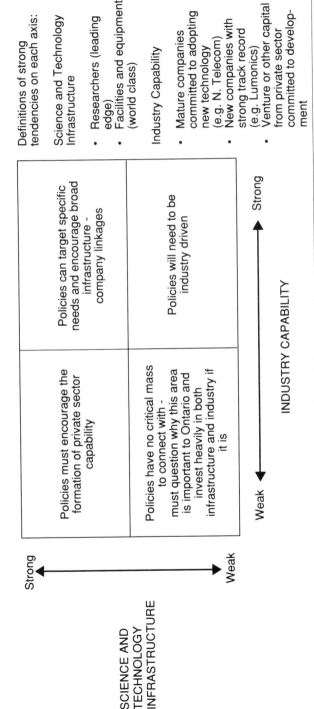

Definitions of strong tendencies on each axis:

Science and Technology Infrastructure

- Researchers (leading edge)
- Facilities and equipment (world class)

Industry Capability

- Mature companies committed to adopting new technology (e.g. N. Telecom)
- New companies with strong track record (e.g. Lumonics)
- Venture or other capital from private sector committed to development

SCIENCE AND TECHNOLOGY INFRASTRUCTURE

Strong ←→ Weak

INDUSTRY CAPABILITY

Weak ←→ Strong

Policies can target specific needs and encourage broad infrastructure - company linkages

Policies will need to be industry driven

Policies must encourage the formation of private sector capability

Policies have no critical mass to connect with - must question why this area is important to Ontario and invest heavily in both infrastructure and industry if it is

143

144

EXHIBIT V.6

TAX AND NON-TAX GOVERNMENT SUPPORT FOR INDUSTRIAL R&D AS A PERCENT OF R&D PERFORMED IN INDUSTRY

COUNTRY	NON-TAX SUPPORT	TAX SUPPORT	TOTAL SUPPORT
United States	33%	7%	40%
United Kingdom	29%	8%	37%
France	22%	7%	29%
Germany	18%	6%	24%
Canada	**12%**	**8%**	**20%**

Source: Canadian Manufacturers' Association, February 1986 Discussion Paper.

them the loss in R&D tax incentive could equal as much as 20 percent of their after-tax earnings. The Council is dismayed by this cut-back in federal incentives, which flies in the face of all the supposed commitments to greater industrial R&D promised by the federal government.

Traditionally, most government non-tax funding of R&D carried out in the private sector has been done at the federal level. The primary mechanism for funding industrial R&D is the National Research Council's Industrial Research Assistance Program (IRAP). A total of $110 million in grants went to industry through this program in the 1986-87 fiscal year. IRAP is highly regarded by the private sector, in part because of its flexibility: it allows industry wide scope in defining the research projects funded by the program. However, compared to the non-tax level of assistance to industry for R&D purposes in other countries, Canada's level of support is very low (See Exhibit V.6).

The markedly low level of Canadian government non-tax support for industrial R&D causes very significant difficulties for Canadian firms competing against U.S., Japanese, or European corporations. For example, much of the non-tax support for R&D in the U.S. comes from the Department of Defense. Many U.S. companies have large percentages of their total R&D paid for by the U.S. Department of Defense - in some cases 90 percent (Exhibit V.7). This defence supported R&D benefits even purely civilian projects since it often funds core technologies common to both military and civilian applications and in any case helps amortize the fixed overhead of R&D operations. Defence R&D also helps to stabilize the cyclical nature of technological spending in some businesses. Three examples[1] illustrate the competitive problems that U.S. defence spending can pose for Canadian firms:

145

- On average, Canadian aerospace firms receive 50 percent of all their R&D dollars from government sources; in the U.S. their competitors average 75 percent of R&D paid for by government. Several Canadian aerospace firms reported that their American competitors offer lower prices for similar products simply because they do not have to recover nearly so large an investment in product R&D
- Despite being the third largest laser company in the world, Lumonics has been effectively shut out of U.S. defence research. The U.S. government is spending over $200 million a year on various types of laser research. Lumonics' two main competitors

1. Based on Telesis and Canada Consulting interviews and analysis.

EXHIBIT V.7

U.S. GOVERNMENT SUPPORT TO THE TOP TEN U.S. DEFENCE R&D CONTRACTORS
($MM Canadian)

COMPANY	DEFENCE R&D CONTRACTS	R&D OF OWN FUNDING	DEFENCE R&D AS % OF TOTAL R&D
Lockheed Missiles & Space	$ 2,048	$ 678	75%
Martin Marietta	1,788	302	86%
McDonnell Douglas	1,281	697	65%
General Electric	1,275	1,794	42%
Grumman	1,256	109	92%
Rockwell International	857	563	60%
Boeing	835	1,045	44%
TRW	740	221	77%
Bell Boeing, Joint Venture	711	N/A	N/A
IBM	683	5,486	11%
Hughes Aircraft	558	N/A	N/A
United Technologies	552	1,177	32%
Total	**$12,584**	**$12,072**	**48%**
			(8 Firms)

Source: Telesis and Canada Consulting based on data from U.S. Department of Defence and *Business Week* 1987, U.S. R&D Survey

in the U.S. (respectively two and three times Lumonics' size) are each receiving from the U.S. government direct research monies well in excess of Canadian $15 million. This support is on top of their own R&D expenditures. Lumonics' entire R&D effort is $10 million

- AT&T is Northern Telecom's key competitor in the U.S. market. Bell Northern Research, Northern Telecom's research arm, has less than one percent of its R&D paid for by government through non-tax measures. At AT&T about five percent ($125 million) of all research is paid for directly by the U.S. Department of Defense. AT&T also receives substantial government R&D contracts and grants from other federal agencies.

Canadian firms which receive a significantly lower level of public non-tax R&D support than their U.S. competitors find it increasingly difficult to stay in the competitive race. This problem will require a national solution since it is international differences that must be compensated for. But Ontario can improve the industrial R&D climate in the province, and in the process help make up some of the competitive disadvantage facing Ontario firms.

Currently, Ontario is doing less for R&D intensive companies than Quebec, which unlike Ontario, does not tax the federal R&D tax credit. Quebec also has introduced a special provincial R&D

EXHIBIT V.8
AFTER-TAX VALUE OF R&D INVESTMENT
TAX CREDITS - ONTARIO vs. QUEBEC

	Ontario	Quebec
Qualifying R&D	100%	100%
Federal ITC @ 20%	20	20
Quebec ITC @ 20% of Direct R&D Costs*		11
Total ITCs	20	31
Less Federal Tax @ 30%	6	9
Ontario Tax @ 14%	3	
Total Tax	9	9
Net After Tax Value of R&D ITCs	11%	22%

* Direct R&D costs (salaries, wages) assumed to be 55% of total qualifying R&D

Note: Assumes a company doing business only in Ontario or only in Quebec. For most companies, the determination of provincial tax is more complicated than the above example. In some cases, Ontario can generate tax revenue from the Quebec tax credit.

Source: Developed by Canada Consulting and Telesis

tax credit for direct R&D costs (salaries and wages). As Exhibit V.8 illustrates, a company doing business only in Quebec would receive 22¢ of every qualifying $1 in R&D back after tax, while an identical firm doing business only in Ontario would receive only half that much back after tax.

The Council believes that Ontario must improve the tax incentives for industry R&D in the province. In keeping with our belief that all incentives should be highly focussed, we would opt for a provincial tax incentive targeted at incremental R&D expenditures by firms.

Recommendation 5: INCREMENTAL R&D TAX INCENTIVES
The Ontario government should institute a special tax incentive for incremental R&D expenditures above a company's three-year rolling average of R&D performed in Ontario.

The incentive could be in the form of a tax credit or a deduction. If it is a tax credit, it should include a provision enabling R&D performing firms which pay no taxes to take advantage of it, by making it refundable. The advantage of using a deduction, of course, is that a tax credit will itself be taxed by the federal government, thus diminishing the benefit to companies receiving it.

148

The Procurement Opportunity

Governments at all levels in Canada recognize that procurement is an important industrial development tool. With close to $80 billion in purchases annually, the public sector's combined buying power makes it the largest potential customer by far for thousands of Canadian businesses. Yet neither the federal nor provincial governments (with the possible exception of Quebec) have effectively harnessed this purchasing power to the benefit of Canadian industry.

One of the most significant problems with existing Canadian procurement efforts is that they are based on a 'local content' approach of giving a price preference or quota to local suppliers. Unfortunately, such an approach does very little to build internationally competitive Canadian firms. In technologically advanced products and services, it does not even result in local procurement because very often a Canadian supplier is not deemed capable.

The Ontario approach to procurement is also oriented toward the awarding of many small contracts for pieces of projects rather than large awards to a few suppliers which could help those suppliers to get to a sufficient scale to compete in export markets. An example of this is the procurement of the ICON computer. At a total cost to the government of over $100 million, the investment in educational computer hardware and software should have been one of the province's greatest opportunities to use procurement to develop high-growth industries. However, the project so far has failed to achieve its industrial development objectives, largely because of Ontario's local content and small contracts approach to procurement. Today, there are approximately 200 software writers in Ontario sustained by small, single contracts from the Ministry of Education. No companies of scale have developed because the procurement process was designed to spread the contracts among as many small shops as possible.

The hardware was developed by local firms, but was made incompatible with computer industry standards and was thus not exportable. Cost pressures also resulted in the hardware manufacturing being moved offshore. The ICON is reported to be a good, inexpensive, educational computer with effective software. However, because insufficient attention was paid to developing specifications for the hardware and software to enable it to be sold outside Ontario, and because no software firms were developed of a scale sufficient to serve export markets, the entire development effort was a botched opportunity for the province. What makes this especially discouraging is the fact that the scale of Ontario's educational hardware and software development effort was unique in North America.

149

The Council recommends that the province move from its current form of 'local content' purchasing to a new approach which we call 'strategic procurement.' In strategic procurement, the goal is to assist local suppliers, through procurement, to broaden or deepen their experience, improve their product, reduce their costs, and/or gain sufficient scale to be more competitive in world markets. Strategic procurement requires understanding the international competitive environment facing domestic suppliers and recognizing the most critical leverage points for gaining a competitive advantage in their businesses.

In some businesses, new product development is a critical competitive tool. Strategic procurement can help by funding the development of new state-of-the-art techniques, testing prototypes, and making the initial purchases of new products. In other businesses, economies of scale in product or after sales service may be critical to competitive success. Strategic procurement can assist companies in those businesses by helping them build scale. In still other businesses, close relations with a major customer for application engineering developments and other product refinements may be a significant means of gaining a competitive edge. Strategic procurement can create a close, preferential, ongoing relationship with critical local suppliers, enabling them to test new applications and perfect product enhancements.

Other countries have used the procurement lever very successfully. France's industries in nuclear equipment, off-shore oil services, high speed trains, and aerospace have all built world-leading competitive positions in various products on the strength of French procurement policies. Canada has seen a few successes, too, particularly in the use of defence offset contracts discussed earlier. But overall, the procurement lever remains largely untapped in Canada. Ontario can change that locally through the comprehensive and more strategic approach described below.

Recommendation 6: STRATEGIC PROCUREMENT PLAN

A strategic approach to procurement should be adopted throughout the Ontario government, including Ontario Hydro. Such an approach should include three initiatives:

• A Strategic Procurement Committee to be composed of independent business, academic, and labour leaders, as well as senior government representatives to lead the initiative

• A Health Care Procurement Commissioner to focus on pulling together Ontario's substantial buying power in the health care field to assist in the development of Canadian medical equipment and pharmaceutical firms and in attracting foreign multinationals to carry out R&D and locate manufacturing facilities in the province

• An Enabling R&D Contract Fund which, under the direction of the Strategic Procurement Committee, would receive proposals from all arms of the Ontario government and provide a means for developing competitive Ontario suppliers by awarding small developmental contracts prior to tendering major contracts.

The role of the Strategic Procurement Committee would be to identify major purchase requirements of the Ontario government over the long-term (perhaps the next ten years) and develop a strategic approach to procurement in selected high potential areas. This approach would involve early identification and notification of Canadian firms, providing these firms with enabling research and development contracts to expand their technical capability, and defining how Ontario's needs and the demands of the international marketplace could be meshed in the development of procurement specifications. The Committee would also act as a watchdog over the entire government procurement system and report regularly to government on how well industrial development objectives are being met. This would require an overall procurement plan from the government with specific goals to be achieved each year.

The Strategic Procurement Committee would use the Enabling R&D Contract Fund to award small, developmental (i.e., enabling) contracts prior to tendering a major contract. This would require anticipating major purchases years in advance and making this information known to the appropriate Canadian companies that might, perhaps with some technical help, be able to bid on related contracts eventually. Small contracts for researching current technologies, writing specifications, and developing and testing prototype designs could then be awarded to one (or perhaps several) Canadian firms. This would give these firms an opportunity to develop a strong position in that product and increase the likelihood of their becoming the most qualified bidder once a contract is tendered to make a major purchase. Eventually, with the experience and scale gained from the major contract, the firms could become significant exporters of the products developed originally through the Enabling R&D Contract Fund.

CHAPTER VI
BACKING THE THRESHOLD COMPANIES

The competitive challenges discussed in the preceding chapters have pointed to an important structural weakness in the Ontario economy: the lack of indigenous world-scale firms largely outside the province's resource-based industries. The development of such firms must become a central goal of Ontario economic policy.

The growth of new world scale competitors from an Ontario base will take many years. The group of companies from which new world scale Ontario competitors could emerge is alive today and already meeting with some success in export markets. We call these " threshold companies." This is because they are on the threshold of becoming leading multinationals in their respective businesses. They run the gamut from metal stamping auto parts manufacturers to developers of high technology lasers.

Threshold firms are generally middle-sized companies with $40 - $400 million in sales and a high degree of exports. Their success in international trade indicates that they have mastered the basic competitive demands of their businesses. Generally, though, they are subject to strong additional competitive pressures because they are up against larger foreign firms with vaster resources. All of the Ontario threshold firms interviewed in our research had major opportunities for growth, but in most cases were faced with tough decisions about allocating their scarce resources to those growth opportunities. Ontario's threshold companies offer tremendous promise to the provincial economy. The following story of one threshold company illustrates some of the characteristic challenges such firms will have to overcome to fulfil that promise.

THE DILEMMAS OF A THRESHOLD FIRM

The executive committee of a $100 million equipment manufacturing company, a large employer in a small western Ontario city, spent much of its fourth quarter last year wrestling with a difficult set of strategic alternatives.

The company has a 25 percent share of the U.S. market in its major product segment and, although not low cost, commands a price premium mainly due to a reputation born of its experience in serving Canadian resource industries. Internationally, the company operates as one of the few medium-sized firms in a business dominated by divisions of huge multinationals, three from the U.S., three from Japan, and four from Europe. Furthermore, the market is crowded with a number of small niche players who operate regionally in North America and Europe. In this difficult competitive playing field, the firm has had to scramble to stay even, but it still maintains a 25-30 percent share in all major markets.

The executive committee is composed of members of the management team and representatives of a U.S. venture capital fund. Together, this group put together a leveraged buyout of the firm from its U.S. based parent five years ago. The firm is profitable but still highly leveraged, and additional capital is not readily available.

Strategic options facing the board include the following:

• Despite its high U.S. market share, the firm is not represented in major market areas such as the Pacific Northwest or some rapidly growing southern states. They take the occasional order from these regions, but cannot push the product. Additional sales offices should be opened, but each one would represent an investment of up to a half-million dollars over a two-year period of building sales during which little return could be expected.

154

• The firm has been an innovator in its major product line, which accounts for 70 percent of total sales, but its engineers have ideas for new products in secondary segments which could represent significant growth areas. Developing a new product, however, can eat up $4-5 million before a single sale is made, and there is no guarantee that the efforts will succeed.

• Of over $60 million in exports last year, about $8 million went to countries other than the United States. The major overseas sales were in Europe with a sprinkling in Africa and South America. The world's fastest growing markets are in Southeast Asia, but the firm does not participate at all in this region. Another overseas sales office should be opened, but that effort would require a commitment of more than a million dollars in an area where the Japanese competition is particularly well entrenched.

• The board strongly feels they cannot remain a competitive international company unless they grow to at least $300 million in sales by 1994. There are a number of smaller start-up companies, particularly in Quebec and in the southern states, which would make excellent acquisitions to help achieve this goal quickly. Capital is the problem.

This company faces challenges, problems, and choices which are common to many Ontario threshold firms. It is a small to medium-sized company in a world of multinational giants. It is a successful exporter, but needs to reinvest constantly just to maintain its position, to say nothing of the imperative to grow. It likely will have to forego some promising opportunities because it does not have ready access to adequate capital. Unlike its larger competitors, making the wrong choice will result in more than a temporary negative blip in total operating revenues. It can set the company back several years, or even spell disaster.

But on the positive side, making a couple of good investment choices can bring the kind of growth which will turn the company into a stable, formidable competitor on the international scene for years to come.

This firm is a typical Ontario threshold company. It is headquartered in Ontario and has had success in exporting and creating high value-added jobs in the province. Threshold firms are relatively strong companies compared to many Ontario businesses, but often they are relatively fragile compared to many of their worldwide competitors. They face opportunities - such as developing new products, entering new foreign markets, growing by acquisition, obtaining new technology through internal development or joint venturing, or improving manufacturing productivity - which could improve their competitiveness and bring them closer to parity with the large multinationals they most often compete against. But they normally do not have the capital to make all the promising investments they could or probably should to keep up. We believe that Ontario must focus special industrial development efforts on aiding these threshold firms to improve their competitive strength and become truly world scale.

155

WHO ARE THE THRESHOLD FIRMS?

Our analysis of industry sectors in Ontario has led us to the conclusion that the class of companies we are calling threshold firms are a largely invisible segment of the province's economy. This is partly because economic analysts look mainly at industry categories, and threshold firms can be found in dozens of industries. Also, much public attention is lavished on high technology start-ups on the one hand and multinational branch plants on the other. Threshold companies usually attract attention only when they are in high technology fields, yet many of them are in more mature manufacturing businesses.

The following is a set of characteristics which can help to define and identify threshold firms more precisely:
- The company will be an indigenous firm, which means that

product development, manufacturing, and overall strategy are directed from a Canadian base

• The sales of threshold firms will generally be in the range of $40-$400 million

• Exports will be a relatively high percentage of the company's sales - at least 25 percent - but will usually be in the range of 60-80 percent[1]

• The firm will have a significant international market share in the core products that it produces

• Management will measure the firm's success against a few definable international competitors, most of whom will be larger in total sales than the Ontario company

• The firm will maintain overseas sales offices, but usually will not be represented in all major international markets

There are probably 40 to 50 firms in Ontario which will meet all of these criteria. We have listed some 25 in Exhibit VI.1 that were identified during the Council's research program. Many of these threshold firms are in high growth areas like telecommunications equipment, software, and lasers, but others are fast growing companies in more mature industries like auto parts, machinery, and forest equipment. We have included companies as big as Magna International and Mitel in the list even though they are over our size criteria because they still have many of the characteristics of threshold firms and in many of their businesses are competing against foreign multinationals which are much larger.

156

The important role these types of companies play is somewhat masked by the fact that their total exports amount to only five percent of the total value of exports from all leading Ontario manufacturers.[2] This low percentage, however, is primarily a reflection of the dominant role of multinational companies in Ontario industry. As a group, threshold firms export more than 70 percent of their Ontario production while maintaining their core research, marketing and management functions in Ontario.[3] They also account for 25 percent of Ontario exports from high growth companies. (See Exhibit VI.2) Even within the mature manufacturing sector, threshold firms are easily among the fastest growing companies. Several Ontario threshold automotive parts companies have growth rates of over 15% per year, making them high growth businesses within a slow growth industry.

---

1. In the case of a few threshold companies like Lurnonics, foreign sales are very high, but exports from Ontario are not over 25 percent of sales due to the servicing of foreign markets from foreign production operations.
2. Based on Canada Consulting and Telesis analysis of the 336 leading Ontario exporters in 1985 (exports over $10 million).
3. ibid.

EXHIBIT VI.1
EXAMPLES OF ONTARIO THRESHOLD COMPANIES
1987 ($ Millions)

	Exports from Ontario	Total World Sales	Country of Ownership	Product Lines
Magna [1]	$454	$690	Can.	Auto Parts
Mitel	385	453	U.K.	Telecom Equipment, Integrated Circuits, Switchboards
De Havilland [1]	242	300	U.S.	Commuter Aircraft and Assemblies
AG Simpson	190	280	Can.	Auto Metal Stampings
Spar [2]	109	191	Can.	Satellite, Communications, Aviation Products
Husky	102	113	Can.	Plastic Molding Machinery
Menasco	79	85	U.S.	Aerospace Components - Flight Controls, Landing Gear
VME Equipment [1]	76	80	U.S.	Bulldozers, Trucks
Timberjack	75	142	U.S.	Logging Equipment
Long Manufacturing	74	78	Can.	Radiators - Auto, Truck Tractors and Oil Coolers
Linamar	68	80	Can.	Machine Castings
Woodbridge Foam	64	287	Can.	Automotive Foam and Plastic Molded Parts
Fleet Aerospace [2]	64	92	Can.	Aircraft Components, Antennae
Electrohome [2]	62	161	Can.	Video Displays, Printed Circuit Boards
Cognos	57	68	Can.	Software
Leigh Instruments	27	53	Can.	Control Systems, Recorders
Devtek	26	104	Can.	Aerospace, Defence and Electronics
Fisher Guage	23	40	Can.	Mini Zinc Die Castings and Machinery
Navtel [1]	22	25	Can.	Data Communications Test Equipment
Lumonics [2]	13	65	Can.	Lasers
RBW Graphics	10	61	Can.	Books, Directories, Catalogs, Publications
GEAC	8	64	Can.	Computer Hardware, Software
Gandalf	8	130	Can.	Computer Data Communications Equipment
CAE Electronics	N/A	486	Can.	Aerospace, Electronics, Auto Parts
Galtaco [2]	N/A	94	Can.	Castings, Auto Parts

157

1 1987 Data not available; 1985 Data used   2 1987 Data not available; 1986 Data used   N/A = Data not available
Source: Canada Consulting and Telesis Interviews and Analysis

EXHIBIT VI.2

THRESHOLD COMPANY ROLE IN ONTARIO EXPORTS

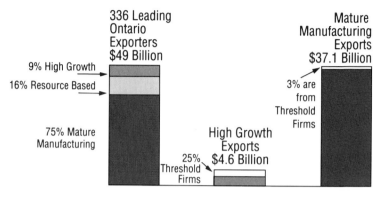

Source: Canada Consulting and Telesis analysis. See Exhibit II.1 for details

THE ORIGINS OF THRESHOLD COMPANIES

Threshold companies spring from a variety of sources. Some begin as entrepreneurial start-ups, often on the basis of a technological innovation. Mitel, GEAC, Lumonics, Cognos, and Gandalf are all threshold firms that began as technology start-ups. Other threshold firms have been around for a long time, but under more aggressive management in recent years have started expanding in new markets and developing new products and services.

Some of the most interesting threshold companies were created by leveraged management buyouts of divisions of U.S. multinationals. Timberjack in forest equipment and Woodbridge Industries in auto parts are examples of firms originating from such buyouts. In the hands of new owner-managers, these firms embarked on aggressive expansion programs by building off the competitive strengths of their established Canadian operations.

Some multinationals based in Canada have become increasingly indigenous in their Canadian operations and have bestowed on their Canadian subsidiaries progressively greater autonomy. These subsidiaries are encouraged to undertake R&D and product development in support of the products manufactured in Canada. Strategic product decisions are increasingly centred in Canada to the point that some of these firms eventually have the characteristics of indigenous threshold companies. Menasco, a U.S. owned maker of jet landing gear, is a threshold company in this vein.

A final type of threshold company which may emerge more frequently in the future is a "resource cross-over firm". Some of Canada's resource-based indigenous multinationals, like Alcan and Noranda, have been investing heavily in new technologies and businesses. At Alcan, this investment has been mainly through subsidiaries; Noranda has used a venture capital fund. These investments in non-resource businesses could lead to the development of new threshold companies owned by Canada's large resource-based firms.

Another example of the cross-over variety could be Ontario Hydro's New Business Ventures Division (NBVD), which Hydro created to bring together its non-utility businesses. In 1987, New Business Ventures had estimated sales of $48 million, most of which were in materials or services destined for export markets. Central among its products is irradiated cobalt for medical and public health purposes, but NBVD also sells Hydro expertise to other countries in areas like consulting engineering, nuclear plant simulation and inspection services, and power systems management and training. NBVD is investing in R&D in many new product areas where Hydro's nuclear by-products or utility expertise could provide the basis for creating sustainable businesses in international markets. The New Business Ventures Division of Hydro could become another significant threshold company for Ontario.

THE COMPETITIVE CHALLENGES

To foster and encourage the success of more threshold firms in the province, it is important to have a clear sense of the competitive challenges they face. Threshold firms are playing from certain strengths. They have managed to develop products which meet market needs, produce them with costs that are competitive, and market them to obtain a significant share of the international market. However, they have not yet reached the size or scale which allows them to grow as quickly as their competitive situations demand and sustain all the major investment vital to their future success. We have found that Ontario threshold firms share one or more of four common strategic challenges for the growth of their companies. These challenges are described below.

The "Bet The Company" Risk

For most small-to medium-sized companies which are not diversified, the development and introduction of a new product imposes costs which could put the entire company at risk if that new undertaking is not successful. For a huge multinational firm such as Philips or General Electric, the failure of a new product introduced by one of its divisions will translate into losses, but it will barely alter the corporation's bottom line. In a $100 million Ontario company, however, such a failure will cause massive disruptions in carrying out a company's short and long-range business plans. In the most extreme cases, management has to "bet" the company's future, in effect, on the success of a multi-year development effort which could cost several million dollars. If the product fails, the company could fail with it. Several of the firms on the threshold company list in Exhibit VI.1 have come close to bankruptcy in such situations.

The Move From "Cloner" To Innovator

In many mature manufacturing and some high growth businesses, some Ontario firms have succeeded by being exceedingly good low cost manufacturers of products more or less "cloned" from the competition. These firms have copied the basic designs and product features already on the market and added perhaps a few changes to aid in manufacturing the product. Northern Telecom in the 1960s was such a firm, which basically "cloned" its product designs from AT&T in The United States.

A low cost "cloning strategy" can be successful up to a point. But in many businesses, long-term competitive success eventually requires the development of true innovative capability. Northern Telecom eventually moved beyond the "cloning" stage to real innovation in the 1970s with the development of digital telephone switching technology. The development of this leading innovative capability made possible Northern Telecom's rapid expansion in global markets. But in the 1960s and early 1970s, Northern was still a threshold company.

A number of Ontario's threshold firms today are in a position similar to Northern fifteen years ago. Several automotive parts companies in the province have been very successful at manufacturing low cost, high quality components to the specifications of the vehicle companies. Now these firms are being asked to do more of the actual product design and development themselves, and they must build an R&D capability they did not require before. They must also take on the risks associated with innovation. If their designs fail to sell, no one will pay for their development costs or compensate for the lost manufacturing opportunities.

The "Simultaneous Markets" Challenge

Particularly in high technology businesses, a company must

attempt to introduce a new product in all major markets simultaneously. High technology firms cannot expect to build sales at home for a few years before tackling export markets. In one to two years, those markets will be full of competitors' products, and those overseas competitors will soon start attacking the company in its home market, perhaps with the next generation of product. Even in less technology sensitive businesses in the international context, it is important to meet competitors in all major markets nearly simultaneously. This need to have a world-wide presence poses difficult cost and resource problems for Canadian companies of the size of our threshold firms. A relatively small threshold company like Cognos in software is compelled by the global nature of its software markets to maintain 35 sales offices on four continents.

The "Stuck In A Niche" Problem

Small companies can successfully dominate a small niche in world markets. To grow, however, the niche must grow or the company must create additional niches. These options carry considerable risks and costs as they require developing new products and marketing skills in different businesses than those which the company started with and knows best. Threshold firms can often grow to $30 million in sales on the strength of success in one or two niches only to stall as they saturate those markets. GEAC ran into this problem after it came to dominate the world's large library software business and the Canadian small bank software market. GEAC then took the leap of investing $30 million to develop a U.S. mid-size bank software program which nearly put the company under when it failed in its first installation.

161

SHARING THE RISKS WITH THRESHOLD FIRMS

Because threshold firms are so critical to Ontario's future prosperity, it is important that government policies take account of the special strategic challenges such firms face. Unfortunately, most provincial and federal programs offer little assistance to these threshold companies. The bias toward fixed asset assistance in government programs is a particular problem since most of the strategic investments of many threshold firms are in product development, design, testing, marketing, and other areas which derive little benefit from fixed asset financing.

In order to help speed the growth of Ontario threshold firms into more stable international competitors, we recommend the development of a program which will share the risks associated with these companies seeking to develop new products or markets.

Recommendation 7: Ontario Risk Sharing Fund

The government should create an Ontario Risk Sharing Fund to provide conditionally reimbursable matching loans to successful, established exporting companies for investments in new product development, prototype placement in export markets, and the establishment of new marketing offices outside North America.

The fund should be focussed on threshold firms, although multinationals would not be turned away if they were indigenous and had suitable export oriented projects. The fund would have the following characteristics:

• Loans would be available for up to 50 percent of total project costs, including new product development, design and placement of prototypes, and/or establishment of marketing offices outside North America

• Loans would be repayable on a sliding scale, depending on the success of the project. There would be no payback if the project fails and an above-market payback rate if it succeeds. The above-market rate would ensure that companies were not merely coming to the Ontario Risk Sharing Fund for low cost capital

• Since the goal is to build on strengths, only companies with a successful record of exporting would be funded

• The fund should also have the flexibility to share the costs with companies (on a conditionally reimbursable basis) of feasibility studies for high Ontario value-added opportunities in new products or overseas markets

• Based on the experience of other countries such as Sweden and France, which have similar funds, this program would aim to be financially self-sufficient after its initial capitalization.

In most threshold firms, investment in a new product is often traded off against the opening of another marketing office, and full prototype testing of a new model may be dropped in favour of funding the marketing of existing products. A threshold firm's limited financial resources cannot accommodate more than a few major investments at one time. The purpose of the Ontario Risk Sharing Fund is to allow a larger number of worthwhile projects to be carried out. With access to this fund, the executive committee of a threshold company faced with six well-conceived investment projects could now do four of them instead of perhaps just two. This ability to intensify a firm's investment program would accelerate the growth of the company, while the risk sharing concept would reduce the immediate cash demands of new proj-

162

ects and the threat posed by any single failure to a firm's overall stability. The requirement that successful projects pay back the loan principal and a high rate of interest would ensure that companies come to the fund only for those projects that they would not undertake otherwise.

There should be a tough, professional review of all proposals to the Ontario Risk Sharing Fund to ensure that each project is an inherently risky one that a company would have difficulty taking on alone. The experience of the Swedish Industrifunden, which operates on a similar basis, suggests that the use of an independent staff drawn from people in industry who have been involved in product development efforts themselves can result in much more informed review of all proposals. In the Swedish experience, this review process also drew on international expertise and consultants as appropriate. Companies found that the high quality of the review process often yielded major improvements in the business proposals themselves.

REFOCUSSING THE ONTARIO DEVELOPMENT CORPORATIONS

The major industrial assistance agencies in the province are the Ontario Development Corporations (ODCs). Charged with encouraging and assisting in the development and diversification of Ontario industry, the ODCs make available loans and investment monies mainly for new business start-ups, capacity expansions, and high risk ventures. They also provide a variety of business advisory services and play a major role in regional development efforts.

163

Unfortunately, the ODCs have exhibited many of the problems of government assistance to business discussed in Chapter III. They have assisted non-traded and traded businesses alike; focussed mostly on very small businesses; lent heavily for fixed assets and not R&D or marketing efforts; and emphasized assistance to slower growth industries and firms which have experienced or are likely to encounter further financial difficulty. The government has already begun to address these issues and refocus the ODCs activities on middle-sized and threshold firms that have strong export performance or prospects. Although the ODCs will continue to serve regional policy objectives, they can and should move away from non-traded, fixed asset, and slow growth firm financing.

The Council has a number of recommendations to offer with respect to the refocussing of the ODCs and how this process should be carried out to enable the Corporations' goals to dovetail with the needs of threshold firms and the creation of the Ontario Risk Sharing Fund.

Recommendation 8: REFOCUS THE ONTARIO DEVELOPMENT CORPORATIONS
The government should accelerate the refocussing of the Ontario Development Corporations according to the competitive priorities identified in this report.

Specifically, this will require adjusting the ODCs' own priorities to:

* Provide assistance only to businesses in manufacturing and tradable service sectors
* Build an active relationship with successful middle-sized companies and assist these firms to make the leap into world export markets
* Improve ODC response times for reviewing and processing applications to match the best industry standards
* Assist the development of Ontario's high growth industries by providing needed funds for prototype development and overseas marketing as opposed to emphasizing fixed asset lending
* Orient all assistance to encourage companies to move to higher value added products
* Emphasize these strategic priorities even when pursuing regional development objectives.

164

The shift in ODC priorities is already underway. Once completed the ODCs should be able to play a complementary role to the proposed Risk Sharing Fund. The ODCs could have two objectives: assisting in regional development and helping middle-sized Ontario companies in traded goods and services move into world markets and over time attain threshold company status. In that sense, many firms might begin as clients of the ODCs and later, as they grow and develop, become clients of the Risk Sharing Fund. Because of their regional priorities, the focus of the ODCs will always be much broader than that of the Ontario Risk Sharing Fund.

CHAPTER VII
FOSTERING AN ENTREPRENEURIAL CULTURE

Ontario start-up companies in traded, high growth sectors will be important to the long-run prosperity of the province and require special attention. It is in the ranks of start-up companies today that we will find many of the threshold firms of tomorrow and possibly the indigenous Canadian multinationals of the next century. New businesses in Ontario, as in any jurisdiction, face a unique set of challenges that are not well addressed by broadly based economic development policies. These businesses tend to be financed outside the mainstream of banking and other financial institutions and often do not have access to marketing and distribution channels routinely used by larger competitors. Yet a disproportionate share of important new products and services, as well as new employment creation, comes from these companies.

An entrepreneurial culture in which start-up companies can flourish does not just happen. It must be fostered. Studies of entrepreneurs, including original research done for the Premier's Council, show that several factors combine to create an environment that spawns successful new businesses. Risk-taking must be valued by society, and its accompanying rate of failure tolerated. Access to start-up capital is essential, as are customers willing to try a new product. Governments can play a role in fostering such a culture through well-focussed incentives and high-profile acknowledgment of successful entrepreneurs.

Almost 90 percent of businesses created in Canada today are in the service sector. With a few important exceptions, these tend to be non-traded businesses serving only local markets. There is a high degree of turnover in the population of these non-traded start-up companies. But in most cases, the demise of one local business is usually followed by the creation of a new, perhaps more productive, local business. However, if a Canadian traded service or manufacturing company fails, all too often it is replaced by a foreign competitor simply importing goods into Canada. For this reason, the success of traded start-up companies, especially those in higher value-added and technology intensive sectors, must be the focus of Ontario policy.

THE STATE OF ENTREPRENEURSHIP IN ONTARIO

To understand the phenomenon of new business creation in Ontario's traded sectors and the constraints and opportunities faced by these companies, interviews were conducted for the Council with 71 Ontario companies established since 1979. [1] A special effort was made to interview another dozen technology based start-ups which were spun out of Northern Telecom and Bell Northern Research in the last ten years. The results of these interviews provide an understanding of the environment in which Ontario start-ups operate and the reasons for their success or failure.

Ontario's community of entrepreneurs in traded, high-growth industries is a relatively small and surprisingly closely linked group. Some entrepreneurs start one company and stay with it for the long term. Others - approximately 50 percent of the 184 entrepreneurs in the Premier's Council survey - start one company and then a few years later go on to begin another. A profile emerged in the survey, particularly among the "technology entrepreneurs", of a small, integrated community of highly trained and motivated individuals who form alliances to pursue a new venture and then, a few years later, may regroup differently to pursue a new technological idea.

There is a high level of business formation and dissolution in all types of start-up companies. The annual failure rate of companies in Canada with less than five employees is 40 percent, compared to only 4 percent in companies with over 500 employees. One lesson drawn from close analysis of the successful start-ups is that many entrepreneurs have failed once, twice, or even three times before succeeding. Tolerance of failure is a necessary part of an entrepreneurial culture that fosters successful start-up companies.

166

Where Entrepreneurs Come From

Ontario entrepreneurs come from all walks of life. A few graduate from school and immediately start their own businesses. Many more work for another firm for several years to gain experience and then strike out on their own, often in a business related to that of their former employer. Some "technology entrepreneurs" become self-employed simply because there is no Canadian firm in which they can pursue their specialized field of research.

Ontario's new businesses most often arise out of other fully integrated Ontario businesses; only a handful of entrepreneurs surveyed came from subsidiaries of foreign-owned companies. The best incubator of new businesses is generally another fully integrated company in which senior employees are exposed to all

---

1. Companies were interviewed by Canada Consulting, Telesis, and staff from the Ministry of Industry, Trade and Technology (MITT).

aspects of business, including R&D, new product development, marketing, and general management. Non-indigenous firms in Ontario are not usually integrated businesses, but simply sales offices or have limited manufacturing facilities operating as branch plants or under world product mandates. Executives in such firms do not have exposure to a broad set of skills unless they join the parent company's operations abroad, in which case they are more likely to create a start-up in that country. Dozens of U.S. start-ups have been created by ex-patriot Canadians in just such a manner.

The outstanding example of the "incubator" phenomenon in Ontario is Northern Telecom, and particularly Bell Northern Research, which together have spawned more than 50 spin-off companies (see Exhibit VII.1). While most of the entrepreneurs in these companies started up independent of Northern Telecom or BNR, a few began with financial backing from their former employer. Typical of these firms is Orcatech, a computer workstation company whose founders had designed the product while employed by Bell Northern Research. When BNR decided not to pursue the project, they gave the technology and a $2 million order for the product to the founders in exchange for 20 percent of the new company. Most of the Northern Telecom and BNR spin-off companies, however, acknowledge them as a source of technology and training, but not as an active player in the formation and success of their businesses.

The Cost of Getting Started

In the Premier's Council survey, entrepreneurs identified raising capital as the most serious challenge facing start-up companies. Lack of equity capital was identified as a constraint to growth by 74 percent of the firms interviewed and lack of debt capital at an affordable cost by 59 percent of the firms (See Exhibit VII.2). For a technology intensive firm, millions of dollars of capital are likely required before the company is profit or even revenue producing. Some firms interviewed had incurred development expenses of as much as $5 million just to get to a product prototype. Although R&D grants and tax credits can assist in the early phases of product development, most entrepreneurs found their post-R&D commercialization costs higher than their basic R&D costs, and no government assistance was available to help at that stage. In fact it was quite common for many of the firms to spend as much as ten times their cost of product R&D in bringing the product to full commercialization.

EXHIBIT VII.1

EXAMPLES OF SPIN-OFF COMPANIES FROM BELL NORTHERN RESEARCH

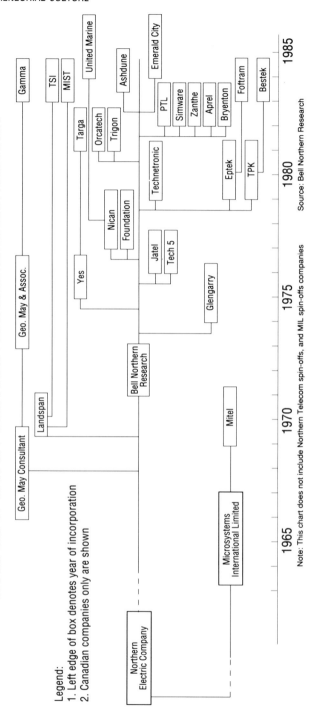

Legend:
1. Left edge of box denotes year of incorporation
2. Canadian companies only are shown

1965   1970   1975   1980   1985

Source: Bell Northern Research

Note: This chart does not include Northern Telecom spin-offs, and MIL spin-offs companies

EXHIBIT VII.2
CONSTRAINTS TO GROWTH IDENTIFIED BY START-UP COMPANIES IN PREMIER'S COUNCIL SURVEY

Constraints Identified	Percent of Companies
Lack of equity capital	74%
Lack of debt capital at an affordable cost	59
Slow product development	52
Lack of marketing expertise	52
Lack of qualified personnel	42
Problems penetrating foreign markets	37
Lack of technical or scientific expertise	33
Aggressive competitor responSe	21
Lack of new product ideas	17

Source: Canada Consulting and Telesis analysis of the Premier's Council Start-up Survey

169

Developing The First Product

The high risk nature of technology-intensive firms is dramatically illustrated in their product development activity. Product development in these companies is often lengthy and results in a relatively short sales life. All of the firms in the Premier's Council survey had product development costs of at least $100,000 and usually much more. The combination of long and costly product development with a volatile, rapidly changing marketplace creates a high risk dynamic that spurs competition among these small technology driven firms.

A few of the new businesses interviewed had turned to universities or other public sector science and technology facilities to assist in the development of their products. In some cases, this was an informal exchange of ideas and information with peers or former associates. Others established an R&D or other consulting contract with a university. However, many of the entrepreneurs interviewed found that the long time frames of university or government lab research simply did not fit with their fast-paced environment where technology and opportunities are shifting daily.

Making The First Sales

Very few new companies in Ontario start with a ready customer for their products. Only a third of the companies surveyed began their business with a product development contract or order. Many companies have to spend most of their early capital in developing their product so it can be sold. Many new businesses finance the launch of their first product by doing consulting or contract research. Some of these firms continue to combine product and service businesses, while for others consulting is a start-up strategy discontinued after the first product is launched. Most successful firms decided it was important to get past the service business stage quickly if they hoped to achieve rapid growth in their product markets.

Developing Successive Products

Initially successful start-ups face "bet-the-company" risks in developing successive products. Although the small firm gains strength at each stage, the development of each new product remains a make-or-break process. The size of the market segment grows; marketing and product development investments become more significant; and the competitors are stronger in each new growth phase. The following example illustrates the dilemma faced by many firms.

170

In the competitive field of microelectronics, one $10 million Ontario company interviewed in the Council research faced just such a situation. The company had a relatively painless start-up and achieved initial success in the early 1980s. Start-up funding was provided by private investment and a regular bank loan supported by an IRAP grant and a line of credit from the Ontario Development Corporations. The company quickly achieved dominance in a small, defensible market niche, and by 1985 had 60 percent of the worldwide market for this specific product. Exports were over 95 percent of sales. But this market segment ended up growing more slowly than the target of 30 percent per year for company growth, forcing the company to seek a new product in another market segment.

Financing of the second product development, costing several million dollars over three years, was provided by an initial public offering of shares and by internally generated funds. As well as the one-time initial development cost, the ongoing marketing and development cost burden for a small company to maintain competitiveness in a rapidly changing technology business can be high. For this small microelectronics company, annual R&D now averages over 20 percent of sales, an extremely high proportion when compared to other companies, even in high technology businesses.

Despite this significant expenditure, this small Canadian company is at a competitive disadvantage compared to its American, Japanese, and European competitors. The American competitors are larger and have access to U.S. defence R&D contracts which subsidize their civilian products. The Japanese and European competitors have opportunities to share in cooperative research programs and in joint ventures with larger firms. This Canadian company has had to go it alone and build its technological strength on applied research and careful market analysis. None of its R&D expenditure is what could be "leading edge" technology, but rather represents the application of existing technologies to new uses.

This strength in applications engineering provided the impetus for development of the second product line, started in 1983. By 1985 the company had competitive products on the market. However, the rules of competition were now very different in this new business. Rather than being the dominant player in a $15 million market segment, they were the new entrants in an $85 million market, growing at over 30 percent per annum. The high growth rates had already attracted medium-sized international firms with R&D expenditures many times as high. The firm's entry into the market took longer and was more expensive than expected. The prospects have not yet been played out, but it will be a difficult struggle for this firm to join the ranks of Ontario's threshold firms.

171

Competing In Global Markets

High technology firms in Ontario face the "small country" problem of a limited domestic market. They often must begin exporting their product without the benefit of a solid domestic sales base. Some firms meet the challenge of producing and distributing products for world markets by selling under contract to original equipment manufacturers who, in turn, sell to the end user. Although these relationships do assist start-up companies in gaining financial stability in their early years, the OEM route can sometimes limit their ultimate growth prospects. Our research indicates that companies selling to end-users have a much better understanding of market demand, adapt products more quickly to suit customer needs, and are better able to differentiate themselves from their competitors. For some companies, though, selling through OEMs is the only alternative. As one Ontario software firm competing in a high volume, price sensitive market put it, "Everyone in our business is trying to figure out how to sell to the end-user, but one [end-user] call to our service desk would wipe out our profit on that sale."

Companies that have been successful in building their own international sales network have found it an invaluable competitive resource. One Ontario telecommunications equipment company that began employing its own sales staff while the company was still quite small now considers this a major reason for its success. In the words of the company's president, "Every year we are faced with the decision whether to continue to employ our own sales force. It is by far the most expensive route, but for us it's the only way customers will continue to determine the development of our products. Without that contact, we can't control how the product is marketed or respond quickly to customer needs."

Marketing and sales costs in this firm are 35 percent of the total cost of the product. They have followed a strategy from the outset that allows them to build this cost into the price of their product. They feel it would be almost impossible to begin to build a direct sales force today without having laid the foundation from the beginning.

THE ROLE OF VENTURE CAPITAL

Venture capital in Canada is a small but critical element of the Canadian financial system. With a total annual investment of less than $250 million, the entire venture capital industry in Canada is comparable in size to half the R&D budget of Northern Telecom or the cost of a new Japanese auto plant in Ontario. However, venture capital is of special importance to the entrepreneurial and high technology sectors; it fills a critical role of providing capital for high risk ventures with potentially high return. As we saw in the discussions above, the major problem facing entrepreneurs is the acute need for equity financing.

Venture capital investment can take place at various stages of a new firm's growth. (See Exhibit VII.3) Funds invested at the seed and start-up stages of a company usually do not earn a return for five to seven years. (We group seed, start-up, and development financings under the heading "early stage financings".) Many venture capitalists prefer to invest in later stage start-up companies requiring expansion financing or in leveraged buyouts of fully established companies. Investing in companies with proven track records, of course, entails much lower risks. Early stage venture capital investors often see themselves as investing in the entrepreneur and his potential rather than in a business. Successful early stage investors generally take a partici-

EXHIBIT VII.3

FINANCING STAGES FOR A TYPICAL TECHNOLOGY-BASED START UP

	EARLY STAGES			
	SEED	START-UP	DEVELOPMENT	EXPANSION
Earnings				
Focus of New Company Activity	• Initial R&D • Marketing feasibility studies	• Product development, prototyping, and initial marketing • Begin commercial manufacturing	• Market expansion • Manufacturing scale-up	• Full market development • Full scale manufacturing
Role of Venture Capitalist	• Capital to develop concept or technology	• Capital to move product into market	• Capital for expansion	• Preparation of company for public offering or sale
Size of Financing	$100,000 - $1 million	$1-5 million	$2-10 million	$5-20 million

173

Source: Developed by Telesis and Canada Consulting

pative role in assisting the general management of the company, whereas later stage investors often monitor their investments primarily through regular financial reports and a seat on the Board of Directors.

Canadian Venture Capital Is Increasing

The primary source of venture capital in Canada is pension funds. Other sources of venture capital include corporations, insurance companies, individuals, and government. Most venture capital funds are managed by dedicated staff.

The amount of money invested in Canadian venture capital funds has increased significantly in the past two years from $124 million in 1984 to $206 million in 1986. A greater proportion of the investments by these funds are taking place in Canada. As recently as 1984, 40 percent of all Canadian venture capital funds were invested outside of Canada. By 1986 this figure had declined to only 14 percent. A number of new funds have been established, and firms are beginning to specialize in certain types of financing or industries in which they have particular expertise.

A Shortage Of Early Stage Funding

174

In spite of the growth in the venture capital industry as a whole, the proportion of funds directed to seed, start-up, and development stage funding is declining (See Exhibit VII.4). On average between 1979 and 1984, these investments made up 47 percent of private venture capital financing. By 1986 the proportion was only 23 percent. In fact, the absolute amount of funds invested in this early stage financing actually declined from $38 million to $36.5 million. The less than $40 million per year invested by all private venture capital firms in early stage financing is not an impressive amount.

Many Canadian funds first tried making investments in new, high technology companies in the 1970's, but got badly burned. In many cases both the investor and entrepreneur were charting new territory and neither had the expertise to make the venture succeed. Today a handful of Canadian firms have built successful track records investing in new high technology businesses. Two Ontario ones, Helix Investments and Noranda Enterprises, have found that the key to success in early stage venture financing is to be a participative, "value-added" investor (See Exhibit VII.5). In fact, the Council's research found that their experience was not unique; all over the world successful early stage venture capitalists take a participative, as opposed to passive, approach to their investments.

EXHIBIT VII.4

PRIVATE SECTOR VENTURE CAPITAL INVESTMENT IN CANADA
By Type of Financing

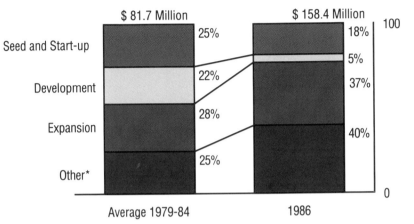

$ 81.7 Million — $ 158.4 Million — 100

Seed and Start-up: 25% / 18%

5%

Development: 22% / 37%

Expansion: 28% / 40%

Other*: 25%

Average 1979-84 — 1986 — 0

* Includes leveraged buyouts, turnarounds, and other special situations

Source: Venture Economics Canada

The Helix and Noranda experience has taught them that the most important role of the participative venture capitalist is to know when to bring outside managers into the company and to assist in making this transition. A second important role of participative investors is to anticipate and deal with problems generic to most early stage high growth companies. Both Helix and Noranda have found that while each business is unique, there are commonalities in the problems most businesses face in each stage of growth. Very often problems that are not initially discernable within the company are more easily recognized by a seasoned investor.

The Council research effort established that participative, early stage venture capital funds are very rare in Ontario. Most of Ontario's venture capital has been more passive in its approach. Quite naturally, more passive investors have tended toward expansion and leveraged buyout financing where the risks are lower. The problem in Ontario is not a shortage of venture capital per se, but a shortage of knowledgeable early stage financiers. This shortage is confirmed by what Ontario entrepreneurs repeatedly identified as a lack of sophisticated venture capitalists in Ontario comparable to the ones they have encountered in the U.S.

The United States does have a much stronger community of early stage venture capitalists than Ontario does. Training in these U.S. firms is on an apprenticeship basis, with new recruits

EXHIBIT VII.5

THE ROLE OF PASSIVE VERSUS PARTICIPATIVE VENTURE CAPITALISTS

Stage Of Investment	Role of Passive Venture Capitalist		Role of Participative Venture Capitalist
Seed	Reviews and selects among a large number of unsolicited proposals	vs.	Actively uses contacts to encourage and solicit the formation of new ventures
Start-up & Development	Conducts due diligence on entrepreneurs' business strategy but leaves them primarily on their own	vs.	Assists in development and selection of alternative strategies, structures, and personnel; carefully monitors expenditures
Expansion	Monitors the progress of new ventures primarily through financial review	vs.	Actively provides ongoing strategic, operational, and financial advice and assistance

Source: Telesis and Canada Consulting interviews with venture capitalists in Canada, U.S., and Europe

spending five or more years working under the direction of an established professional. Individual early stage venture capitalists usually specialize in a few industries, although a number of different industry specialists often jointly manage a diversified fund. The best early stage venture capitalists in Canada and the U.S. actually act as catalysts in many of their deals by bringing together the principals in the first place from their contacts in various companies. In Silicon Valley, less than ten key venture capital firms in the 1960s and 1970s accounted for most of the major successful new businesses. This is not unusual: in Israel, which has a very active high technology sector, a single major participative early stage venture capital firm was involved with almost every one of the most successful start-ups of the 1970s. The challenge for Ontario is to build a stronger core of participative, early stage venture capitalists.

The Difficulty With Initial Public Offerings

An important factor in any venture capital investment is the "exit route" by which the investor can sell out. An initial public offering of stock is usually a preferred exit route for venture capitalists. Such an offering can not only raise sufficient funds to buy the venture capitalist out at a healthy premium, but it can also provide an additional infusion of equity to assist the company which is going public in its continued growth plans.

In the U.S., public stock issues are the primary exit route for venture capitalists, whereas in Canada, repurchase of shares or acquisition of the company by another firm predominates. These latter exit routes are more difficult for a venture capitalist to find and generally do not attract as large a premium on the value of the original investment as public stock offerings. Because opportunities for initial public offerings are more limited in Ontario than in the U.S., the attractiveness of venture capital investments in Ontario is diminished relative to the U.S.

Initial public offerings present more difficulties in Ontario mainly because of the structure of the brokerage industry in Canada. In the U.S., most initial public offerings are handled by second tier "regional brokers" which specialize in such offerings. Hambrect and Quist in San Francisco, for example, specializes in initial public offerings for high technology firms on the West Coast. The large national underwriters do not play such a major role in the U.S. new issues market. In Canada, there are very few second tier brokers which could play a role similar to a Hambrect and Quist in the U.S. Most of the large national Canadian underwriters do not want to spend much time on relatively small capitalization initial public offerings when they can be doing large debt or equity issues for established companies or the government.

Moreover, high technology new issues have not performed well on the Toronto Stock Exchange (TSE). Of 23 small and medium-sized high technology stocks on the TSE between 1983 and 1987 (prior to October 19), only one increased in value. All the rest fell and a few went into bankruptcy. Meanwhile, the TSE Composite Index rose 23 percent. The across-the-board decline in technology stocks partly reflects inflated expectations on the part of investors and partly the very hard time that most high technology companies in Canada have in getting to the threshold company stage.

The problem of having few participative early stage venture capitalists and the lack of initial public offering opportunities are actually two sides of the same coin. If initial public offerings were more accessible in Canada, more experienced venture capitalists might invest in early stage opportunities; and if there were more good early stage investors, the competitive prospects of high technology firms making it to the initial public offering stage might be improved, thus resulting in better stock market performance after the offerings.

178

Given the importance of equity financing to start-up companies, addressing these issues is a critical priority. More participative early stage investing is needed, as is investment in initial public offerings for exporting firms, especially those in high technology. While the Premier's Council does not recommend direct involvement by the government to fill this gap, mechanisms must be found to make investing in early stage opportunities by the private sector more attractive and more viable.

THE CURRENT ROLE OF GOVERNMENT

Government's objective in fostering the entrepreneurial sector of the economy should be twofold: it should encourage more people to try starting their own traded businesses and foster the success of more of those that do. To meet these objectives, governments around the world often act as investors, lenders, customers, advisors, or suppliers to start-up companies. Many entrepreneurs surveyed identified a government contract, agreement, loan, or other assistance as the turning point in the early development of their firms.

In Ontario, assistance to start-up companies is primarily through loans, direct pre-venture equity investments, and grant incentives to investors in SBCDs. The government also plays an advisory and informational role in such areas as exporting and technology licensing (See Exhibit VII.6).

The federal government assists start-ups mainly through the Federal Business Development Bank (loans and venture capital), the Small Business Loans Administration (bank loan guarantees), and the Program for Export Market Development (conditionally repayable loans for export sales trips). All of these government programs do play a role in developing start-ups, but they lack a focus on the traded and especially, high growth sectors of the economy. Other government programs misunderstand the needs of small high growth firms. The fixed asset orientation of much of the financing, for example, is of little use to companies trying to sustain large product development and marketing efforts.

SBCDs in Ontario indicate a different kind of role the government can play. Private investors in these registered corporations receive a grant or tax credit on their investment. Program regulations limit the size of the investee firm and the size of SBDC investment capital such that the program attracts small private investors who seek out secure, relatively low risk investments in small Ontario firms. The program is now in its eighth year and has achieved apparent success in attracting $360 million into Ontario small business during that time. However, the program precludes investment in high growth firms which require substantial capital and, if successful, will soon outgrow the SBDC's size requirement. Venture capitalists do not consider participating in the program because of regulations that would restrict their investment decisions. Most of the SBDCs are actually small business investment vehicles set up by lawyers, and as such, they do not serve the early stage financing role discussed earlier.

179

In general, start-up companies surveyed on behalf of the Council considered government assistance valuable, but noted that pursuing government funding was often a time-consuming activity that put other vital business activities on hold. Several entrepreneurs reported that they had spent so much time chasing federal and provincial assistance programs they neglected their customers and consequently lost sales. In a small firm where the founder is frequently both head scientist for product development and the key marketing representative, time away from these functions to obtain supplementary funding is very costly indeed. Software writers who stop developing programs to spend literally weeks looking for government assistance can never recapture that time, even with additional financial help. Without exception, every company interviewed asked that simpler, more effective ways be found to make government assistance available.

Another common observation offered by many start-up firms was that it is much easier to find R&D money than assistance for

EXHIBIT VII.6

FEDERAL AND ONTARIO ASSISTANCE PROGRAM USED BY START-UPS

PROGRAM	FOCUS	DEGREE OF ASSISTANCE TO TRADED START-UPS
ODC: Ontario Development Corporations	Loans and equity investments for new businesses and small business. (80% of loans to companies with less than 11 employees). 50% of funds are for fixed assets (building and equipment). Focus on mature industries and services rather than high growth industries.	**Moderate-** Valuable source of new business financing, but focus is on fixed assets. Because of extensive small business financing, the ODCs are not frequently used by rapidly growing firms past the start-up phase
Innovation Ontario: (Part of the ODC)	Financing of up to $250,000 for new high technology businesses for product and market development. Pre-venture funding of up to $30,000 for business plans, prototyping, and patenting	**Moderate-** Program is well targetted and fills a need, although the $250,000 ceiling on funding excludes many ventures. Because each application has to be thoroughly reviewed by government staff, the program served only 50 companies in its first year
FBDB: Federal Business Development Bank	Loans and venture capital equity investment for small-to-medium sized companies - 35% of customers are classified as "start-ups"; 50% of loans for fixed assets; small business counselling and training	**Moderate-** Important source of new business financing, but focus is again on fixed assets rather than development costs; some counselling considered valuable.

Program	Description	Impact
Small Business Development Corporations (Ontario)	Grant or tax credit incentive to investors in small businesses	**Minor-** Fills a need but restricted in scope. Tends to be lower risk financing of small but mature businesses
Small Business Loans Administration (Federal)	Guarantee up to 85% of bank loans to small businesses	**Minor-** Most of the firms are local service businesses and again the loans are for fixed assets
PEMD: Program for Export Market Development (Federal)	Conditionally repayable financing up to 50% of the cost of penetrating a new market	**Minor-** Program used by new businesses; mostly small amounts for trade missions
IRDP: Industrial & Regional Development Program (Federal)	Grants and loans primarily for plant establishment or upgrading; bias to regionally disadvantaged areas	**Minimal-** Mostly for fixed assets; little for start-up companies. Could encourage companies to establish in areas that will limit their growth and profitability
DIPP: Defense Industry Productivity Program (Federal)	Program finances the development and maintenance of defence-related production capability and technology	**Minimal-** Program is useful for companies targetting defence-related markets; a small number of Canadian new businesses

181

Source: Canada Consulting and Telesis analysis based on government and company interviews

commercializing a new product. Unfortunately, assistance programs offer hundreds of thousands of dollars for qualifying R&D and almost nothing for marketing and product launches. For many small firms, it is simply not practical for them to carry out basic R&D. The focus of their work is frequently on product development and new generations of existing products.

In spite of these concerns, our survey analysis indicated that use of government programs probably does contribute to start-up firm success. Rapidly growing companies showed a high use of government programs, while struggling companies had used them less frequently. However, the lack of focus in the allocation of government funds continues to be a concern. Programs such as the SBDC and the Ontario Development Corporations' small business loans do play a role in fostering the entrepreneurial community overall. However, 90 percent of all start-ups, as we have seen, are non-traded and therefore should not be a priority. Without an emphasis on high value-added traded sectors, a substantial proportion of government financing will continue to flow to firms other than those which can become the threshold firms of the future.

A NEW ONTARIO STRATEGY

182

The lessons we have learned from our research on entrepreneurship in the province have specific implications for Ontario's efforts to foster a better entrepreneurial culture. Any new Ontario initiatives for start-up companies should:

• Focus on manufacturing sectors and clearly traded services only

• Create a climate that tolerates failure; many entrepreneurs start several companies, often succeeding only the second or third time around

• Support the success of growing indigenous Canadian firms which are the most likely incubators of new companies

• Encourage new businesses to sell to end-users as much as feasible; success by selling to OEM's can be short term and generally does not build a firm foundation for sustained growth

• Encourage more venture capital to be directed to the early stage financing of start-ups

• Foster a more participative venture capital industry in which fund managers take an active role in advising and sustaining the firms they fund, like the participative funds that are at the heart of the U.S. entrepreneurial successes in Silicon Valley and Boston

- Create symbolic recognition of the importance of entrepreneurs in society and encourage more individuals to learn about entrepreneurship and take the risk of becoming one.

Increasing Early Stage Venture Capital

Past efforts to aid start-ups have focussed mainly on a direct government role in venture capital. Such an approach does not yield much leverage on the government investment. Moreover, it does not put the emphasis on development of the participative venture capital expertise which Ontario lacks and needs. Instead of focussing on direct assistance to start-ups, the best and most highly leveraged help the government can give would be incentives to increase the sophistication of the venture capital industry and encourage its funds to flow to early stage financing in traded businesses.

Recommendation 9: EARLY STAGE VENTURE CAPITAL INCENTIVES
The Government should provide tax exemptions for investments in a special class of early stage venture capital funds.

These funds would be established by private sector venture capitalists specifically to invest in qualifying businesses for which investors would receive a tax exemption. Qualifying businesses would include manufacturing or traded service businesses committed to achieving substantial export sales over the next five years.

183

A minimum of 20 percent of each fund would have to be set aside for seed capital investment, and the balance for investing in businesses of up to $10 million in sales (although follow-up second and third investments in firms would be allowed after they had passed that size). The fund could only invest in firms committed to maintaining significant production, R&D, and a head office presence in Ontario. Full-time professional management with an equity stake in the fund would be a requirement in order to encourage participative management assistance and active monitoring of the firms financed.

By structuring the incentive as a capital gains exemption (rather than as an up-front incentive, as in an SBDC) the investor would be encouraged to stay in for the long term and maximize the return on his investment. Whereas a grant program assists a small private investor who is limited to investing his available capital, a capital gains tax exemption appeals more to a venture capital firm which would far prefer the possibility of a large tax break later to a small guaranteed grant today. A capital gains tax exemption has the added benefit to the government of not requiring any subsidy until the benefits of the assistance have been proven. If the venture capital fund fails in its investments, no subsidy will be given.

A capital gains tax exemption will be an incentive for individual and corporate investors to support these early stage funds, but it will not attract pension funds which already pay no income taxes on their investments. The Council recommends that the government give careful consideration to developing an acceptable mechanism which would encourage the flow of pension fund money to those licensed early stage venture funds. One possibility is a requirement that all pension funds over a certain size invest a very small portion of their monies in these early stage funds. An additional few million dollars of pension monies for early stage venture financing will represent a tiny investment for Ontario's largest pension funds, but twenty to thirty such investments could make a tremendous difference to the development of Ontario's early stage venture capital industry.

Assisting Initial Public Offerings

184

Assisting public stock offerings (as happened, for example, in Quebec under the Quebec Stock Savings Plan) would enhance the liquidity of venture capital investment in Ontario, thereby making it more attractive to investors. The Council recognizes that the Quebec plan was far too broadly designed and benefitted mainly large companies and non-traded sectors, and consequently recommends a much more limited and focussed approach for Ontario.

Recommendation 10: INITIAL PUBLIC OFFERING INCENTIVE
The Ontario government should offer investors in the initial public offerings of Ontario companies in traded sectors an incremental tax incentive significantly above the base level tax credit or deduction offered under the Ontario Recapitalization Incentive Plan described in Recommendation 1.

The Initial Public Offering Incentive would apply to first time offerings for firms meeting the requirements of the Ontario Recapitalization Incentive Plan. The incentive would be easy to administer as part of the plan. Its benefits would be to:

• Encourage early stage venture capital investment in traded start-up businesses
• Increase the capital available to threshold companies

- Foster a more entrepreneurial culture in Ontario which would lead to a higher formation of start-ups in traded businesses in the future.

The importance of symbolism in building an entrepreneurial culture in Ontario should not be overlooked. In Chapter XI we will discuss how successful entrepreneurs in Ontario could be better recognized. In addition, the government should take the opportunity to encourage the study of entrepreneurship in the schools. Until recently, government policies and programs did not address the opportunity to encourage an entrepreneurial culture by teaching the concepts and advantages of starting your own business. In 1987, the Premier's Council recommended and the government established six Centres of Entrepreneurship in Ontario universities and colleges. These institutions receive funding to sponsor leading experts in entrepreneurship, both academic and actual practitioners, to offer courses in entrepreneurship at business schools and in local communities. These centres represent a unique learning opportunity for potential entrepreneurs to develop and enhance the skills and knowledge associated with entrepreneurship.

These two recommendations - tax exempt early stage venture capital funds and a tax subsidy for investors in initial public offerings - are tightly focussed on the points of maximum leverage in the whole start-up financing system. As such, they would provide the government with the greatest value for its investment in this area. Monies spent on these programs would enhance the success rate of start-ups in traded sectors more than direct assistance now being meted out by the federal and provincial governments in their current programs aimed at start-ups.

185

CHAPTER VIII
REFINING THE ROLE OF SERVICES

In recent years the service sector has gained increasing recognition for its importance to the economy. It is by far the largest part of the economy and the sector in which the bulk of employment has been created. As the significance of the service sector has increased, so have the efforts to understand it better. Ontario has been at the forefront of this effort, having provided valuable insights into the role and function of the service sector in a recent provincial study.[1]

The Council has drawn on this work and focussed on a specific aspect of services - their traded nature. At issue is the way in which services are traded and domestic value-added is created by that trade. We have not attempted a comprehensive review of traded services, but have dealt primarily with financial services as a case study of how services are traded internationally.

Services in general are not widely traded. Because of the nature of service businesses, most of their value-added must occur in the markets being served. McDonald's Restaurants, for example, operates a world-wide network of fast-food outlets, but most of the value-added in that business occurs in the countries where the restaurants are located. The only significant value-added which flows back to the U.S. headquarters is the share of international profits not re-invested abroad. Of course, headquarter jobs which support the international operations also represent value-added which accrues from McDonald's international activity, but these are very small in number compared to the jobs they support abroad.

In total, only about three percent of all service sector businesses actually compete in an internationally traded context where revenues flow across borders to create value-added in another country. The only service industries with significant traded aspects are transportation and communication businesses, consulting engineering, software, and a few smaller business service areas. Tourism is not an industrial category per se, and its revenues are actually accrued under dozens of other categories such as restaurants, hotels, and personal services. Analyses of

---

1   Ontario Study of the Service Sector, Ministry of Treasury and Economics, 1986.

services trade sometimes overstate their traded nature today because they mistake foreign expansion of essentially domestic-type operations for trade. When most Canadian service businesses expand abroad, they do not significantly increase trade.

This is not to say that the government should ignore traded services. Service trade is growing rapidly, and Ontario must support its traded service companies and industries as aggressively as it supports traded manufacturing. However, given the current public enthusiasm for the shift to the so-called service economy, it is important to re-define our expectations of the role it can play. The foundations of wealth creation in our economy lie in the traded industries; the much larger non-traded portion of our economy that is mainly in services will thrive if our traded sectors are healthy. Japan, which has a much less efficient domestic service economy than we have, has surpassed our level of wealth creation because of its competitiveness in high value-added traded goods. An efficient non-traded service sector contributes significantly to our standard of living, but it is no substitute for high productivity in our traded businesses.

Non-traded services do, of course, affect the competitiveness of traded businesses when their output is used by such businesses. The efficiency and effectiveness of our transportation system, our business services, and our communication networks all contribute to the competitiveness of our traded sectors.

188

THE SIZE OF TRADED SERVICES

The service sector encompasses more than 100 distinct types of activity that can be grouped into six broad divisions: construction; transportation, communication, and utilities; retail and wholesale trade; finance, insurance, and real estate; community, business, and personal services; and public administration and defence. The service sector represents the largest part of the Ontario economy in both output and employment terms. In 1985, it represented 75 percent of Ontario employment, or almost four million people. In terms of real gross domestic product, it represented 67 percent of the total economy. Obviously, the service sector on average has lower value-added per employee than does manufacturing.

According to the Ontario Task Force on Employment and New Technology, at least 80 percent of all new jobs created in Ontario over the next decade will be in the service sector. Schools and hospitals represent Ontario's leading sources of service sector employment, but recent fast growth in employment has been in areas such as brokers and dealers, private household workers, dentists, computer services and educational services. Services also represented over 85 percent of new business creation between 1974 and 1982.

Despite the major role that the service sector plays in the domestic economy, services play a far lesser role in the traded dimension of the international economy. Total service trade is a small component of total world trade. Services account for an estimated 17 percent of total international trade, with a U.S. dollar value of over $350 billion a year.[2] But while small, such trade has been growing rapidly. Total world services trade grew at an annual rate of 6 percent in 1978-84.[3]

In 1984, Canada had $8 billion in service exports, ranking tenth in the world, and ninth in the value of its service imports.[4] The U.S. $8 billion in service exports and U.S. $11.4 billion in imports created a Canadian deficit of $3.4 billion in services (see Exhibit VIII.1). In each of the last forty years except one, Canada has had a deficit situation in services, with interest and dividends representing one of our major imports. Exports of services in Canada account for the equivalent of 3 percent of total gross domestic product, compared to 24 percent for manufactured goods.

THE CASE OF FINANCIAL SERVICES

189

In examining financial services, the Council focussed on the internationally traded dimension of this sector. While research into the service sector is relatively new, research into the value created by traded services activity has not been done at all. Therefore, the Council sought to acquire an initial understanding of this area before deciding whether to pursue it further. Several case studies and analyses were conducted in traded financial services in the banking, life and casualty insurance, investment and brokerage, and trust industries.

Ontario's international competitive position in financial services is strongest in banking and life insurance. In banking, traded activity includes trade finance, some foreign exchange, and cross-border lending. In the life insurance business, reinsurance, individual life, and group life can be traded activities, while in property and casualty insurance, most activity is non-traded, except for certain international activities such as insuring foreign industrial plants or shipping equipment and activities. Within the

2 International Competition in Services,Office of Technology Assessment,1987
3 Ibid.
4. Services exports as used here is a balance of payments definition which includes some interest, royalties, fees and other revenues which do not correspond to industrial categories per se. The largest industry contributor to service exports is transportation. Tourism is a large category as well, but tourism revenues flow to dozens of other industrial categories including domestic transportation, retail, and community and personal services.

EXHIBIT VIII.1
LEADING EXPORTERS AND IMPORTERS OF SERVICES
1984

Value of Services Exports

Country	Billions of U.S. Dollars
United States	$41.1
France	35.5
Germany	27.0
United Kingdom	26.2
Italy	21.3
Japan	20.9
Netherlands	14.4
Spain	12.6
Belgium/Luxembourg	11.3
Canada	8.0

Deficit $3.4 Billion

Value of Services Imports

Country	Billions of U.S. Dollars
United States	$41.5
Germany	40.1
Japan	35.0
France	27.1
United Kingdom	20.7
Italy	15.2
Saudi Arabia	14.4
Netherlands	13.9
Canada	11.4
Belgium/Luxembourg	10.2

Note: Excludes investment income

Source: World Invisible Trade, London, 1986. Based on Data Compiled by the International Monetary Fund

investment business, international securities trading activities and underwriting can be traded, but most of the value-added is in domestic trading and retail operations, and is thus not traded. In the trust business, almost nothing is traded.

International Dimension Of Banking

Canadian banks engage in two main types of internationally traded activity. The first relates to the operation of overseas subsidiaries. These operations result in two types of value-added in Canada: the repatriation of profits and the domestic employment generated in Canada from services performed for those international operations. The second internationally traded activity relates to trade financing for Canadian manufacturing.

Although 10 to 15 percent of a major Canadian banks' staff are located internationally, the value-added of this employment typically accrues to the host nation, not to Canada. At home, no more than one percent of staff located in Canada are directly involved in international operations of any kind, including administration, economic analysis, information systems, agency trading, and other areas.[5] The total employment value-added created in Canada from international activities is thus very small compared to the level of value-added created in the host countries.

The other dimension of value-added from international operations is profit or net income generated abroad which is repatriated to Canada. During 1986, Canadian banks earned more income from international operations than did foreign banks from Canadian activity. This surplus amounted to $227 million.

Trade financing for Canadian manufacturing is the other primary traded activity of the banks. The banks are the principal providers of trade finance services to exporters, which accounts for 85 percent of total trade finance in Canada. To the extent that Canadian exporters could get financing abroad for their shipments, this represents a traded business activity. However, the value-added accruing to Canada from it is tiny.

The degree of international activity in which Canadian firms can engage depends on non-tariff barriers erected by the host countries. In banking, these barriers can often be formidable: in the European Community, foreign ownership of domestic banks is restricted; in Japan and in some Far Eastern countries, entry barriers are particularly onerous; and in the U.S., while entry is not closed, administrative complexities are a burden.

191

---

5. Based on case studies, interviews, and analysis by Canada Consulting and Telesis.

The Importance Of Trade To Insurance

Life insurance is the most internationalized of the financial service industries. Over two million people outside of Canada own policies with Canadian life insurance companies in the amount of $275 billion. During 1985, people in other countries bought $76 billion of life insurance from Canadian companies and paid $5.6 billion in premiums. Eleven countries host operations of Canadian life insurers, with the United States being the most important among those. Canadian insurers have some existing business in a further 25 countries, but this involves writing little or no new insurance.

Some of the major Canadian life insurance companies have large staffs involved in international operations. In companies with substantial international activity, 30 to 50 percent of their personnel are located outside of Canada, generally indicating that employment value-added resides in these host countries. In a few companies, 10 to 20 percent of the domestic staff, although located in Canada, are involved in international operations - a figure substantially higher than that for the banks.

The foreign operations of Canadian life insurers are an important source of premium income. For life insurance companies, premium income generated outside of Canada was 40 percent of total premium income in 1985. For health insurance, it was 26 percent. During 1985, the total revenues earned by Canadian life, property, and casualty insurers from international operations amounted to $2.5 billion. Very little of this revenue flowed back to Canada in the form of repatriated profit. Foreign companies in Canada earned substantially less revenue ($1.5 billion) and as a consequence Canada had a small surplus in traded life insurance activity. In a few cases studied, Canadian life insurers conducted the back-office processing and administration of accounts and claims for their foreign operations from a Canadian base. In such cases the value-added to Canada of international operations is greatly increased. However, competitive trends and foreign government regulations are encouraging firms to put their processing activities in the host country markets, thus limiting this opportunity for Ontario.

The extent of international activity in which Canadian life insurance companies can engage depends on non-tariff barriers. These barriers to trade vary by country, but generally they involve establishment issues, exchange and repatriation of profit controls, and the desire to keep insurance under domestic control to protect local value-added. These measures tend to minimize the value-added created in Canada by the international operations of Canadian firms.

The Limited Role Of Trade In Investment Dealing

Canadian investment dealers have limited international involvement. Only ten firms conduct international business through foreign branches and subsidiaries. One such firm with a substantial international presence has roughly 700 people abroad, representing 30 percent of total staff. Although profits are repatriated to Canada, the value-added of the employment is captured in the host country. A 1984 survey of the international activity of investment dealers indicated that total revenues of the foreign operations of these firms amounted to 16 percent of total commission and principal revenue. Only a small percentage of this foreign revenue would represent traded value-added accruing to Canada.

Another indication of the limited role of international activity for Canadian dealers is their limited presence in the Eurobond market. During 1986, only two Canadian firms, Orion Royal Bank and Wood Gundy, appeared among the top 50 firms in the Eurobond market.

Typically, Canadian investment firms derive practically all of their revenues from domestic business, primarily retail operations. Case studies and analyses done for the Council found that in Canadian investment businesses, the proportion of a firm's revenue deriving from traded business activity was small in all business segments, including retail operations, corporate and government finance, institutional equity and bonds, and money market activities. In fact, this limited international presence accounts in part for the industry's movement to pursue linkages with better capitalized organizations and stronger international networks.

193

Non-Traded Financial Services

In two of the financial service pillars, property and casualty insurance and trust companies, traded activity is virtually nonexistent. Canadian property and casualty insurers conduct little business outside of Canada. In 1984, less than four percent of total net premiums were written outside Canada. This can be largely explained by the high degree of foreign ownership of the Canadian industry. Seven of Canada's eleven largest property and casualty insurance companies are foreign-controlled. More than 70 percent of Canadian property and casualty business is written by foreign-controlled companies. Only 27 percent of the business was written by Canadian companies. This compares to

66 percent in the life and health field.

Trust services are not typically traded, although one large trust company has established an international presence. For the most part, trust companies do not have international offices.

DIMENSIONS OF AN ONTARIO SERVICE SECTOR STRATEGY

Even though services have, to date, played a comparatively minor role in Canada's traded activity, growing internationalization or globalization of services is occurring. International Monetary Fund statistics reveal that growth rates in global service trade almost approach growth rates in merchandise export trade. Other signs point towards increasing international competition in service industries as well.

This globalization presents opportunities and challenges for us. If we fail to achieve a greater degree of competitive strength in service exporting, we may be left with a branch plant traded service sector. Competitor nations, such as the United States, Japan, and Great Britain, are focussing attention on their service industries. Financial institutions and business service companies are actively merging and building stronger international capabilities. Furthermore, major corporations such as General Motors, which bought Electronic Data Systems, and General Electric, which purchased Kidder Peabody, are aggressively pursuing international service sector strategies.

194

The strategic importance and opportunities for the development of the traded service sector cannot be overlooked. The importance of the non-traded service sector to industrial development is also critical. Service industries provide crucial markets for Canadian manufacturers and traded service suppliers. The domestic communications industry has helped foster the growth and development of Northern Telecom and Bell Canada International. Ontario Hydro played a major role in the emergence of the Canadian nuclear energy industry. The rail transportation industry has given rise to a large manufacturing supplier industry. Offsets in defence contracts have increased the aerospace manufacturing base.

In the public policy area, government procurement can play an important role in providing a domestic market for traded service firms which better positions them to compete abroad. The emergence of three large internationally active consulting engineering firms in Quebec is a case in point. The rapid growth of Lavalin, SNC, and Monenco in the 1960s and '70s is largely attributable to the fact that Hydro Quebec's massive hydro-electric projects were contracted out to the private sector. In a variety of other professional and technical fields - data processing, software development and specialized consulting - the Ontario government and its agencies could assist the growth and export potential of Ontario firms by contracting out work in preference to doing it in-house or to buying small quantities of services from a variety of firms. Preference should be given to indigenous firms, which have a greater tendency to export than do non-indigenous firms.

Service industries can support the competitiveness of traded business activities. The banking system has given vital support to the international activities of Canadian firms. Educational networks are important to the traded activities of Britain, France and the United States. The education of foreign students can lead to future business relationships with Ontario in areas such as engineering and construction, as well as in the development of future markets for Canadian manufactured and agricultural goods.

Although the Council has made no specific recommendations with respect to the service sector, our investigations into services have yielded several important findings. The role of trade in services is overstated, but there are some higher value-added segments of the service sector, notably engineering services and computer software, where increased traded activity could reap major benefits for Ontario. Our proposals with respect to a new Ontario procurement policy in Chapter V could represent a first step in building greater capability in this regard. Furthermore, the Ontario Risk Sharing Fund proposed in Chapter VI could have particular application in the computer software industry, and the market development component could be useful to several other traded services. The programs proposed in the venture capital area have selective application to the traded service sector as well.

Any Ontario strategy for the service sector as a whole must also take into account its non-traded dimension. Non-traded services contribute to the competitiveness of companies in traded sectors through purchasing their products and by supplying necessary domestic services in an efficient manner. While the Council is strongly opposed to providing non-traded businesses with the industrial assistance we have recommended for traded businesses earlier in this report, there is a role for provincial initiatives which encourage efficiency in non-traded sectors through competition policy or improved training and technical infrastructure. The recommendations we propose in the following chapters on improving our education, training, science, and technology policies could thus be broadly applicable to our service industries as well.

195

CHAPTER IX
MEETING THE SCIENCE AND TECHNOLOGY IMPERATIVE

The industrial competitiveness of a nation today, more than ever before, is influenced by its capabilities in science and technology. The industrial leadership of the United States can be attributed in large part to its research and development efforts, much of it carried out for defence purposes. Japan's rapid rise to international competitiveness has been traced to its rapid ability to adapt existing technology to new applications.

Research and development spending in Canada has not kept pace with the international requirements for competitive success. Our technological effort is concentrated within government labs and lacks strategic focus. The industry R&D base is limited and fragile. Industry research and development is concentrated in a relatively small part of Canadian business, and a significant portion of it is performed by small and medium-sized firms that must put their entire company at risk with each new major technological investment.

The Council believes Canada is at a critical point in meeting the science and technology imperative. The old approaches are no longer viable. New strategies are not yet in place. This chapter reviews where we stand and begins to chart a fundamentally different course of action for the future.

THE CENTRAL PROBLEM: INADEQUATE INDUSTRIAL R&D

The correlation between science and technology and industrial competitiveness is well documented: countries which support their science and technology effort with substantial and well-targetted resources are more competitive in international markets. As we have seen, a country's competitiveness can be measured in its balance of trade. OECD comparisons of science and technology expenditures as a percent of GDP find that countries with a positive balance of trade in high growth industries are those which make substantial investments in research and development. In a comparison of trade balances in selected industries, Canada was one of only a handful of OECD countries found to have a negative balance of trade in both medium and high R&D intensity industries. It is sometimes argued that

Canada's poor performance in industrial R&D is because of its natural resource industries, which do not need to invest heavily in research and development. But science and technology does not just apply to new industries like biotechnology or advanced ceramics. Scientific and technological advancement is increasingly important to competitiveness in all sectors of the economy, including natural resources.

Yet in forest products, a sector of traditional strength in Canada, the nation's five largest companies (Abitibi-Price, MacMillan-Bloedel, Consolidated Bathurst, B.C. Forest Products, and Crown Forest Products) spend less than 0.4 percent of their sales on research and development - a level less than half that of their major U.S. competitors, which spend 1 percent of sales on R&D. In chemicals, our low R&D spending has resulted in Canada competing with low wage countries for market share in commodity chemical products, while other advanced nations are creating new specialty products for growing markets. Food processing exhibits a similar disregard for the R&D imperative. The Canadian food processing industry, in spite of a few large indigenous companies, invests in research and development at less than half the U.S. rate (as a percentage of sales).

In other Canadian high technology industries, like computers, science equipment, and drugs, Canadian firms spend in most cases less than five percent of sales on R&D. To some extent, this limited commitment to research and development can be explained by the structural problems described in earlier chapters, particularly the high foreign ownership levels. While it is true that indigenous firms often do spend more on R&D than do non-indigenous foreign subsidiaries, this is only part of the problem. The pulp and paper industry has low R&D expenditures despite very high Canadian ownership. In the steel industry, which is almost 100 percent Canadian-owned, spending on R&D is half the U.S. level of expenditure. In the chemical, drug, and automotive sectors, however, low R&D spending in Canada probably is a direct function of high foreign ownership.

In a few high growth industries, Canadian firms outspend their U.S. counterparts in R&D relative to their size. In telecommunications, for instance, this outspending is due to Northern Telecom's aggressive pursuit of international leadership in telecommunications technology and the fact that a large part of its R&D spending is in Canada, while its sales are spread around the world. In the aerospace industry, indigenous firms like Pratt and Whitney Canada have no choice but to spend more of their own funds on R&D to make up for their competitors' much greater U.S. defence R&D subsidy.

The poor industrial R&D performance in Canada cannot be dismissed simply by pointing to the resource intensity of the industrial structure or the high level of foreign ownership. It is a systemic problem that has many facets, both economic and cultural. At its most fundamental level, the nation is confused about who should do what to improve the industrial R&D performance. Industry, government, and universities largely work separately and often at cross purposes.

The appropriate R&D roles in industry, government, and universities need to be agreed upon and their activities directed at achieving not only their own, but national goals. In the view of the Council, it is difficult if not impossible to set a science and technology spending target (as a percentage of GDP) without examining each industry in light of its global competitive position and requirements. National targets should be the sum of appropriate industry, university, and government targets. This chapter describes the base of knowledge from which broader directions and accompanying targets can be derived. The Premier's Council recognizes that the issues related to science and technology in Canada go far beyond its impact on industrial competitiveness. The public sector role in R&D for the protection of the environment, for example, while absolutely vital, is outside the scope of this report. We have focussed only on the role of science and technology in increasing the competitiveness of Ontario industry.

199

CANADA'S OVERALL SCIENCE AND TECHNOLOGY PERFORMANCE

By almost any measure, Canada's science and technology performance is below the level of other leading industrial economies. Canada's spending on R&D as a percentage of GDP is less than that of most other OECD countries (Exhibit IX.1). At 1.3 percent of GDP, Canada's rate is about half the U.S. and Japanese rates of spending, and well below the rates of Germany, Sweden, Switzerland, the U.K., France, and the Netherlands.

To evaluate Canada's R&D performance in a global context, we have constructed a number of comparisons between Canada and seven leading competitive countries which have living standards at least 69 percent of the Canadian level. The competitive countries selected are the United States, Japan, Sweden, Germany, France, the Netherlands, and the United Kingdom. We have chosen this group because they represent a logical competitor class of countries with high living standards and sufficient economic diversity to make comparisons relevant.

Science and technology comparisons between Canada and

EXHIBIT IX.1

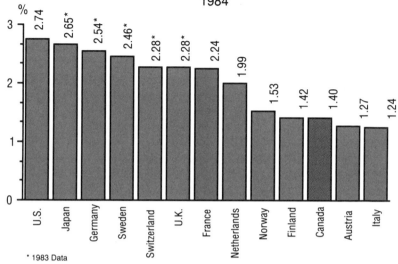

GROSS R&D EXPENDITURES AS A PERCENT OF GDP
1984

* 1983 Data

Source: OECD, Recent Results, 1979-86; OECD, Main Economic Indicators, March 1986

these seven other countries reveal Canada coming in last in many categories of science and technology performance and results (See Exhibit IX.2).

Both industry and government R&D spending in Canada are clearly below internationally competitive standards. At 0.57 percent of GDP in Canada, industry-funded R&D is little more than half the level of the second lowest country in the comparison group, the Netherlands. Government-funded R&D in Canada - only 0.76 percent of GDP - is lower than that of all the comparison countries except Japan. Although government research levels are higher than industry R&D levels, governments in Canada are still funding R&D to a much lesser degree than their counterparts in most competitive countries. Canadian government funding of R&D, for example, is only 59 percent of the U.S. rate.

It is sometimes suggested that comparisons of government-performed R&D put Canada's position in a better light. To some extent that is true as government performed R&D in Canada is 0.39 percent of GDP, which is higher than in the U.S., Germany, Japan, and Sweden. Only France and the U.K., with their substantial state research institutes, are significantly greater government R&D performers than Canada. But such comparisons lose their relevance in measuring the comparative contribution of

EXHIBIT IX.2

SUMMARY OF CANADA'S SCIENCE AND TECHNOLOGY PERFORMANCE

Measure of Science and Technology Competitiveness	Canada's Rank Among Eight Comparison Countries*
Gross expenditure on R&D as a percent of GDP	Lowest
Industry funded R&D/GDP	Lowest
Government funded R&D/GDP	2nd Lowest
Government performed R&D/GDP	Middle
Higher education R&D/GDP	2nd Lowest
Domestic patents granted per 100,000 inhabitants	2nd Lowest
International patents granted - by population	Lowest
Advanced degrees awarded - by population	Middle
Scientists and Engineers in labour force - by population	Lowest
Number of technology intensive industries with positive trade balance	Lowest

* France, Germany, Japan, Netherlands, Sweden, United Kingdom, United States and Canada
Source: Canada Consulting and Telesis, based on OECD and other international sources

201

national R&D efforts to that of our industrial competitors. Research done in laboratories in Canada transfers only slowly and fitfully to industry in most cases, if it transfers at all. Indeed, the Council is of the view that the current proportion of total R&D performed by government is probably too high.

Canada's funding of university R&D again places us at the low end of our comparison countries. Canada spends only 0.3 percent of GDP on university research versus significantly higher rates in Sweden, Japan, and the Netherlands, and marginally higher rates in Germany and the U.S. France and the U.K. spend at the same rates as Canada.

Comparisons of Canada's performance in realizing the fruits of its R&D efforts once again indicate weak Canadian performance. Canada scores very poorly in terms of the number of domestic patents granted to residents per 100,000 inhabitants and the number of international patents secured by Canadians per 100,000 inhabitants. Only eight percent of all patent filings in Canada are made by Canadians. Low resources devoted to R&D correlate, as one might expect, with low numbers of scientists and engineers in the workforce. Despite relatively high numbers of technical graduates, Canada has only 2.7 research scientists and engineers per thousand people in the labour force, which is well below the comparison countries and only one-third the rate of the highest country, Japan.

GOVERNMENT SURROGATES FOR INDUSTRY RESEARCH

The low level of research spending within Canadian industry has contributed to the formation of a relatively large government science and technology infrastructure in Canada. With a 1987 budget of $4.1 billion, the federal government is by far Canada's largest investor in science and technology. The fact that 75 percent of those funds are spent internally indicates how heavily government re-invests in its own R&D capability (See Exhibit IX.3).

This massive and self-sustaining public sector research effort was created partly as a surrogate for the research and development which is lacking in industry. However, experience has shown that this approach is far from effective. Government department priorities differ dramatically from those of industry, and even when the research focus is complementary, there is very little transfer of technology to the private sector.

R&D performed within government tends to be based on broad areas of study determined by government departments rather than being focussed on problems of strategic significance to Canadian industry. An analysis of Ontario and federal govern-

202

EXHIBIT IX.3
FEDERAL EXPENDITURES ON SCIENCE AND TECHNOLOGY
1985-86

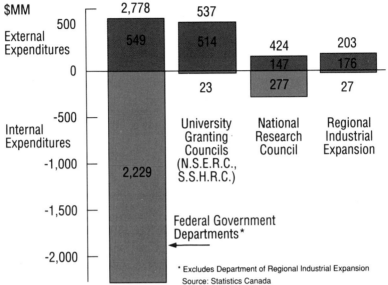

ment R&D spending shows that the majority of it is neither industry directed nor targetted on core technologies (Exhibit IX.4). Canada is a small country with very limited R&D resources and cannot afford to distribute those resources without targetting critical technological needs.

The Case Of Advanced Materials Research

Since most of the advanced materials research in Canada is carried out by the National Research Council (NRC), the problems encountered here are illustrative of the difficulties of public-private sector linkage in R&D. The NRC research programs in advanced materials are the largest in the country. Direct costs are nearly $20 million per year, and indirect capital and overhead to support the program are several times that. Research areas include electronic materials, metals, polymers, composite materials and ceramics. Given the importance of the materials industry in Canada, it would seem natural that companies would pursue all avenues to remain current with new materials technologies. In spite of the apparent size of NRC's research effort, the Premier's Council research found that most firms view it as a facility for routine testing and solving very specific technical problems, not as a source of important product or process development assis-

EXHIBIT IX.4
DISTRIBUTION OF ONTARIO AND FEDERAL GOVERNMENT R&D, 1986-87
($ Millions)

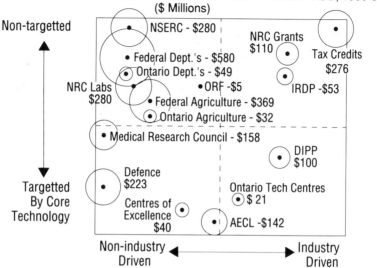

Note: The area of the circle represents R&D expenditure, as reported by Statistics Canada, 1986-87

Source: Canada Consulting and Telesis analysis for the Premier's Council in Ontario based on Statistics Canada data and hundreds of interviews with government departments and industry

tance.

About fifty "industrial collaborators" were identified by the NRC as being involved with one or more of their areas of materials research. Thirty-one of these collaborators were interviewed and their interaction was characterized in a hierarchy ranging from passive, informal contact to product testing, major R&D projects, and technology licensing. The interviews found that the level of interaction of these firms with the NRC was surprisingly low, given that they were selected by NRC as industrial collaborators. The most common form of interaction was simply materials testing; only 12 of the 31 companies had actual R&D projects with the NRC or had licensed technology developed by NRC. Very few of the companies viewed NRC as being on the leading edge in materials research or as an important source of new product or process ideas.

An exception to this pattern is the NRC/Bell Northern Gallium Arsenide (GaA) research program in which a major research commitment has gone hand in hand with participation by a major Canadian industrial client. The NRC awarded Bell Northern Research a $7.5 million PILP grant to do GaA research. Despite the considerable size of this grant relative to most Canadian R&D

funding, it is a small commitment in comparison to U.S. and Japanese spending levels on comparable technology. Northern Telecom is clearly Canada's best hope in entering this industry, but it will probably need to focus on a well-defined niche where Canada can gain competitive advantage.

Unfortunately, Canadian materials companies ranging in size from small start-up companies to billion dollar businesses generally do not look to the NRC for fundamental assistance in competing in world markets. This is all in sharp contrast to Japan, the U.S. and several European countries where government sponsored precompetitive research is critical in creating new industries and restructuring old ones. To be effective, public sector research will need to become much more responsive to the needs of industry. It cannot act as an industry research surrogate; without productive interaction with the private sector, government-run laboratories cannot be expected to contribute to industrial competitiveness.

DEFINING THE APPROPRIATE R&D ROLES

Industry, government, and universities are all active players in setting the science and technology agenda in Canada. Their respective roles have emerged through a history of experience and adaptation. Current pressures of rapid technological change, industrial adjustment, and economic survival have focussed attention on a central policy question: is the role of each player appropriately defined and are we adequately funding the right efforts?

205

The public and private sectors have, separately and in combination, shaped Canada's economic development. Some Crown agencies have played an important part in industrial development; Polysar, AECL, and the provincial hydro corporations have been research leaders in their fields. Private sector firms such as Northern Telecom, Pratt and Whitney, Alcan, and Gandalf have all established internationally recognized competitive advantages through their science and technology efforts. But as we have seen earlier in this chapter, the combined efforts of our industries in science and technology are not at a level adequate to assure Canada's future prosperity. In fact, we have consistently lost ground to our leading competitors in science and technology. Neither private nor public sector resources today are adequately meeting the science and technology imperative. The challenge is to redefine the role of each player and coordinate these efforts to maximize Canada's industrial competitiveness.

The Lessons From Abroad On Appropriate Roles

Having studied the science and technology policies and experiences of the United States, Sweden, Germany, France, the U.K., and Japan, we have found some fairly clear role expectations which are consistent across most of these jurisdictions. The following observations on science and technology roles in other countries are instructive in our search for the appropriate Canadian model.

Industry abroad is perceived as the primary competitive vehicle for the development of science and technology. The commercial marketplace is too far removed from public sector players and research resources are not well expended by them for competitive ends. In other jurisdictions, public resources for industry-related research and development tend to be allocated mainly to the private sector. This is especially true of Japan. But the United States also clearly follows this direction, and the Europeans are increasingly moving this way as well. For example, industry in the United States receives 52 percent of the federal government research and development funding versus only 18 percent in Canada.

Universities are seen as playing a central role in basic research and providing a vital function in developing advanced technical graduates. In the United States, universities receive 60 percent of the federal government funding for basic research.

Governments are playing a key policy coordination role and a more targetted applied research role. Their primary concern is with economic growth and helping to build essential industry research scale in key emerging technologies. Often this means greater long term planning. The Japanese experience in very large systems integration (VLSI) technology is a classic example of industry and government identifying the critical long-term applied research problems facing the industry and attacking them jointly. Governments are also active in finding ways to accelerate and intensify the transfer of technology towards commercial ends. Europe, Japan, and the United States have all launched major science and technology projects with industry. Better linkages are being encouraged between industry and universities and cooperative pre-competitive research is being sponsored between companies. In-house government research is becoming more mission-oriented. Well over half the spending in United States government labs is on development work, and over 80 percent is on applied research and development. Research in Japan is even more commercially driven. In virtually all the major OECD countries efforts to link government research organizations with private sector clients are intensifying, and increasingly industry is shaping the research programs of these organizations.

While research institutions in other jurisdictions have relatively well-defined roles, all are endeavouring to build flexibility into their systems. They are identifying the strengths of their various institutions, seeking ways to build more effective integration among organizations, and using these linkages as important competitive tools. The overriding objective for all is to allocate science and technology resources in the ways they will be used most effectively.

The experiences of other countries suggest the acute need for clarification of roles in Canada:

- There can be no substitute for research done in industry by industry. Decisions on resource allocation must be made in a way that increases applied research and development in industry
- Expectations of the capabilities of universities in terms of commercially-related research are too high. While coordination and linkage between industry and universities will need to be continually strengthened, applied research and development should be based in industry. Basic research should continue to be the preserve of universities
- Government research that is not dedicated to clearly-articulated public missions (environmental protection, and defence, for instance) will increasingly need to be tied to an industrial client base and driven by market needs and specific long-term national missions. Government resource allocation should be redirected in favour of industry, and research that is carried on in government settings should be subject to re-examination.

207

THE CHAIN OF INDUSTRIAL R&D

Understanding the stages of industrial research and development is critical to identifying where public sector assistance can be used to advantage. Industrial R&D ranges from pre-competitive basic research, which is concentrated in a few of the largest companies, through to product development that is little more than clone-making (See Exhibit IX.5). Effective government support must be responsive to the needs of industry at various stages in the chain.

At the earliest stage of the chain - basic research - the goal is simply to study areas of science and technology of clear industrial interest and to test broad concepts and directions. Only companies developing products that depend on advancing the frontiers of science engage in research in this early stage. It is extremely costly and, by its very nature, involves a high degree of uncertainty. Most large companies cannot afford to carry out basic

208

EXHIBIT IX.5

THE CHAIN OF INDUSTRIAL RESEARCH AND DEVELOPMENT

	PRE-COMPETITIVE		CLEARLY COMPETITIVE	
	Basic research	**Solving defined gaps in knowledge**	**Original product design and development**	**Derivative products "clone making"**
Goal:	To study areas of clear industrial interest and test broad concepts and directions	To solve defined problems that relate to specific product or process innovations	To apply existing scientific knowledge to the design and development of new products and processes	To copy basic designs and features from competitors
Company Examples:	In the U.S.: Bell Labs General Motors IBM (Few, if any, Canadians)	Northern Telecom Allelix (Few other Canadians)	Northern Telecom Lumonics Pratt & Whitney (Many other Candian firms)	Many Canadian firms

research. There are few, if any, Canadian firms in this category and in the U.S., only a few companies such as Bell Labs, General Motors, and IBM carry out basic research.

At the second stage - solving specific gaps in knowledge - the R&D is still pre-competitive, but now more narrowly defined. Some of this type of research is market driven in the sense that the anticipated value to the customer of solving specific technological problems usually justifies the research. However, R&D at this stage still involves a high degree of uncertainty in outcome, and is therefore far from industrial product design. Allelix and Northern Telecom are among the few Ontario firms engaged in this level of research. Non-industrial labs in governments and universities are carrying out research relevant to this type of technological problem-solving.

Most Canadian industrial research begins at the third link in the chain: original product design and development. Here the goal is to apply existing scientific knowledge to the design and development of new products and processes. This type of research, which is clearly oriented to winning in the competitive marketplace, is carried out by a number of Canadian firms such as Lumonics, Spar, Pratt and Whitney and IBM Canada. This R&D relies on a publicly available body of scientific knowledge. For Canada much of this knowledge comes from other countries via journals, conferences, and individuals coming to Canada.

209

The final phase of the chain of industrial R&D is the development of derivative products and clones of existing products. The goal of this type of R&D is to enhance the next generation of an existing product or to duplicate the basic design and features of a competitor's product. There are many Canadian firms carrying out this development work.

SUMMARY OF THE PROBLEMS WITH CURRENT GOVERNMENT R&D INFRASTRUCTURE

The current government role, both in direct research activity and in providing incentives for increased private sector R&D, falls far short of its potential as a tool to leverage Canada's overall science and technology effort. The reasons for this weakness are manifold.

There has been a misunderstanding of the role of government science and technology infrastructure, which has resulted in substantial internal government R&D with no linkage to industry. Furthermore, only a small amount of government science and technology funds are distributed to industry, compared to government funding available in other countries. This leaves Canadian firms at a competitive disadvantage in financing R&D.

Not enough targeting of research and development is done in government. Broadly-based government department research lacks strategic focus. Priorities for public sector research are also not industry driven. There is little consultation between industry and government on priorities for public sector research. Maximum leverage is gained when public and private sector strength are combined. The $190 million Canada spends on biotechnology, for example, barely allows us to be in the race. Focussed on areas of traditional Canadian strength, however, such as solving specific agricultural or forestry problems, or innovative solutions to waste management issues, might put Canada at the forefront in those specific fields.

Procurement policies are not well used as a lever to increase industrial R&D. As discussed in Chapter V, enabling R&D contracts, and outsourcing, are among the mechanisms for intensifying a country's R&D effort that are significantly untapped in Canada. In some cases, the dollar value that could be invested in private sector R&D through procurement is even greater than through grants and other incentives. It also carries less cost to the government since it is simultaneously fulfilling the government's own purchasing requirements.

TOWARDS A NEW TECHNOLOGY STRATEGY

In the previous chapter on high growth and emerging industries, two recommendations were made to promote the R&D efforts of firms in those industries: incremental R&D incentives and a strategic procurement plan. The additional recommendations offered here are intended to broaden the scope of R&D incentives to meet the needs of innovative firms in all sectors of the economy.

The overriding recommendation is to shift the performance of R&D out of government departments and labs and into industry to the greatest extent possible unless the research serves clearly-defined public missions.

Recommendation 11: RE-DIRECT GOVERNMENT RESEARCH TO INDUSTRY

The Ontario and Federal Governments should involve the private sector more effectively in university and government research and ensure that industrial priorities play a much more important role in guiding such research.

Specific steps that can be taken include:
- Ensure that 100 percent of R&D in government labs is mission-oriented and if the R&D is oriented to business, it should

be directed and co-funded by industry
- Shift a significant percentage (say 20%) of the current federal government in-house research effort to industrial research under the direction of the private sector
- Where feasible, source necessary government research and development from private sector firms capable of building on it in developing commercial products
- Encourage universities to orient more research to industrial priorities but dampen overall the expectations of what universities can do in short term commercial research - their primary role should be to train world class graduates and be pre-eminent in longer term pre-competitive research.

Our second recommendation is to establish an R&D personnel assistance program to help small and medium-sized firms build the capability to do R&D and use the public science and technology infrastructure. Programs like this have been used with success at two of Ontario's Technology Centres, in Germany, and recently in Quebec. Among the hundreds of small to medium-sized Ontario companies in core industries like auto parts, metal fabrication, and plastics are many firms which do not yet have any substantial technological capability on staff and which are not fully aware of the technological opportunities open to them. In fact, over 70 percent of Ontario manufacturing firms do not employ any full-time engineers or scientists. In some cases, firms know they need to do more technologically, but cannot justify the hiring costs.

211

Recommendation 12: TECHNICAL PERSONNEL ASSISTANCE PROGRAM

Ontario should establish a Technical Personnel Assistance Program to encourage small and medium-sized firms to accelerate their hiring of R&D, engineering and other technical personnel.

Qualifying firms would have less than $100 million in sales. Priority would be given to exporting firms, but it is also recognized that import replacement firms may become exporters and should also be given consideration. For each new incremental technical job created, the employer would receive a subsidy of 50 percent of the new employee's salary in the first year and 25 percent in the second year. Positions qualifying for the subsidy would include qualified technicians as well as engineers and scientists.

The Premier's Council has already recommended and the government has established six Centres of Excellence designed to stimulate advanced research in Ontario's critical areas of scientific endeavour. The Centres will draw on Ontario's best scientists and are expected to play a role in training and developing world-class researchers, both from Ontario universities and abroad.

Each Centre is comprised of both university and industry participants to encourage the transfer and diffusion of technology into industry. The Centres will receive a total of $200 million from the Technology Fund over a five-year period.

The seven Centres of Excellence are:

- The Ontario Centre for Materials Research
- Telecommunications Research Institute of Ontario
- Ontario Laser and Lightwave Research Centre
- Waterloo Centre for Groundwater Research
- Information Technology Research Centre
- Institute for Space and Terrestrial Science
- Manufacturing Research Corporation of Ontario.

Canada's ability to meet the science and technology imperative will depend on having a full fabric of industrial research and development. Gaps due to a lack of linkage between early stage research, competitive research and actual product development must be closed. The critical final stages of commercialization cannot be overlooked in our definition of R&D for tax purposes. The roles of government, universities and industry must be redefined and clarified. Like other countries, Canada must adopt a coordinated industrial research and development strategy to meet the demands of global competition.

The Premier's Council recommendations on science and technology, taken together, offer support to all stages of the industrial research and development chain (see Exhibit IX.6). The Centres of Excellence will advance basic, pre-competitive research (Stage 1) and supply advanced technical manpower to Canadian industry. The Strategic Procurement Plan will target pre-competitive applied research (Stage 2) and original product design and development (Stage 3). The recommendation to shift more R&D from the public sector into the private sector will also assist pre-competitive applied research (Stage 2). The Technical Personnel Assistance Program will assist small and medium-sized firms to increase both original product design (Stage 3) and "cloned" products (Stage 4). The R&D tax incentives will benefit all stages of industrial R&D activity. In short, the Council program is comprehensive enough to advance the R&D capability of all industry in the province whatever their level of current technical capability.

EXHIBIT IX.6

THE CHAIN OF INDUSTRIAL RESEARCH AND DEVELOPMENT

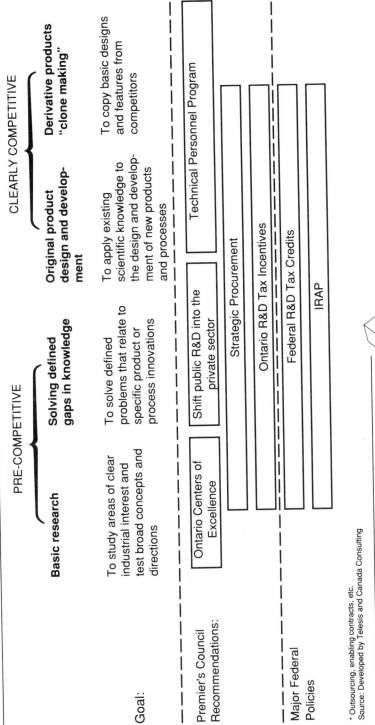

	PRE-COMPETITIVE		CLEARLY COMPETITIVE	
	Basic research	**Solving defined gaps in knowledge**	**Original product design and development**	**Derivative products "clone making"**
Goal:	To study areas of clear industrial interest and test broad concepts and directions	To solve defined problems that relate to specific product or process innovations	To apply existing scientific knowledge to the design and development of new products and processes	To copy basic designs and features from competitors
Premier's Council Recommendations:	Ontario Centers of Excellence	Shift public R&D into the private sector	Technical Personnel Program	
		Strategic Procurement		
		Ontario R&D Tax Incentives		
Major Federal Policies		Federal R&D Tax Credits		
	IRAP			

* Outsourcing, enabling contracts, etc.
Source: Developed by Telesis and Canada Consulting

213

CHAPTER X
INVESTING IN PEOPLE

Developing a strong, dynamic human resource base is a precondition to achieving and sustaining economic growth. Without an educated, skilled, motivated, and adaptable workforce, productivity will suffer and efforts to compete in the global economy will be undermined. One of the key competitive challenges Ontario faces is developing our most fundamental natural resource: the minds and skills of our workers.

While education and training are often seen as social programs, they are really investments in our economic future. Most major industrialized nations have long recognized and capitalized on the connection between people and productivity growth. Japan's strong economic performance in the past 20 years has been widely linked to human resource development; Germany's to its intensive investment in skilled trades training; while Sweden's labour market policies and commitment to full employment are an implicit acknowledgment of the value of investing in people for industrial revitalization.

215

Ontario's competitive position has been seriously challenged in recent years. While the province has made gains in real economic growth and job creation, our competitiveness in several industries has been eroded by our major trading partners. Those economies that have invested in the basic and advanced skills of their workforces have achieved stronger economic performance through superior worker training and labour market responsiveness.

As industries become more technologically sophisticated, they also become more knowledge-intensive, placing new demands on the skills and capabilities of the labour force. Human capital is therefore a critical factor in achieving the full transition to an advanced industrial society. Because education and training provide workers with the knowledge and capabilities to function effectively in the technology age, these people expenditures are an essential complement to investments in facilities and equipment: both increase output and productivity. Similarly, both people investments and fixed capital investments, if neglected, lead to deterioration and obsolescence, seriously impeding our ability to compete in changing world markets.

The rapid introduction of new technologies, coupled with changing demographic trends in the labour force, have made continuing education and increased training an economic imperative for Ontario. Ontario used to rely on immigration and the inflow of recently trained young people to supply specialized and up-to-date skills. With fewer young people and skilled immigrants joining the labour force, there will be a growing reliance on training and retraining of the existing workforce to meet industry demands. By 1990, the majority of the Ontario workforce will fall into the 25 to 44 age group, making skills upgrading a necessity to ensure a competitive labour force. Meanwhile, the upgrading and retraining needs of older workers - those 45 to 64 years of age - will also have to be satisfied as they represent the fastest growing segment of the population. The emergence of the second-generation baby boom will call for continued youth programming support from the mid-1990's and beyond.

STRIVING FOR EXCELLENCE IN EDUCATION

Investing in people is a matter of aiming for excellence in all stages of education. Early education, where young people acquire the fundamental skills upon which they will later build, is just as important as the career training they receive prior to or during their working life.

It is for this reason that the Premier's Council chose to include an initial, but by no means comprehensive, discussion of education in this report. Obviously, education serves many public purposes; in this report we have focussed on its role in providing people with the skills and talents necessary to contribute in a meaningful and productive way to our economic system. While we have deliberately limited our remarks on the education system to this area, the task of reviewing the education system within this role as a support to our economic system is far from complete. The Council intends to revisit the education issue, along with training and other "people concerns" in its agenda for next year.

The importance of basic or formative education is underscored by what employers tend to identify as the main deficiencies in Ontario's current workforce: inadequate reading, writing, analytical, and interpersonal skills. A recent survey of managers in the automotive parts industry revealed that 29 percent found their current workers' literacy skills inadequate, while 36 percent perceived their workers' mathematical skills to be insufficient (See Exhibit X.1).

An underskilled workforce is frequently one that is undereducated. The problem begins early, while young people are still in the school system, but surfaces late - perhaps too late - when they make the transition to work.

The few available studies comparing achievement in basic

216

EXHIBIT X.1

MANAGERS' PERCEPTIONS OF BASIC LITERACY AND
MATHEMATICAL SKILLS IN THE ONTARIO AUTO PARTS
INDUSTRY WORKFORCE

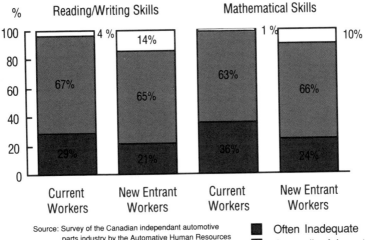

Source: Survey of the Canadian independant automotive
parts industry by the Automative Human Resources
Task Force, 1985.

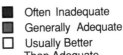

■ Often Inadequate
■ Generally Adequate
☐ Usually Better
Than Adequate

217

skills suggest that Ontario students are not meeting their own
past performance standards, nor are they on a competitive footing
with students from the highest achieving industrialized nations.
Measurements of language and mathematical skills on the
Canadian Tests of Basic Skills reveal that Ontario student
achievement in the 1980s was appreciably lower than it was in
the sixties. The greatest drop in student achievement was in
language skills, which test administrators attribute to a declining
emphasis on the teaching of basics during the late sixties and
early seventies. Equivalent standardized testing in the United
States shows a similar decline in student achievement over the
last two decades.

A 1985 study comparing mathematics and reading comprehen-
sion test scores of Japanese, Chinese, and American elementary
school children suggests that the problem of underachievement
often begins early. In that study, U.S. first grade children placed
slightly behind Japanese and Taiwanese students in mathematical performance tests; U.S. students in the fifth grade, however,
performed much more significantly below their Asian counterparts.[1]

1. *Cognitive Performance and Academic Achievement of Japanese, Chinese and American Children*, Child
Development VO/86, 1985, p. 718.

EXHIBIT X.2A

SCORES FOR FINAL YEAR, SECONDARY SCHOOL

Statistics		Analysis		Calculus*		Trigonometry		Geometry		Algebra	
Hong Kong	73	Hong Kong	71	Hong Kong	68	Hong Kong	75	Hong Kong	65	Hong Kong	78
Japan	70	Japan	66	Japan	62	Japan	62	Japan	60	Japan	78
Sweden	64	England	58	England	57	England	62	England	51	Finland	69
England	64	Finland	55	Finland	49	Sweden	57	Sweden	49	England	66
Finland	58	New Zealand	51	New Zealand	47	Israel	55	Finland	48	Flem. Belg.	61
New Zealand	58	Sweden	48	Sweden	47	Finland	52	New Zealand	43	Israel	60
Scotland	47	**Ontario**	**46**	**Ontario**	**43**	Flem. Belg.	51	**Ontario**	**42**	Sweden	60
Ontario	**46**	Flem. Belg.	46	Flem. Belg.	42	**Ontario**	**50**	Scotland	42	**Ontario**	**57**
Flem. Belg.	43	Israel	45	Fr. Belg.	41	Scotland	49	Flem. Belg.	42	New Zealand	55
Fr. Belg.	42	Fr. Belg.	43	Israel	40	New Zealand	48	Fr. Belg.	38	Fr. Belg.	55
U.S.	41	Scotland	32	Scotland	28	Fr. Belg.	44	Israel	35	Scotland	48
B.C.	38	U.S.	28	U.S.	23	B.C.	34	U.S.	33	B.C.	47
Israel	38	Thailand	26	Hungary	21	U.S.	34	B.C.	33	Hungary	45
Thailand	34	Hungary	26	Thailand	21	Hungary	31	Hungary	30	U.S.	43
Hungary	29	B.C.	21	B.C.	14	Thailand	29	Thailand	28	Thailand	38

* Some countries do not have calculus available in all school districts
Source: SIMS, unpublished data, 1984

These early performance problems become intensified in later stages of education, as the results of the recent Second International Mathematics Study (SIMS) confirm. This authoritative comparison of secondary school student achievement in some 20 countries placed Canadian and American students well below their international competitors in applied mathematical skill levels.[2] Ontario students' consistently average performance on SIMS was in stark contrast to the consistently superior performance of students from Hong Kong and Japan (See Exhibit X.2).

Ontario's students did outperform students from the U.S. and British Columbia, among other locations, but such success should offer us little comfort when all jurisdictions in North America trailed so far behind some of our leading competitors in Asia and Europe. Average educational performance may have been good enough in the past, but as we attempt to make the transition to higher value-added products and services in our core industries and accelerate our participation in high growth sectors, we will find average performance entirely inadequate. The SIMS results clearly signal a need for Ontario's education system to foster higher levels of achievement in both basic and advanced mathematical skills.

Early underachievement in education also manifests itself later in high rates of adult illiteracy. Statistics Canada figures reveal that 22.3 percent of the Canadian population and 19.6 percent of the Ontario population over age 15 and not attending

219

EXHIBIT X.2B
AVERAGE INTERNATIONAL SCORES
Second International Mathematics Study

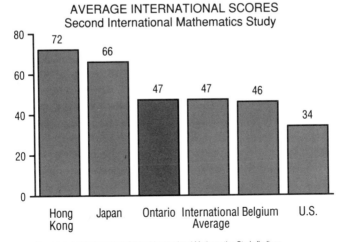

Source: Averaging based on Second International Mathematics Study findings

2. SIMS assessed performance of Grades 8 and 12 students in core mathematics subject areas. Conveniently, Ontario and one other province - British Columbia - were assessed as separate "countries" for precise comparison with the other nations surveyed.

school are illiterate or functionally illiterate.[3] The functionally illiterate population in the 20 to 24 age group is 5.5 percent for Canada and 3.7 percent for Ontario (See Exhibit X.3). Surprisingly, illiteracy is even a problem among college and university students. The failure rate on literacy tests administered to first-year post-secondary students in Canada ranges from 20 percent to over 40 percent, while the average failure rate in Ontario's 22 colleges of applied arts and technology is 25 percent.

The problem of inadequate student achievement in basic skills is compounded by a lack of commitment to educational completion. Ontario has the dubious distinction of leading much of the industrial world in the percentage of students who fail to complete high school. Roughly 30 percent of Ontario students drop out of the formal education system before receiving a secondary school graduation diploma or a certificate of training from a publicly or privately funded school (See Exhibit X.4).Canadian participation rates of people aged 17 in formal education and apprenticeship are only 72 percent, compared with participation rates of 94 percent in Japan and 89 percent in Germany (See Exhibit X.5).

Of those students who do complete their basic education and

220

EXHIBIT X.3
LEVEL OF SCHOOL ACHIEVEMENT OF POPULATION 15 AND OVER
Those Not Presently Attending School
% of Total Population
1981

	Illiterate Grades 0-4	Functionally Illiterate Grade 5-8	Total
Canada	4.7%	17.6%	22.3%
Ontario	4.1%	15.5%	19.6%

LEVEL OF SCHOOL ACHIEVEMENT OF POPULATION 20-24
Those Not Presently Attending School
% of Total Population
1981

	Functionally Illiterate
Canada	5.5%
Ontario	3.7%

Source: Statistics Canada 1981 Census

---

3. Functionally illiterate is defined as reading at below ninth grade level.

EXHIBIT X.4

JURISDICTION	Percentage Of Students Not Obtaining Qualification At Post Compulsory Or Upper Secondary Level (Ages 16-19) (1980-84)
Canada	31%
Ontario	**30%**
Sweden	31%
Italy	28%
United States	25%
France	23%
United Kingdom	15%
Germany	14%

Source: Education and Training After Basic Schooling, Table II.6, page 63 for U.K.; 1981 Census and Projections, and Analysis Section of Education, Culture and Tourism Division of Statistics Canada; Education Statistics, Ontario, 1984; and U.S. Bureau of Census.

EXHIBIT X.5

PARTICIPATION RATES OF 17-YEAR OLDS IN FORMAL EDUCATION

Country	Participation Rate
Japan	94%
Germany	89%
United States	87%
Sweden	78%
Canada	**72%**
Italy	70%
France	69%
United Kingdom	53%

Source: Education and Training After Basic Schooling, OECD.

go on to achieve advanced degrees in post-secondary institutions, the vast majority in Ontario enter the social sciences and humanities streams. This creates a healthy supply of service professionals ultimately, but does little to expand our pool of skilled scientists and technologists. For every 400 engineers in Japan, there are only 112 engineers in Ontario. Meanwhile, Ontario's output of service professionals, such as accountants and lawyers, far exceeds Japan's (See Exhibit X.6).

If there are too few scientists and technologists to serve our growing research and development needs, it is probably because our education system is not equipping students to enter these fields. The SIMS results suggest that our students' mathematical skills need improvement, and a 1984 Science Council of Canada study shows that science is rarely taught adequately, if at all, in elementary schools across the country. The Science Council study attributed this failing to teachers' reluctance or inability to deal with the subject: most of the teachers surveyed had not taken a college or university-level course in a subject other than education in the last ten years; over 50 percent of elementary school teachers had no university-level mathematics; and almost 75 percent had no university-level science. It is not surprising then that inadequate background in the subject was widely cited by teach-

222

EXHIBIT X.6

NUMBER OF ACCOUNTANTS, ENGINEERS AND LAWYERS
JAPAN AND ONTARIO
(Per 10,000 Workers)

Source: Lester Thurow *Zero Sum Solution*, Law Society of Upper Canada, Canadian Institute of Chartered Accountants, and Association of Professional Engineers of Ontario

ers among their reasons for preferring not to teach science, though they conceded that the amount of time allocated to science teaching in early and middle grades was insufficient.

Addressing The Education Challenges

Increasing the commitment to educational achievement and completion is the central education challenge facing Ontario policy makers, educators, and students. All partners in the education system must respond to the fact that student performance on basic skills tests is sliding or comparatively mediocre, that illiteracy rates among those in and out of school are alarmingly high, that almost a third of our students are dropouts, and that our students need earlier and more effective exposure to an expanded scientific and technological knowledge base.

The strengths and weaknesses of the education system must also meet the test of how well young people are being prepared for the world of work. Any rethinking of the system must therefore be responsive to the standards being set by industry for today's and tomorrow's workforce. Employers expect their workforce to have a strong fundamental skills base; the education system must respond with a renewed emphasis on the teaching and mastery of core subjects, a concerted effort to lower illiteracy rates, and incentives for students to complete their formal education. Employers also require a growing proportion of their workforce to have advanced science and mathematical abilities; the education system must respond with effective early education in these subjects so that students will develop the competence and confidence to enter these demanding fields.

223

Some of the shortcomings of Ontario's education system have been examined in recent reports and are already being addressed by Ministry of Education initiatives. The reduction of class sizes in early grades will permit teachers to work more effectively and individually with grades 1 and 2 students in developing their early reading, writing, and numeracy skills. The establishment of new provincial benchmarks to measure achievement is a much-needed return to the setting of standards for system performance. The increased use of computer and educational software in early grades, along with new requirements for updating teachers' computer skills, will help broaden the technical knowledge base of young students.

However, the Council has serious concerns that, despite these improvements, the education system is not delivering value for the money it receives. Of the countries in Exhibit X.7, Canada is the highest spender next to Sweden on public education as a percentage of GNP. From 1981 to 1987 total public expenditures

EXHIBIT X.7
INTERNATIONAL COMPARISON OF PUBLIC EXPENDITURES ON EDUCATION
1980

COUNTRY	Public Expenditure On Education/GNP	SIMS Average Score Position
Sweden	9.1%	Top third
Canada	7.7%	Middle third
United States	6.9%	Lower third
Belgium	6.0%	Middle third
Japan	5.9%	Top third
United Kingdom	5.7%	Top third
Hungary	4.7%	Lower third

Source: UNESCO, Statistical Digest, 1985 and SIMS, unpublished data, 1984.

on elementary and secondary education in Ontario rose from $5.1 billion to $8.5 billion, an increase of 67 percent. But that increased spending on education has raised teachers' salaries and overhead costs without necessarily yielding better scholastic achievement, lowering dropout rates, or generally improving the system. Even with expanding budgets, insufficient funds have been allocated to training teachers and principals. The research we have examined indicates that high educational achievement, rather than being the result of higher spending, seems to be more systematically linked to rigorous performance expectations, curriculum content that concentrates on mastery of core subjects, highly motivated students, and a highly trained teaching body.

These findings reinforce the importance and urgency of raising the government commitment to achieving excellence in education in the province. The Council sees the need for some specific actions to enhance the level of achievement throughout the school system:

• Provincial standards for educational performance should be maintained and regular province-wide testing should be undertaken

• The province should initiate and participate in national and international performance comparisons of its students and school

systems

- Public accountability should be fundamentally strengthened through the reporting to parents and guardians of the performance of individual schools and the province in comparative testing

- A thorough review of the overhead cost structure of the educational system should be undertaken with a view to reallocating greater resources to the training of educators

Although these initiatives will heighten Ontario's commitment to building a leading education system by international standards, Ontario must also recognize the importance of its education system and the outstanding individual and group efforts that are part of it. Later in this report we will propose that a broad program of Ontario Excellence Awards be established. Applying this initiative to the education system would recognize and inspire higher achievement on the part of teachers, principals, students, and schools.

Facilitating The Transition From Education To Employment

The distinctions between education and work are becoming increasingly blurred as colleges and universities develop industrial linkages and industry develops more in-house educational programs. Efforts to combine education and work experiences must begin earlier, though. In many European jurisdictions, high school education often includes a working term in industry, so that students acquire an early familiarity with the working world they will enter later.

225

An interministerial committee has been addressing the school-to-work transition issue. This committee or the Ministry of Skills Development, with its lead responsibility for provincial youth job creation and training activities, should consider expanding school co-op programs, possibly by twinning schools with companies or introducing internship programs at the high school level. This early exposure to the work setting would make the transition from school to work less jarring for young people and ultimately more successful.

Although the Premier's Council is keenly interested in educational issues, it has been unable to pursue this area intensively given the breadth of its mandate. In its next agenda, the Council proposes to work in cooperation with the Ministries of Education, Colleges and Universities, Skills Development and Industry, Trade and Technology, as well as other relevant public policy groups to pursue an in-depth review of the education issues discussed here and devise strategic policy approaches to meet the challenges identified. Similarly, the Council will be undertaking a more thorough review of training issues in its future work program; in the next section we offer a brief review of the major issues in training which require further study and action.

INTENSIFYING THE COMMITMENT TO TRAINING

Training in industry is a substantial and growing activity in Ontario. In its 1985 Survey of Employer Sponsored Training Programs, the Ontario Manpower Commission estimated that formal industrial training in the province amounts to about $1 billion annually. Thus, training expenditures in Ontario are slightly less than the $1.1 billion spent on research and development, only half of the $2 billion spent annually on advertising, and considerably less than the $22 billion of capital expenditures in the province.

The business commitment to training is growing as it gains recognition as a vital competitive factor. Training is increasingly being looked upon as an investment rather than a cost. For example, international competitive pressures and quality standards are forcing the automotive industry to increase its training expenditures from $75 million in 1984 to an estimated $200 million in 1990. While GM Canada provided 800,000 hours of training (an average of 20 hours per employee) in 1984, training is expected to increase to 2,000,000 hours by 1990 at a cost of $80 million per year. Meanwhile, employees at IBM are receiving a minimum of 40 hours of training per year to keep pace with changes in the manufacturing system.

226

The training intensive companies are often the high performers in their industries. They are also organizations that are committed to the long term employment of their people. These companies almost invariably point out that their same workforce has been through several fundamental changes in manufacturing technology and that proper training has enabled workers to meet the next challenges readily. As one company observed, "With the changes taking place in the work place today, training has become critical to maintaining our competitive edge. We know our workers can always adapt, so it's our responsibility to help them get there."

Industry today invests the majority of its training effort in building basic skills that workers lack. Workers are increasingly being expected to participate in solving production problems and applying their expertise to improving product quality and lowering costs. Both modern problem solving techniques, such as statistical process control, and advanced technologies, such as programmable machines, require new levels of competency in literacy and mathematics. Furthermore, the growing use of quality circles and other worker involvement groups is increasing the importance of team problem solving and communications skills. Many organizations in Ontario find that before they can train workers in these specific skills, they must first make up for the educational system's failure earlier to provide workers with adequate basic skills. For example, shop floor implementation of statistical process control often requires hourly workers to construct and interpret graphs - a skill which Ontario auto firms found they could not assume their workers had mastered.

Despite widely professed industry support for training, the training effort is being carried out primarily by major employers in selective industrial sectors. Formal training rates in Ontario companies vary from 9 percent in primary industries to 51 percent in durable goods manufacturing and 60 percent in public administration. For many of these companies, the commitment to training is no more than five years old. In fact, serious training efforts only started in most of the automotive parts industry when it became a precondition to having the skills to maintain supply contracts with the major vehicle companies.

One of the most surprising revelations of a 1986 Ontario Manpower Commission survey was that business and industry had little knowledge of or reliance on government training programs to supplement their own provision of training. Even the best known provincial training program, the now-lapsed Training in Business and Industry (TIBI), was known to only 12 percent of the establishments surveyed. This indicates that government has not been seen by many companies as a partner in training.

Advancing Ontario's Training Strategy

The Government of Ontario has provided a single focus for training in the province. The Ontario Training Strategy (OTS), launched in 1986, has doubled the province's training commitment from $50 million to $100 million annually. Training in Ontario now has the same level of financial support as the Premier's Council Technology Fund.

The major focus of the OTS is short-term training in industry. Firms with fewer than 200 employees receive subsidies covering 80 percent of training costs, while larger firms receive 60 percent subsidies. Over half the program money is allocated to smaller firms. The industrial component of the Ontario Training Strategy (OTS) represents $68 million, while "access" or social programs directed at improving basic skills to facilitate workforce re-entry account for the remaining $32 million. (It should be noted, though, that the province's training effort also includes institutional training, apprenticeship, specific older worker training, and other initiatives in addition to the OTS.)

An important complement to the Ontario Training Strategy will be the Technology Adjustment and Research Program, a Premier's Council initiative described earlier in Chapter IV. This program will play a central role in identifying critical skills shortages and changing training requirements by anticipating the effects of technological change on the workforce and the workplace. The technology impact studies sponsored by the program will help guide the development and ensure the relevance of education, training, and retraining efforts.

Gaps in the Apprenticeship System

The Council's preliminary investigations into apprenticeship in Ontario have raised questions regarding whether the apprenticeship system is keeping pace with the needs of industry. A number of factors appear to inhibit the province's apprenticeship system from fulfilling its objectives of providing a skilled workforce to employers and providing the skills necessary for individuals to achieve trades completion. Lengthy training periods of up to five years for some trades, coupled with inadequate wage provisions often prevent apprentices from achieving full journeymen's status, thus contributing to a significant dropout problem among apprentices. The outdated equipment in some colleges also makes it difficult for apprentices to keep their knowledge current and their skills up-to-date.

As Exhibit X.8 illustrates, the emphasis on apprenticeship and employer-sponsored training is considerably weaker in Ontario and Canada than in other major industrialized nations. In Germany and Japan, for instance, the substantial emphasis on apprenticeship and employer support for training in industry reduces the need for extensive government support for training in industry. And in Sweden, where there is considerable government support for training in industry, industry-sponsored training and apprenticeship still manages to exceed Ontario levels.

The Premier's Council supports the province's current efforts to revamp the apprenticeship system. Several innovative approaches announced in August, 1987 and now being implemented include: the development of pre-apprenticeship programs; greater use of co-op models to allow for alternative timing ratios of in-school to on-the-job training; establishment of a pilot mechanism to enable employers to take on entry-level employees and provide formal, on-the-job training; and expanded support for skills upgrading of journeymen through a trades updating program. In

EXHIBIT X.8
COMPARITIVE EMPHASIS ON ASPECTS OF TRAINING IN SELECTED COUNTRIES

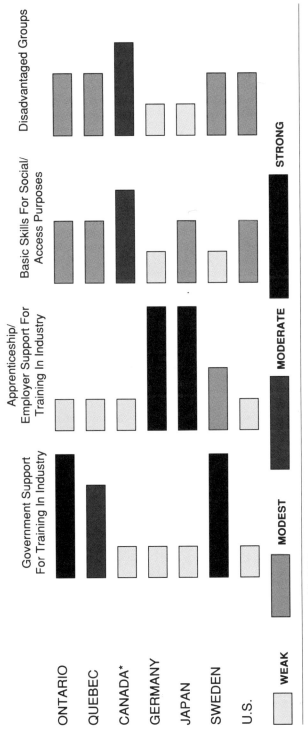

229

* Refers to federal government training initiatives
Sources: Analysis by Canada Consulting, based on interviews, country visits, and published sources.

addition to these efforts, the outdated wage provisions, training ratios, and guidelines in the provincial Apprenticeship and Tradesmen's Qualification Act could be reviewed to allow for greater flexibility in dealing with new and changing training and apprenticeship needs.

Providing Stronger Federal Leadership

Ontario has recently advocated the creation of a Canada Training Allowance as a collective effort on the part of the provinces and the federal government that would provide a more rational system for offering income support to adults undertaking long-term training. It would also offer apprentices an incentive for completing their programs by supplementing their income, at least while they are engaged in the institutional portion of their training. Furthermore, it would remove the stigma associated with the requirement that apprentices declare themselves unemployed while they are taking their classroom training. The Premier's Council strongly supports the advocacy role assumed by the province in this area.

The research prepared for the Council clearly demonstrates a need for the federal government to offer training allowances to unemployed youth as an alternative to the "keeping them off the streets" approach of the Unemployment Insurance system. Government spending on U.I. for youth in 1985 amounted to $2 billion, nearly one-third of total federal spending on youth programs. Although 1971 amendments to the Unemployment Insurance Act have permitted U.I. funding to be used to assist job creation or to pay benefits to people attending training courses, spending for these efforts has been marginal. Only 10 percent of U.I. funding (6 percent for youth) has been devoted to increasing employability through training. The Premier's Council therefore urges the federal government to restructure its Unemployment Insurance scheme by offering the training allowance as an incentive for the unemployed, particularly the young unemployed, to enroll in basic and job specific training programs that would improve their chances of gaining productive employment.

While the federal government generally matches provincial government expenditures on training in Ontario[4], the bulk of the federal training funds are committed to access programs. The federal training mandate emphasizes the social rather than the industrial side of training. Almost 90 percent of individuals in

230

---

4. With the Ontario Training Strategy and other programs included, Ontario's total training expenditures roughly equal federal expenditures on job creation and training. For example, in 1985-1986, the Ministry of Skills Development spent $392.3 million on training and labour market development, whereas total Canadian Job Strategy expenditures in Ontario were $391.1 million.

federally-sponsored programs throughout Canada were unemployed, indicating that a major objective of the federal training initiative is to allow people to enter or reenter the workforce, rather than develop industry-specific skills. It is also worth noting that institutional training in the colleges of applied arts and technology accounts for $155 million or 55 percent of all federal training expenditures, while training in industry has been cut 40 percent from previous levels and now represents only 9 percent of all federal training monies. (See Exhibit X.9)

Until the advent of the Canadian Jobs Strategy (CJS) in 1985, federal training dollars were more strongly committed to developing skills in occupations deemed to be in short supply. But consistent with the CJS objective of focussing training expenditures on those members of the labour force most in need, spending has been redirected to ensure equitable representation of social target groups, with secondary emphasis on benefits accruing to employers and industry. This shift in focus has been accompanied by a reduction in the level of federal funding for training.

The Premier's Council believes that weaknesses in the industrial and competitive aspects of the national training program weaken the training effort at the provincial level. Because of the federal government's predilection for using training as a tool to

EXHIBIT X.9

FEDERAL EXPENDITURES ON INSTITUTIONAL AND INDUSTRIAL TRAINING IN ONTARIO SINCE 1982-83

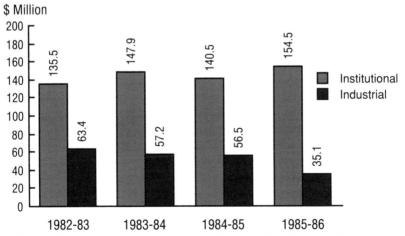

Note: Industrial training includes general industrial training, critical trade skills training and the non-institutional component of Skill Shortages and Skill Investment in 1985-86. Figures for 1985-86 represent best forecast, July 1986.

Source: Canada Employment and Immigration Commission

alleviate unemployment and improve access to the labour market for disadvantaged Canadians, Ontario must take the lead in creating an environment in which more and better industrial training will take place. The province must concentrate on establishing and maintaining programs that develop strong linkages with the private sector and organized labour to increase the awareness of and commitment to training in those constituencies.

The priorities of the federal government in Canada stand in sharp contrast to the national policies of other countries such as Japan, Germany and Great Britain, where training is seen as primarily part of an economic rather than social strategy; policies and programs are aggressively pursued to this end, and institutional structures reinforce the national commitment. The current institutional arrangements at the federal level work against an effective national commitment to investing in people. Institutional structures force a compromise among immigration, unemployment, and manpower development policies. No single advocate, such as the Manpower Services Commission in Great Britain, exists to symbolize the national economic importance of human resource development. In the view of the Council, training for competitiveness is too important a matter to be left off the national agenda. Getting it there will require the firm and focussed commitment of governments at all levels. It is with such backing that industry can indeed be expected to take the initiative of investing much more heavily in the training necessary to secure our future well-being.

232

DEVELOPING A COMPREHENSIVE PEOPLE STRATEGY

The economic strategy we have laid out in this report will not succeed if the human resource programs in the province do not support it. A much more intensive commitment to R&D will require significantly more qualified graduates and technicians. Successful restructuring of our core industries will depend upon our ability to retrain displaced workers and broaden and deepen the skills of those who remain in our resource-based and mature manufacturing sectors. The development of a larger base of high growth industries and threshold companies will require a well-educated supply of workers in those industries and firms. In short, if we are not capable of providing a flexible workforce with basic and applied skills at the level of our leading competitors, the agenda we have set out in this report cannot succeed. The Council's work to date on education, training, and labour adjustment has only provided us with enough understanding of these "people issues" to realize that Ontario has serious problems in these areas that must be addressed. To build on that work and develop the necessary human resources strategy and programs to support the economic policy agenda we have set forth, we offer the following recommendation:

Recommendation 13: Comprehensive People Strategy
The Premier's Council should work with appropriate areas of government to develop a comprehensive people strategy that would address vital education, training, and labour market policy issues as an integral part of the council's next agenda.

The Council proposes to undertake a new research and policy development program that will permit full discussion of the education and training initiatives now underway, identify critical issues that require further exploration, and establish a work plan that draws on the expertise of government to examine these issues.

Having carried out some preliminary research into the education and training areas, the Council sees an immediate need to delve further into a number of key issues:

- The low literacy and basic skills levels of the workforce, and the availability of basic skills upgrading opportunities to meet their needs
- The various shortcomings of the apprenticeship system and how they can best be addressed
- Methods of increasing the amount and quality of training in industry through incentives or a regulatory framework
- The special training needs of older workers in restructuring industries and types of employment undergoing major adjustments
- The role of training in industrial adjustment, particularly in comparison to the training for adjustment experience of other jurisdictions.

The Council would expect that if this program is pursued, it will be able to put before the government next year a comprehensive people strategy and set of initiatives which build on the existing provincial efforts in education, training, and labour adjustment. This strategy should not be seen as a new or additional mandate for the Council, but rather as a natural and necessary complement to the economic initiatives recommended in this report.

233

CHAPTER XI
BUILDING A NATIONAL CONSENSUS

THE NATIONAL IMPLICATIONS

In the foregoing pages, the Premier's Council has identified the central challenges facing the Ontario economy, set the direction for future wealth creation in the province, and mapped out a practical course to follow. This chapter extends this agenda for change beyond the province's borders and brings it into a national context. It argues strongly for the need to build a national consensus around what the challenges are and how to address them.

The Premier's Council firmly believes that building and sustaining international competitiveness must be viewed as a national goal and achieved cooperatively by the provincial and federal governments. Moving towards that goal is a matter of adopting, at both levels of public policy, a consistent, compatible and complementary approach.

There are several key areas in which a unified approach to policies and programs would serve the combined provincial and national interests particularly well. These key areas include science and technology, industrial support, training and industrial adjustment, and tax incentives.

235

NATIONAL SCIENCE AND TECHNOLOGY POLICY

No one area speaks to the need for strong national leadership and complementary federal and provincial policies more than science and technology. It is the area where the national government influences most of the nation's policy levers and public sector expenditures. It is also the area in which the Premier's Council has come to believe that substantial changes in policy, direction and approach are warranted.

As Chapter IX clearly demonstrated, Canada is undergoing a crisis in science and technology. Of particular concern is Canada's comparatively low level of industrial research and development. Traditional reasons for this disturbing performance - the heavy branch plant structure and the dominance of resource industries - do not fully explain the situation. Branch plant spending on research and development is frequently lower than that of comparable Canadian-owned operations, but in other indigenous industries, such as pulp and paper and non-ferrous metals, R&D spending in Canada is also considerably lower than in other countries.

This low level of research and development in industry is paralleled by the amount of R&D spending by government: Canada ranks near the bottom of all OECD countries in terms of government-funded R&D as a percent of GDP. But Canada ranks above such countries as the United States, Japan, Germany and Sweden in terms of the proportion of government-funded R&D that is carried out within government. Low overall spending and the bias towards in-house research leave the Canadian private sector at a severe competitive disadvantage in terms of the level of government funding for R&D in industry.

Government's counter-argument to the extremely low level of direct industry R&D funding in Canada is that the tax incentives for R&D are more favourable. While Canada's R&D tax incentives are among the most generous, when direct program support and tax support are combined and compared with total support in other countries, Canada's ranking drops to the bottom. The single focus on the level of tax expenditures addresses only part of the R&D funding issue and fails to recognize the considerable public funding disadvantage that industry faces in this country. Moreover, with the recent cuts in federal tax support for industry R&D, the outlook for industry will only become bleaker (See Exhibit V.6).

236

The federal government, under its tax reform proposals, has reduced the investment tax credit for R&D from 100 percent to 75 percent of taxes payable, which will cut companies' cash flow for R&D by $30-40 million in Canada. This will have the effect of limiting the capabilities of some larger firms in competing against foreign firms that operate in a more favourable domestic R&D policy environment.

The Council has also found that the rules prescribing what can be claimed as R&D tax credits are viewed by industry as overly restrictive and tediously applied. The definitions of research favour an academic interpretation, and efforts to resolve disagreements are time consuming, costly, and frequently unresolvable. As one company commented, "No one in Canada should feel apologetic about doing R&D, but that is certainly the message the tax system sends to industry."

The Council is also concerned about a continuing policy bias that assumes the low level of industry R&D can be offset by the R&D activities of government labs and university research programs. In fact, one of the rationales for government research in resource and emerging industries has been the lack of a strong industry research base. Universities in recent years have also supported research funding proposals with arguments of competitiveness and limited corporate capabilities.

However, the Council regards much of the research carried out in government and university settings as a surrogate for industry research and development and one which falls far short of building industry capability. In fact, research surrogates divert the scarce funds needed to expand the level of industrial research in Canada. It is in the national interest that the excessive level of support for these research and development surrogates be diverted to industry, where it properly belongs. The message for Ontario and even more so for the federal government is that significant commitments need to be made to moving in-house government research to the private sector.

There is no continuing justification for either the amount that is carried on within government nor the amount that is carried out without a clear mission (See Exhibit XI.2). The R&D which remains in government labs must be directed and managed with a strongly-defined mission orientation. The overall goal must be to build industry capability, and resource allocation decisions should reflect this orientation.

The Premier's Council, through the Centres of Excellence Program and the University Research Incentive Fund, has put in place substantial funding to build new research capabilities in Ontario and to improve industry-university linkages. But the Council also believes that the role of the universities in commercially related research needs to be re-examined. Universities play an important role in advancing basic research and provide an invaluable training ground for research minds and capabilities. But universities cannot substitute for industry-based research and development. While university-industry linkages improve the transfer of technology, they will not make up for the serious limitations of Canada's comparatively low industrial R&D levels.

237

The Council endorses the federal government's recently announced initiative to establish national Centres of Excellence. At the same time, we caution against any interpretation that this commitment advances the development of today's industrial R&D capability in the country. This continues to be a strategic gap, and we encourage the federal government to join Ontario in focussing its future commitments on increasing support for R&D in the industry setting.

Having considered R&D policies and efforts in other countries, the Council has also come to believe that Canada falls far short of initiating science and technology programs that are central to our national interests. Japan with its Fifth Generation Computer Project, the United States with Sematech, the European Community Esprit Project, and the U.K. Alvey Programme all provide examples of countries endeavoring to advance the research horizons of industry, reduce the risk associated with longer term industry research, and gain lasting competitive industrial advantage. These advanced technology projects reflect their respective national interests and demonstrate the significance which these countries attach to leading-edge technologies in industry. They also reflect a belief that the industries of the future and the continued creation of wealth require an ongoing national commitment to helping industries maintain or advance their strategic technologies. Such recognition of the future importance to industry of strategic technologies has not been a national priority in Canada. The Council believes that we should be aggressively advancing those technologies that will be critical to our economic well-being and working with industry to transform research into competitive capability. As a nation, we have yet to recognize how critical being at the forefront of certain technologies will be to our future.

Proposals to enhance the science and technology capabilities in Canada typically call for more spending. Our investigations led us to the conclusion that private sector spending on R&D must increase. More public funding is required as well, particularly in support of strategic technology development for Canada. In total, these efforts will still place the government commitment to R&D in Canada at a level lower than that of our competitor nations for some time to come. But these proposals will build for the future, reinforce our competitive structure and increase substantially the effectiveness of public funding for science and technology.

238

Federal Industrial Support

The Council has focussed its recommendations on key areas of public policy that provide competitive leverage to Canadian industry. The two areas that require particularly coordinated federal and provincial policies are strategic procurement and risk sharing with industry.

1. Strategic Procurement - The Council reiterates the importance of strategic procurement in the development of emerging industries and technologically advanced firms. The United States, Japan and Europe all utilize government procurement as a key lever in the development of indigenous capabilities. It is not uncommon to find that 50 percent or more of the research and development effort of major firms in the United States is financed through some form of government procurement. Although the level of support may differ in other countries, the intent does not.

As discussed in the previous chapter, purchasing policy in Ontario has often missed strategic opportunities and tended either to fragment the contract scope or position Ontario firms as subsuppliers to OEMs. This approach contrasts sharply with the experience of Quebec, for example, where the development of engineering, software, and manufacturing firms has been nurtured through strategic purchases.

At the federal level, the crucial role that purchasing can play in the product development stage has not received sufficient emphasis. In software and computer services, there appears to be a readiness to encourage the entry of large U.S. suppliers into Canada through federal contracts. Rather than encouraging the development of international scale in the Canadian industry, the prevailing concern is to diminish risk by attracting foreign suppliers.

The Premier's Council recognizes that most federal contracting will not provide strategic opportunities. We also fully understand the need to respond to the regional development requirements of this country. Nonetheless, we firmly believe that there is a national responsibility to build selective indigenous capability in Canada in emerging industries. Procurement is one of the main levers our competitors use in achieving this end. Theirs is an aggressive approach we should emulate.

239

We have offered various proposals that would encourage Ontario to use strategic purchasing as a powerful tool for economic development. The outcome of the federal/provincial task force deliberations on procurement may assist in aligning federal policies with Ontario's so that the full force of the national purchasing power can be realized. Again, consistent and complementary policies and programming are required at the provincial and national level.

2. Risk Sharing With Industry - The Risk Sharing Fund proposed by the Council for implementation within Ontario commends itself to careful consideration at the national level as well. This fund could be considered a model by the federal government in how to increase new product development in Canada. This fund, described in Chapter VI, addresses the post-R&D and market launch stages of the commercialization process. Federal definitions of research and development are restricted to early stage product development, where there is still a high degree of uncertainty. Canada has a history of developing new technology that is subsequently commercialized in another country, often with no return on investment for Canada. We need to become much smarter about new product development, prototype financing, and export marketing. The Ontario Risk Sharing Fund ad-

dresses these needs at the provincial level and could fill an important strategic gap in federal program support to industry as well.

The value of this program is that it allows industry wide scope in defining the course of action to be taken and reinforces the national need to move continually to higher value-added products and markets. It also makes government a partner to the risks inherent in technological investments. This relationship between government and industry, based on mutual assumption of risks, is common among most of our competitive trading partners.

NATIONAL TRAINING AND ADJUSTMENT POLICIES

The Council cannot emphasize strongly enough the extent to which the programs and initiatives proposed, particularly with respect to restructuring, depend on people. It depends on people having or acquiring necessary skills and on companies that will invest in people so that they can develop the necessary skills. Two areas of national priority that are directly related to people are training and industrial adjustment: one is building the ability to adjust; the other is having in place the human safeguards in the event that business has not adjusted.

1. Training for competitiveness is one important area where the policies of the federal government are currently not well aligned with those of the provincial government or with the needs of industry. The philosophy of the federal government is substantially different from that of the Ontario government. It focusses on the 'social' aspects of training, and deals primarily with such human resource concerns as training the unemployed, unemployment insurance, and immigration policy. Training in business and industry remains a secondary concern. In fact, recent reductions in the level of funding for job-specific training have diluted the federal commitment to training for industrial competitiveness even further.

The Canada Employment and Immigration Commission is the major federal department which develops and implements the training policies of the federal government. Its prime initiative, the 1985 Canadian Jobs Strategy, focusses on getting people jobs, with training as a means to that end. Training at the national level is only one element of an integrated labour market policy dealing with broader issues, including labour market access, long-term unemployment and community development. This is in sharp contrast to the national policies of other countries, such as Japan, Germany and Great Britain, where training is seen as an economic initiative; policies and programs in this vein are aggressively pursued, and institutional structures reinforce the national commitment to value-added in the development of human resources.

The Government of Ontario has recently made proposals to the federal government that would yield positive advances in its approach to industrial training. Ontario has proposed that the federal government move to create a Canadian Training Allowance to provide income support for adult Canadians undertaking long-term training. Such an initiative would greatly aid Ontario's ability to respond to the combined pressures of new technologies, global competition and industrial restructuring. At present, the federal income support for trainees is restrictive in terms of who is eligible for support and what courses are open to trainees. Current criteria favor the long-term unemployed and the employment disadvantaged. Support programs at present do not encourage the employed to enter long-term training.

From the Councils' perspective, this proposal is only symptomatic of a much more fundamental need for the federal government to give national emphasis to the importance of effective skills development. A single purpose organization with senior ministerial responsibility should be established to recognize the importance and contribution of people to the country's economic future. At the national level, the failure to acknowledge the economic necessity of investing in people has become a significant impediment to progress.

241

2. Industrial Adjustment. The federal and provincial governments have played different but somewhat complementary roles in industrial and technological adjustment programs.

The federal role, which has been largely embodied in the Industrial Adjustment Service (IAS), has emphasized the placing of laid-off workers in jobs as its principal response. This service, established in 1963, operates as a catalyst in the development of labour deployment and redeployment strategies at the plant level to help workers adjust. The program operates through a bilateral committee, which oversees the development and implementation of the solution to the particular adjustment problem. Mobility programs and training have been utilized to round out the federal government response to labour adjustment. The federal government has also introduced specific adjustment programs during times of fundamental industrial restructuring and serious economic downturns in industries. Two cases in point were the Transitional Assistance Benefits Program, established to facilitate adjustment under the Auto Pact, and the Industrial and Labour Adjustment Program, which was designed to help relieve severe unemployment in the early 1980s.

The Premier's Council has proposed several measures that will aid the competitive transition taking place in industry:

- New Directions For Restructuring (Recommendation 3)
- Ontario Shared Ownership Initiative (Recommendation 4)

The Council has also developed the Technological Adjustment and Research Program (TARP), which is already being implemented.

These measures should help bring planning into the adjustment process and provide essential lead times for positive action. Federal programs such as the IAS are already perceived as working well. But adjustment pressures, such as those emerging out of the proposed trade deal with the U.S., will increase the level of funding needed well beyond the current levels in Ontario. A good program such as the IAS is destined to become overburdened or fail unless it is adequately funded. Industrial training efforts that keep workers in the workforce should be the first priority. However, new initiatives at the federal level will also be required to move the worker adjustment approach out from its present reactive mode.

Federal Tax Incentives

242

Incentives such as tax rate reductions, investment tax credits, capital depreciation incentives, capital cost allowances and research and development incentives have become an important part of the industrial support framework of this country since the 1970s. They are attractive to business because the rules in most cases are clear, eligibility generally relates to the activity and not to the firm, and the delivery is by and large non-bureaucratic. Given the tedious and complex bureaucratic negotiations involved in direct program funding, most businesses decidedly prefer the tax route.

While Ontario has some room to manoeuvre in corporate tax incentives, the personal tax regime is mainly the preserve of the federal government. Quebec, which collects, administers and determines its own personal tax base and tax rates, has more flexibility than Ontario does in this regard. Thus, Quebec could institute a system such as the Quebec Stock Saving Plan (QSSP), which allows Quebec residents to deduct the amount invested in newly-issued shares of corporations. In Ontario, such a system, particularly a deduction on the personal tax side, would likely not be acceptable to the federal government.

Of particular concern to the Premier's Council are some of the tax changes that are part of the recent tax reform of the federal government. Some of these changes in fact reduce the incentives that companies in this country require to increase their competitiveness and continue their growth.

The federal government has proposed removal of the inefficient manufacturer's sales tax (MST) set at 12 percent, but has made no commitment to replace it with a more efficient consumption-based tax. Canada is one of the only major industrialized countries to have a tax on inputs. Failure of the federal government to act on stage two of its tax reform by introducing a consumption tax could lead to the implementation of an interim tax system which taxes inputs more and consequently increases costs to business.

Other areas of tax reform which raise the costs of investment to Ontario industries are the proposed changes to investment tax credits and capital cost allowances. These changes, if implemented, will effectively offset the corporate tax advantages which existed in Canada over the United States prior to tax reform. A case in point is the tax reform measure which extends the number of years during which companies can depreciate machinery and equipment. Before the tax reform proposals were introduced, companies could write off machinery and equipment over a three-year period. The tax reform measure would require that companies depreciate their equipment and machines over a seven-year period, a measure which would lead to substantial cost increases, particularly for more capital-intensive industry sectors.

243

At a time when the real challenge in the country is expanding the base of industrial R&D and encouraging new investment in higher value-added production, it is a strategic blunder carrying grave long-term consequences to undertake tax reform that removes key incentives. This is even more troubling in view of the fact that the previous tax regime provided compelling incentives for multinational companies to direct their new investment to their Canadian operations.

Restructuring and reinvestment today are the pass-cards to competitive survival. These pressures will only grow under a changing trade regime with the United States. The Council has serious concerns that the tax changes before us will retard rather than facilitate the competitive restructuring process.

SUSTAINING A CONSENSUS

Having outlined the directions in which Ontario should be moving to achieve prominence as an advanced and competitive industrial society, and having described the need for national policy and program consistency, we now turn our attention to the methods for effecting this transition. Ontario policymakers, in concert with the private sector players in this process, must develop and be guided by an ethic that complements the direction being chartered.

It is essential that a clear and consistent focus be established and maintained in carrying out the objectives set by the Council. The considerable effort expended by the Council in arriving at a set of policy directions for Ontario must be matched by a long-term commitment to carrying them out. Maintaining a strong central focus in a dynamic policy environment must remain uppermost in the minds of those who are charged with the task of reshaping the province's economic and industrial development. A steady course for future prosperity has been charted; an even keel and a consistent direction must be maintained if the province is to arrive at its destination.

A Model For Consensus Building

The Premier's Council is a new initiative in the public policy process in Canada. The Council has been a testing ground for the creation of a broad consensus mechanism that represents the diverse but compatible interests of the Ontario economy. The Council prides itself on having proven that such a consensus building mechanism can indeed be effective in developing success-ful joint strategies. But there is an urgent need to build on the momentum of the Council model by extending and deepening it throughout the system.

The Council's work in providing advice to government has raised the level and quality of debate in all aspects of interna-tional competitiveness. Since the creation of the Premier's Coun-cil in Ontario, comparable initiatives have taken place at the federal level and in several of the provinces. This Council looks forward to discussing and sharing the findings and conclusions of our report as part of building a national consensus around the industrial strengths and opportunities for Canada.

A Process for Consensus Building

In order to clear the way for effective, long-term change, two potential impediments to government and industry cooperation must be overcome. The business world's traditional reluctance to deal with government bureaucracy must be broken down, and government's perceived resistance to involving the private sector meaningfully in public policy development must be dissipated.

The industrial community has long harboured complaints

about bureaucratic barriers to doing business with government. Businesses are discouraged by the costs and excessive time involved in steering proposals through government. Once proposals are in the system, they are often slow to emerge or are altogether lost in the unwieldly maze of program delivery. Bureaucracies in other jurisdictions have made their industrial assistance regimes more accessible and responsive means of stimulating economic growth. Quebec, for instance, has managed to streamline the program delivery process by developing a more results-oriented approach to doing business with the private sector, as well as a stronger marketing orientation.

To become more responsive to the needs of industry in providing incentives, government must also rid itself of the subtle bias against bringing the private sector into its midst as a participant in policy development and program delivery. There is a decided need for more and better public and private sector interface to stimulate new thinking in both arenas and to create common ground for action. The traditional ways in which government and business interact must give way to a more supportive and mutually beneficial partnership. The effectiveness of the business-government relationship can be a competitive advantage. It enhances the quality of public policy and encourages decision making that is more responsive to the client group.

245

Providing Symbolic Leadership

It is important that government use symbolic leadership to inspire higher achievement and strategic development throughout the province. The Council believes strongly that there is a need for leadership and excellence to be recognized and rewarded. Symbolic but highly visible recognition of excellence is an essential form of goal-setting that will provide a powerful incentive for those in the province who are involved in these economic activities to move towards higher achievement.

Recommendation 14: ONTARIO EXCELLENCE AWARDS
The Ontario Excellence Award should be created to give recognition to individuals in the province for their special contributions to making a better economic future for the people of the province.

The Ontario Excellence Awards would be an annual celebration in which people who are making outstanding contributions in their fields are recognized. This will give Ontarians whose special achievements merit acclaim an opportunity to be honoured. Areas for recognition of performance should include:

- Education
- Entrepreneurship
- Worker innovation
- Engineering
- Science

Excellence Awards in these areas would be distinct from the Order of Ontario in that they would recognize the achievements and unique contributions of people in the mainstream of their careers within strictly defined categories.

The changes in the areas that the Council has identified must be approached systematically and effected responsibly. The recommendations that existing programs be restructured or new programs be developed have resulted from extensive consideration and analysis of the issues. There are, of course, major financial implications in implementing many of the recommendations put forward in this report. The Council therefore urges the government in adopting its advice to manage the changes with as much consideration, analysis and recognition of the long-term and financial implications as the Council used in developing these strategies.

GLOSSARY OF TERMS

Business Segment vs. Industry Companies in a "business segment" operate in a common competitive environment and thus face similar competitive challenges. "Industry" refers to the more traditional SIC classification combining companies which provide similar products or services but which may be driven by very different competitive dynamics.

Emerging Industries Those industries in which the base of scientific knowledge is still being developed and the source of competitive advantage is usually a technological breakthrough.

High Growth Industries Developed, high wage industries whose new technology enables them to grow much faster in gross value-added than average high wage industries.

High Wage Industries Industries with internationally traded products in which competitive advantage is not gained primarily on a raw materials cost or low wage basis.

247

Indigenous Refers to a firm whose strategic planning, marketing, R&D, manufacturing, and head office functions are directed from an Ontario base; the firm may or may not be Canadian-owned.

Industrial Restructuring An ongoing process of renewal within the economy in which companies respond to changes in markets and competition by moving to higher value-added per employee activities.

Low wage industries Low value-added industries in which labour is a significant cost component, making low wages the primary means of gaining competitive advantage.

Non-Traded Businesses Those businesses which serve only domestic markets and are not exposed to international competition.

Resource-Based Industries Those industries in which the relative price and quality of the raw material available to a company determines its competitive position.

Risk Sharing A means of reducing the risk of a business venture by involving a number of participants and thereby sharing the profit or loss.

Start-up Company Company which has been in business less than seven years.

Traded Business Those businesses which are exposed to international trade and competition.

Threshold Firms Companies in the $40-400 million size range with a competitive cost position, proven success in exporting, but which have not yet reached a dominant world market position and are therefore still vulnerable compared to diversified multinationals.

Value-added The cost of a finished product minus the raw materials and purchased services required to produce it.

Value-added per employee A company's total value-added divided by the number of employees.

LIST OF MEETINGS

July 10, 1986
Location: Main Legislative Building, Queen's Park.

September 4, 1986
Location: Sutton Place Hotel, Toronto

October 16, 1986
Location: Sutton Place Hotel, Toronto

November 13, 1986
Location: Sutton Place Hotel, Toronto

January 15, 1987
Location: Sutton Place Hotel, Toronto

February 27-28, 1987
Location: Millcroft Inn, Alton

April 2, 1987
Location: Sutton Place Hotel, Toronto

May 11-12, 1987
Location: Four Seasons Hotel, Toronto

June 18, 1987
Location: Sutton Place Hotel, Toronto

Auqust 5, 1987
Location: Four Seasons Hotel, Toronto

October 1, 1987
Location: Four Seasons Hotel, Toronto

November 12-13, 1987
Location: Sutton Place Hotel, Toronto

December 3-5, 1987
Location: Millcroft Inn, Alton

February 17-18, 1988
Location: Four Seasons Hotel, Toronto

March 11, 1988
Location: Sutton Place Hotel, Toronto